From the Grassroots:
Essays Toward Afro-American Liberation

by Manning Marable

South End Press　　　　**Boston, MA**

Cover Design by Ann Raszmann
Publishing and production work
done by the South End Press

ISBN 0-89608-073-0 paper
ISBN 0-89608-074-9 cloth
Library of Congress Card Number: 79-66995
South End Press, Box 68, Astor Station
Boston, MA 02123

Special Thanks

Special thanks are in order for the contributions of three special people. John Schall and Barbara Beltrand helped to transform *From the Grassroots* from a collection of essays to a statement on Afro-American and U.S. culture, economics and politics. Hazel Ann Marable, my wife, has helped to reinforce those inner traditions of Southern black culture and protest thought which, though sometimes dormant, remain the basis for my praxis.

Acknowledgements

Many of these articles first appeared in my newspaper column "From the Grassroots" and were published subsequently in an expanded version in other journals. A version of "Anatomy of Black Politics" appeared in the *Review of Black Political Economy* (Summer 1978). An early version of "Whither a Black Political Party" was published in *Confrontation/Change Review* (Winter 1977/78). The essay "A. Philip Randolph" was published in *Radical America* (March/April 1980). Portions of "The Cultural Dialectic of Violence" appeared in *Endarch* (Augum 1976). "The Psychopolitics of the Movement" was published in *State and Mind* (September/October 1978). An earlier version of "Tuskegee" was published in *The Black Scholar* (May 1977). Portions of "Black Education" were published in *Moving On* (January 1979).

Table of Contents

Forward and Definitions

From The Grassroots is a collection of articles on the prospects for creating a new black common sense for liberation in the years to come. Drawing inspiration from Malcolm X's critical search for a grassroots agenda for black people in 1964 and early 1965, these essays attempt to embrace the totality of the black experience of the nineteen seventies and examine many aspects of white American culture and political society. Originally, the essays were an attempt to analyze issues or questions of a political nature as they influenced the material life and thoughts of black people. As I continued to contribute political articles on an individual basis to a small number of journals and newspapers, I recognized the need to expand the work to reach a larger number of people. At first, the Grassroots column appeared regularly in the *Tuskegee News*, the *Dayton Black Press, Pensacola Voice, Macon Courier,* the *Black Explosion* of the University of Maryland, the *Sacramento Observer, Grass Roots Forum*, the *Amsterdam News* and student newspapers at Tuskegee Institute, Amherst College, the University of Massachusetts, Morehouse College and Fisk University. The column has now become a regular feature of over one hundred papers and journals throughout the country.

Occasionally, more than two million people read a particular Grassroots essay. The readers come from a wide range of income groups and social backgrounds: college students, community organizers, farmers, factory workers, ministers, welfare mothers, intellectuals. Gradually, I have come to appreciate the political perspective of the majority of my regular readers. Most of the readers who vote support the Democratic Party and many of them voted for Carter in the 1976 election. All of them are somewhat cynical of the political status quo, are suspicious of corporate America's rationalizations for increasingly higher profits and feel that their interests are not really represented within the government. The majority are Christians (either Methodists or Baptists) and as such also have the basis for a moral repudiation of capitalist politics and economics. Almost all are high school graduates but often have a difficult time obtaining steady employment and making ends meet. Many participated in marches during the Civil Rights decade but hesitate now to become involved in political activities that might lead to violence. A slight plurality of the more faithful readers could be termed black nationalists. Black nationalism is, within these pages, characterized as including a strong personal pride in one's black cultural and ethnic heritage, an advocacy of separate black economic and social institutions within black communities, a rejection of the tactics and principles of integrationist black leaders, a commitment to struggle against white authority, oppression and racism, and an approach to the world from a cultural frame of reference reflecting positively upon the black human experience.

The basic thesis presented here can be summarized in several ideas. The social progress for blacks achieved during the Civil Rights Movement has been largely halted and in some instances reversed. Black elected officials, traditional black leaders of civic and religious organizations and even their black nationalist critics have not developed an effective strategy to counter these attacks aimed at limiting black economic and political gains. A grassroots strategy of black liberation, a methodology which can achieve a popular consensus among our people, must of necessity combine a materialist critique of existing economic and political inequities within society with a black nationalists' appreciation for the cultural autonomy and traditions of black folk. Any strategy which aims at the fundamental transformation of the U.S. socioeconomic system must be informed also by what Marxist theorist Antonio Gramsci termed the "long view" of historical development. Before an authentic social revolution could succeed within black America, a systematic transformation of black thought, culture and political consciousness must take place. The "long view" of this transformation is what *From The Grassroots* seeks to present.

A brief note on terminology: throughout these articles I have endeavored to speak clearly and precisely to the problems of black America as I perceived them. Occasionally, I have used terms which may mean various things to different political sects and radical groups—petty bourgeoisie, proletariat, means of production, surplus value and classes. This is particularly the case in the longer essays. I have attempted to limit the use of some of what my associates have called "foreign" phrases for the simple reason that a transformation of black politics must take place within the historical traditions of black people, using the language which the majority of black folks will readily comprehend. It is impossible, however, not to employ some essential theoretical concepts of democratic socialism when discussing the kind of economic system which black people must achieve.

When the term bourgeoisie is used it refers to a relatively small group of people who own or control the major economic institutions of society, and who may also dominate political and cultural institutions as well. A class is a designation for a group of people who have a certain relationship to the way in which things are produced within society; that is, the means of production. A working class or the proletariat means a large group of people who sell their labor power, their ability to produce or make things, for a set wage or income in cash. Race connotes a body of people who belong to a broadly defined (genetic) grouping, share a commonly conceived history, ancestral heritage and culture, may speak a common language and who sometimes belong to a particular geographical, national or regional polity or state. Civil society is used to connote a diverse number of cultural institutions, educational and civic groups, ideologies as manifested within social hierarchies of caste and class, aesthetics and popular thought. The state is defined as the combination of two factors—the impact of civil society plus the structural political expression of those dominant social and economic elites which control the most powerful economic institutions.

Historical materialism is an approach toward understanding human life and history which emphaiszes the creation of material goods as central in affecting all other forms of existence and being. The analysis of *Grassroots* emphasizes cultural, ethnic and social relations as being critically important factors in the direction of human society, but also recognizes the ultimately decisive factor of economic relations over the forms of thought and consciousness. Finally, socialism is broadly defined as an economic, political and social movement which advocates the public, collective ownership of the basic productive forces of society, the guarantee of human equality within ethnic, civil and social relations and the democratic transformation of the political system at all governmental levels.

There are many people who have contributed their energies and talents toward the completion of this work. Diane Hoskens, Christine Buchanan, Evelyn Nodal and Crystal Allen helped to type and edit the various drafts of the manuscript. The dedicated assistance of the South End Press collective, and especially the tireless and critical efforts of my editor John Schall, was helpful and essential in preparing the final draft. At earlier stages of this work I was helped in one way or another by the editorial collective of *Radical America*, Haki Madhubuti, Richard Healey, David Plotke, the editors of *In These Times* and the friends and associates of the Institute of the Black World. Carol Berstein Ferry, William Ferry, Ernie Bickerstaff, Henry Wilton, William Lee, Marty Sklar, James Weinstein, Liz Moore, Raymond Boone, Les Humphrey, David Smith, Charles Thrower and my parents June and James Marable, Sr. are only a few of the many editors, publishers and friends who have supported my work and efforts. My wife Hazel has made undoubtedly the greatest sacrifice of all, giving birth to three children and working to support us while I was revising various sections of this or that chapter. If any credit comes from the contributions made in these pages, it belongs to her.

Manning Marable
July 5, 1980

Introduction: Toward a Critical Theory of Grassroots Liberation in Black America

> Hide nothing from the masses of our people.
> Tell no lies. Expose lies
> whenever they are told.
> Mask no difficulties, mistakes, failures.
> Claim no easy victories.
>
> Amilcar Cabral

Prologue

We are approaching the end of a particular historical epoch: the period of struggle for equal black civil rights and limited economic opportunity within capitalist America. It is true that white racism continues to perpetuate itself through America's cultural, political and economic institutions. Nevertheless, through the popular mass struggles for civil rights and the desegregation of public accommodations, open ballot boxes, and complete participation within electoral politics, *de jure* segregation has virtually disappeared. Many important objectives of the black leaders of the first Reconstruction of 1865-1877 were only achieved during the integrationist struggles one hundred years later. Hundreds and subsequently thousands of blacks were elected as mayors, and council people. Thousands more were allowed to enroll into previously all white educational institutions. Churches and civic organizations suddenly were desegregated. But these victories took place within the political economy and cultural framework of capitalism—a system of social relations utterly incapable of destroying racism. The Movement culminated in a series of economic opportunities for the elite. The vast

5

majority of black people continue to be almost as oppressed as before.

Desegregation was perhaps most pronounced within U.S. civil society, that is, within the dominant cultural institutions of white America. Blacks suddenly became familiar personalities on television commercials, promoting everything from McDonalds hamburgers to laundry bleach to jockey underwear. Black actors and actresses appeared on Broadway in well publicized, prominent roles. Black exploitation movies became a major part of the film industry. During this "blackening process," an uneven fusion of cultures occurred—the more whites mimicked aspects of black culture, the more Afro-Americans in turn imitated aspects of white, bourgeois culture.

The leadership of the Civil Rights Movement was grafted onto the U.S. state. In the South, former segregationists and white racist politicians tolerated the entrance of a slender number of blacks into municipal and state government. As a result the gains of the Movement itself began to wither away. The seventies brought a basic cultural and political reaction which reversed many of the gains made during the mid-sixties. The state isolated the demands of the Movement, handing soft jobs to former S.N.C.C. leaders in the government and in university settings. Black nationalists like Imamu Baraka were welcome to lecture at Yale University. Former demonstrators like John Lewis were given high paying positions within the federal bureaucracy. Lesser known activists were absorbed into the state structures at lower administrative and electoral levels. These "successes" produced a stagnant black political and cultural elite, men and women who found it difficult to engage in an ongoing struggle against white racism and political oppression.

In the wake of the turbulence of the sixties, the past decade was a time of frustrations and unfulfilled dreams. Objectively, it is often pointed out that the problems of black people are certainly as great as they were at the height of the Movement. Black unemployment is higher today than in the mid-sixties. The distance in real income, standards of health care and in some aspects of public education are widening between whites and blacks. But the subjective conditions essential for the mobilization of black people no longer seem to be present. On many black college campuses black students are more interested in fraternity and sorority parties than in analyzing the contemporary black political and cultural situation. Fewer students attend serious political debates or lectures. Many black youth seemed preoccupied with their own personal illusions of advancement into graduate or professional school and thereafter into the corporate world of the white bourgeoisie. Black studies programs have declined in number since 1971 and many existing Black studies programs have been watered down by merging them with ethnic studies, women's studies or American studies programs. This malaise and new emphasis upon individualism crosses racial lines. The majority of white youth also seem to indulge themselves with their own personal utopias or pet fantasies. Unemployment is high for Vietnam veterans and for recent college graduates, but one would never know it from the lack of concern expressed on the question of jobs. People avoid conflicts with other people and within themselves; hedonism has replaced social commitment. Black folks are following the irreverent advice of the Isley Brothers: "It's Your Thing."

Many Afro-Americans have internalized daily phenomena according to the general cultural framework in which it is presented. When Walter Cronkite in summing up the daily events that constitute our lives adds, "and that's the way it is," black people all too often turn off their televisions and say to themselves "that's the way it must be." No critical perspective on bourgeois thought is presented within the capitalist media; the problems of racism and class confrontations are discussed in a most superficial manner. Politicians from Carter to local city aldermen bicker about personalities rather than about the basic issues; the media transforms this rhetoric into a popular language of politics for the public. This language is largely internalized by the black population even as it is struggling to transcend the problems which are caused by the media. Thus within what claims to be a free and democratic society there is a virtual dictatorship of opinion and a vulgar permeation of the dominant white, capitalist culture within the educational systems, religious institutions and cultural forums throughout the entire social hierarchy. Anxiety is redirected inward; hostility toward the state and the institutions of law and order are redirected through the popularization of Starsky and Hutch, Barney Miller and Baretta. The common sense of modern capitalism prevails over the more critical perspective of the real world. The hostile mood of the grassroots is skillfully transformed into acquiescent support for the cultural and economic elites.

The Politics of Illusion: Left, Right and Center

This past decade was called many things: a return to the fabulous fifties, a gut reaction to the countercultural catharsis of the sixties; the "me" decade, where every individual seizes control over his or her own life and selfishly manipulates others around his or her own needs. Mostly, it came to represent an end of illusions. Throughout the twentieth century humankind has been a prisoner of various racial, political or economic chimeras. The great "American Century" of Henry Adams in which the United States dominated the world's economic and political order lasted barely two generations. The "War to end all wars" of Woodrow Wilson was followed two decades later by the most costly military conflict in human history. Afro-Americans marched tirelessly in the streets, had their heads busted and were threatened repeatedly with death when they struggled for the illusion of integration. The seventies produced higher unemployment, drug addiction and increased crime for the black community, while its self-appointed leaders were unable to come up with meaningful solutions to current problems. The illusions around which humankind projected its political agendas and social programs proved for better or worse to be bankrupt, unable to withstand the challenges of the transition to a new historical period.

Each political faction, economic interest group and clique operates in the light of its own perceived illusionary goals and perspectives. The conservatives, within the culture and inside the state, demand a return to the capitalist work ethic, an end to state interference within the private economic sector and the reestablishment of state and local governmental hegemony over the Washington bureaucracy. None of these political principles make much sense any longer in the aftermath of the Great Depression. The Right within the U.S. political system, which has become a coalition of businessmen, corporate leaders, and many working class whites, draws its emotional appeal from a psychological desire for social simplicity and political conformity. Even though the material conditions as well as the political climate have changed tremendously during the past forty years, the illusion that somehow the national debt can be erased and that states' rights can return again still commands the support of millions of frightened white voters.

The liberals have their own peculiar illusions which are just as anachronistic as those of the conservatives. The righteous advocates of liberal reform cry out for corrective actions from the federal regulatory agencies—the Securities and Exchange Commission, Federal Communications Commission, Food and Drug Administration and a host of other bureaucracies. The newest demand by the liberals, in the post Watergate years, is a longing for honesty in government. They reason that certain numbers of blacks, Chicanos and poor people must be elevated to positions of nominal influence with the government and on corporate boards of directories in order to "humanize" the processes of the modern state. Percentage increases in the numbers of these historically oppressed groups within the federal bureaucracy and in business are viewed as progress and a fundamentally positive achievement.

What undermines this approach toward politics is, first, the general attack of rightist politicians and corporations like Sears against affirmative action, and second, the powerful opposition of traditionally liberal constituencies against the expansion of the public sector on behalf of minority group interests. The multitude of "Proposition Thirteens" enacted by many of the states and the Supreme Court's *Bakke* decision in 1978 are indications that a majority of white people in the U.S. oppose any additional legislation which will promote the rapid economic advancement of black folks. Certainly the bulk of the white middle class, and its ideological interpreters in both the state and civil society, have expressed an unwillingness to tax themselves simply to provide jobs and welfare for blacks, browns, and the unemployed.

The great illusion of liberal reform within capitalist society embodies a central contradiction; the excesses and oppressive character of the economic system is essential to the maintenance of the system itself. No one can advocate full employment within the framework of capitalism because the system maintains itself only with a certain level of unemployment. The liberal reformers are forced to resort to rhetorical games to mask the inadequacies of their economic analysis. Thus, "full employment" is defined as a level of four percent unemployment within the recent Humphrey-Hawkins bill.

The central illusion of most prominent U.S. socialists, especially non-Marxist intellectual/reformers, is that the process of nationalization and centralized government is fundamentally progressive. Moderate socialists advocate increased federal spending for welfare programs, health care programs, education and other spheres of cultural and social life. All of this centralized planning, even as it occurs under the most enlightened white socialist, is still taking place within the limits of a capitalist state, in which the basic organization of production is private enterprise. Increased federal money into the black community has not ended unemployment, but is has developed a quasi-neocolonial, black professional strata of job seekers and hustlers, perpetuating the New Deal myth that the federal government and the existing system can solve all our problems (if only more Democrats are elected). The social democrats' faith in the omnipotence of the welfare state is pathetically revealed when black Congressmen and Civil Rights leaders run to the White House whenever high black unemployment figures are released. As long as a capitalist economy exists and labor is organized around the concepts of exploitation and racism, black unemployment will remain twice the national average.

The most pervasive myth which burdens the prospects for radical, leftist social change, ironically, is the illusion of revolution. Less than a decade ago, George Jackson projected the blueprint for the coming revolution:

> We must accept the eventuality of bringing the U.S.A. to its knees; accept the closing off of critical sections of the city with barbed wire, armored pig carriers crisscrossing the streets, soldiers everywhere, tommyguns pointed at stomach level, smoke curling black against the daylight sky, the smell of cordite, house-to-house searches, doors being kicked in, the commonness of death.

There are at least three problems with this scenario for revolution. First, in practical terms, a minority revolutionary uprising involving the use of weapons would be tantamount to suicide within this country. Only a tiny fraction of the white working class would be prepared to participate in a violent class confrontation-to-the-death with their bosses and the police. A minority of Afro-Americans and Hispanics are politically open to the use of force or violence to obtain political objectives, but the vast majority of both populations are not and will not be for the foreseeable future.

Second, the historical precedents for change within the framework of U.S. civil and political society have established a tradition of concensus rather than fundamental confrontation. The U.S. working class participates in electoral politics through the Democratic Party, a coalition of diverse interests which is dominated by a section of the capitalist class. There is neither a "labor party" nor a "black party" through which dissent and political unrest can be channelled effectively. The illusion of "democratic choice" of a public office holder is maintained despite the fact that a minority of eligible voters do the choosing, and that the selection is almost always confined to a fairly narrow political spectrum. The U.S. left is outmaneuvered and outnumbered by the powerful right tendency within both capitalist parties. If tommy guns were pointed at stomach level within the black community, it is more than likely that the reactionaries would be doing the pointing, and black folks would be dying.

Third, the image of revolutionary change as a military maneuver obscures the more decisive and problematic question of the process of transformation within the totality of all cultural, economic and social relations. Struggle in one area of human relations, such as the continual battle of labor for higher wages vs. the owner's battle for even more surplus value, inevitably effects all other human activity and concerns. To place the role of the gun at the head of revolution is to minimize the role of competing human questions as being irrelevant to the achievement of socialism. As a result, many older leftists still subscribe to the base/superstructure model of social development, arguing that economics or struggles within the base are always decisive. Many younger leftists, influenced by Regis Debray and Frantz Fanon, argue that the pivotal aspect of revolutionary transformation is the development of an armed elite, a vanguard prepared to die for the cause. In both instances, it is neither clear nor probable that the use of weaponry or the forces of economics are *always* decisive within the evolution of new human possibilities.

The social transformation of any peoples' societies is a gradual culmination of material and ideological conditions building toward a new form of social reality. The violent phase of the American Revolution between 1775 and 1783 was merely the final stage of a profound cultural, economic and political struggle between white colonists and England, which began soon after the founding of the first permanent settlements. When black representatives of the Democratic Party, the Republican Party or some civil societal organization deplore the ultimate goal of complete social revolution, they usually do so to reinforce their basic strategy of gradual reforms within the state. Neither cultural integration within the existing system nor the advocacy of an immediate, violent confrontation between a handful of so-called revolutionaries and the police will create the conditions essential for the liberation of black people.

Black people in the U.S. are, therefore, faced with a monumental task: to struggle against white racism and economic exploitation and in the process, begin the transformation of the entire state and civil society of the present day U.S. There are no preconceived theories that have evolved from the Soviet Union, China or any other country which are directly applicable to our situation. Indeed, both the Soviet Union and China provide examples of the serious contradictions and problems involved in the process of social transformation. Neither Amilcar Cabral nor Frantz Fanon, two black intellectuals who had only brief opportunities to observe racial relations within the United States, equated the complex problem of uprooting racism in the U.S. with the struggle to overthrow colonialism and neocolonialism in Africa. Complicating our struggle is the central factor of white racism. History has provided ample evidence that whites in the U.S. are unable or unwilling to struggle against their deep-seated racism. The black elite defends the illusion of racial integration without directly combatting white racism. Both political parties of capitalist U.S.A. reinforce racism and perpetuate bankrupt remedies for unemployment and poverty. The state is bloated from its own fiscal waste and unplanned economic development, and white bourgeois culture is an empty wasteland of sexual exploitation and banality. Black people, in our generation, must find practical alternatives to these immense social and economic contradictions. If we fail, we must inevitably face the possibility of the complete disintegration of black people as a group, along with the destruction of the total fabric of U.S. society.

Toward a New Common Sense

It is in the nature of all human beings who live within any society to make choices. Such choices usually appear to be determined by the individual, one decision at a time, on rational or irrational grounds. But these choices, when considered within the framework of all human creativity and productivity, are usually made within a common consciousness or sensibility shared by other people within one's immediate class or social group. This consciousness, which is conditioned by a people's material needs and the general pattern of human productive activity, is the basis for any group's understanding of its own history. Such consciousness is often called "mother wit" in the blackbelt South and by my own grandmother. Elsewhere it is known as common sense. Common sense is that popular philosophy or folk consensus of what is right or wrong in the world, moral or immoral, aesthetically pleasing or ugly, possible or impossible. It expresses the final product of specific, collective historical decisions and the forces of material production and their impact upon humanity within a given period of time.

Within contemporary U.S. society, the dominant common sense of the majority of people is directly related to the existence of the capitalist mode of production. Common sense within the modern capitalist state is largely dictated by the internal dynamic for survival and legitimacy of the institutions of government. The process for creating consciousness and common sense is constantly directed and managed by the many agencies of the civil society—by intellectuals, the media, educational and religious institutions, civic clubs, artistic and entertainment industries.

At an unconscious level, individual members of the bourgeoisie do not always determine the contours of the popular mind at a particular given moment in history. But over a broad period of time, the ruling class through its dominant position within the marketplace and the state usually determines the set of human possibilities which ultimately constitute the parameters of popular consciousness.

When an individual states, "You cannot fight city hall," he or she expresses, first of all, an individual judgment, and second, the consensus of those within the dominant particular class and/or caste which has matured within the context of capitalist society and the state. To "fight city hall" is like doubting the law of gravity; in other words, the decisions of the political elite are constructed in such ways that single individuals or groups of individuals do not believe for a single instant that they will be successful in challenging the political decision-making process. Politics is therefore left to the politicians of the capitalist parties. And the decision not to fight a controversial political question is viewed as common sense.

Common sense presupposes a detailed world order, a sense of relationships and a certain material reality which has been reproduced so long that it seems to acquire a supernatural connotation, as if sanctioned by God. During the antebellum slavery period in the South, slavery was commonly held by virtually the entire white population to be a "positive good." It was a system of economic and social relations between the races that was supposedly profitable all the way around. Only one in four Southern whites owned slaves, but the vast majority of nonslaveholders concurred with their plantation owning brothers and marched off to die for the right to hold blacks in perpetual bondage. The notion that enslavement was in itself somewhat immoral did not become popular among the majority of Southern whites until the early twentieth century. This was because the material foundations for popular common sense shifted from an agrarian economic base dependent upon slave labor exploitation to a capitalist economic system rooted in share-cropping and wage labor. The economic transformation of the South's marketplace allowed for the development of new ideas within white civil society, which in turn promoted the ethos of Jim Crow and modern white racism throughout the breadth of the region's culture—in churches, schools, theatres, fraternal organizations, libraries and so forth. This transformation could not have occurred before 1865, because slavery had become completely identified with the white South's common sense and notion of reality. A defense of slavery among white racists was like a defense for the roundness of the earth.

The common sense of Afro-Americans has been pre-conditioned by two historical realities: the factor of white racial hegemony and the factor of economic exploitation. Within the sphere of production, black labor is the most exploited sector of the working class. Within civil society, white racism afflicts the entire set of social relations between blacks and whites. The choices which black people make concerning their work and social behavior are constantly conditioned by these omnipresent factors. Their consciousness, or their "mother wit," is an expression of their material existence and constant social struggle within the realm of ideology and culture. The mind of black America, and the inner logic of its civil society, establishes the parameters of its productive activity. Consciousness and blacks' material existence stand in a reciprocal relationship with each other.

The civil society of Afro-Americans has expressed two warring tendencies which in turn influence black consciousness: a desire for integration within the dominant white culture and a contradictory impetus towards an autonomous Afro-American culture. The contours of black history have been etched permanently by this divided racial consciousness, a strong identification with the values of the white majority vs. an equally strong rejection and revulsion of white America's political institutions, economic system and culture. Ontologically, blacks in the United States have been both a part of the dominant culture and always simultaneously outside of it; a member of the household but never allowed to be a member of the family.

The best expression of this duality is found in W.E.B. Dubois' *Of Our Spiritual Strivings*. "The history of the American Negro is the history of this strife—this longing to attain self-conscious manhood, to merge his double self into a better and truer self," Dubois observed critically. "One ever feels his twoness—an American, a Negro; two souls, two thoughts, two unreconciled strivings; two warring ideals in one dark body whose dogged strength alone keeps it from being torn asunder." Within the veil there have been blacks who have made their respective individual peace within the white world at the expense of their own heritage and historical traditions. On the other hand, many nationalists assume that because our blackness is of prime importance that the negative aspects and oppressive impact of white culture upon black consciousness can be ignored. In either case the groundings for unified black common sense have always been a merger of both the integrationist and nationalist traditions, with strong historical emphasis upon the autonomous racial and nationalist tendencies.

In the pursuit of an ideological consensus, a new black common sense of liberation, it is crucial that the positive elements of integration be merged with the activist tradition of black nationalism. The quest for desegregation carries both positive and negative characteristics—a desire for equal political rights, a demand for human respect and dignity, a willingness to be jailed for these rights and demands, as well as an impulse to deny the continuing African heritage of black people. Some separatists have been too quick to opt for emigration to Africa as a panacea for the racial domestic crisis in the United States, and have become like many sectarian Marxists more unrealistic with the passage of time. On the other hand, integrationists have always underestimated the meaning of race within political and economic formations, and often issue political demands for desegregation which the majority of black people neither want nor will accept. There is no guarantee through a simple reorganization of a capitalist United States toward socialism that racism will be destroyed; indeed, there is every indication that racism as an historical idea is even more powerful than the material institutions that gave it life. What is important for a grassroots analysis is that the traditions of both integration and black nationalism speak to important aspects of the experience and consciousness of black people within the United States and that both have something to offer each other. We must begin building our political agendas upon a comprehensive understanding of our historical and ideological experiences, both nationalist and integrationist. Black nationalists should not hesitate to applaud the legacy of Civil Rights struggles simply because these previous efforts were integrationist oriented.

Building a new black common sense means, in part, a break with our own illusions about strategies for black material and cultural advancement. The opportunity for constructing a Blackbelt nation no longer exists in the United States. An independent league of black-dominated cities or a section of the Deep South would simply replicate the *apartheid* system of bantustans in this country, which definitely would be a step backward. As Part III of *From the Grassroots* argues, the Southern political economy is dominated by a handful of wealthy and powerful white men, a ruling elite which also maintains control over the region's churches, colleges and university systems, entertainment and amusement industries. Individual black people will undoubtedly return to the Motherland, but our people as a whole are destined to remain in America. It is sufficient to state that any model for socialism within Black America will not succeed without taking into account the successful and unsuccessful models for political and economic transformation throughout the entire Black diaspora. However, our struggle for human integrity, for the destruction of white racism, for economic self sufficiency and control over our own communities is inextricably connected with the struggles of other U.S. ethnic groups and oppressed economic classes. The final strategy for liberation must be found here, not through the vicarious experiences of another people. Black nationalists who imitate African socialists at the exclusion of historical and cultural elements that make our own history unique are repeating the same error of some Communists and ultraleftists who imagine that New York and Washington are identical to Petrograd and Moscow of 1917. Each revolution, like each human being, is original and unique.

PART ONE: BLACK POLITICS IN CAPITALIST AMERICA

PROLOGUE TO PART I

Any Negro who registers as a Democrat
or a Republican is a traitor to his own people.

Malcolm X

By Any Means Necessary
New York, 1970

We begin our discussion of Afro-American politics by admitting the obvious: despite major advances in the number of black elected and appointed officials in federal, state, and local government, the historical period between 1970 to 1980 amounted to a political Reaction against black people as a group. Beyond the illusion of mounting electoral successes festers the contradiction of growing black unemployment, a deepened black distrust of all politics, electoral and non-electoral, and a relative loss of group economic power. The gap between black political rhetoric and the real lack of black political self-determination creates cynicism and anger among the black poor, the working class and the oppressed.

Part of our dilemma began with a series of political assumptions which were retained by most black activists, elected officials, community organizers and radicalized black intellectuals. First, most blacks approached the question of political power from the identical perspective of whites in the United States-namely, that real power was within the electoral process. Winning a seat in Congress or in the county government would mean a greater share of influence for blacks as a group within the system. Some veterans of S.N.C.C. were politically astute enough to understand the limitations of electoral politics. These forces usually described their electoral efforts as a "holding action," a temporary or transitional maneuver toward the final goal of black community control in both the public and private sectors. The overwhelming majority of blacks running for offices, however, had played little or no role of leadership in either the Civil Rights or Black Power Movements whatsoever. They gave the appropriate "lip service" to the rhetoric of black group empowerment, but viewed the pursuit of electoral "plums" almost solely in narrow, individualistic terms.

Second, most black politicians were not theoretically inclined. Even the most experienced black member of Congress would have a difficult time trying to define the "state," for example. Thus, when blacks began to compete for electoral positions, they had no independent theory of state behavior based upon the historical relationship between black people and the U.S. state. Usually black activists assumed the neutrality of the state apparatus vis a vis black folks. Their line of reasoning followed from the belief that the lack of black people within leadership positions in the police force, or within municipal government, was what made the police and local politicians racists in their approaches toward the black community. As more blacks were elected to governmental positions, many black folks were surprised to discover that almost none of the basic problems within their cities or neighborhoods were addressed. Having a greater number of black policemen did not provide a guarantee against police brutality and frequent violation of civil rights. Racism within the state did not greatly diminish as more blacks won places within the government.

The number of blacks within the A.F.L.-C.I.O. and other unions had grown sharply during the period after the Great Depression. In almost every opinion poll, black workers say that they view participation within unions more favorably than do almost every other section of the U.S. working class. Through the League of Revolutionary Black Workers, a new militancy spread throughout the ranks of young blacks employed in industry. Black Power and its internalization by the masses forced the traditional labor leaders to increase the number of blacks in positions of responsibility within the unions. Subsequently, as more blacks rose to prominence, the militant activism among certain sectors of black labor declined. As in electoral politics, white leaders had made a tactical retreat before their black critics, giving up certain positions to mostly moderate blacks without fundamentally challenging the racism and political elitism within the unions.

In each instance, black political activism was confined to the Democratic Party or to traditional institutions which perpetuated the racial and economic status quo. By viewing political work as work within the government, and by thinking of politics as electoral office holding, black militants became reformist in outlook, and conservative in their practice. Ironically, many orthodox Marxist political formations contributed to this theoretically backward behavior by defining "revolutionary activity" as seizing power within the state apparatus. Both the leftists and moderates within the black community had little appreciation for the interrelationship between economics and politics, and the crucial role of culture and popular consciousness within both.

These essays in part one cover four specific issues and personalities: the evolution of black political activism on the national level during the 1970s; the attempt to create an independent black political formation, the National Black Political Assembly; an assessment of the activities and social thought of Martin Luther King, Jr.; and a critique of the leading black socialist and trade union figure in Afro-American history, A. Philip Randolph. No attempt is made to cast any individuals, especially the post-Black Power black leadership, in an unduly negative light. The majority of black men and women who compete for political leadership positions usually within the Democratic Party are neither stupid, nor corrupt, nor fundamentally reactionary. Their failure is, more than anything else, a lack of a coherent theoretical understanding of our social history and the role of racism as a central theme in the development of the U.S. state and economy. We can no longer assume, as most black leaders think, that political power is directly transferable from electoral participation and office holding. A narrow analysis of politics is one which condemns black people to yet another generation of wandering in the wilderness of oppression.

Anatomy of Black Politics from 1970

Introduction

Historians will record that November 2, 1976 was an important date in the history of Afro-American politics. James Carter, a Southern peanut farmer and one term Governor from Georgia, was elected President of the United States by a margin of less than two million popular votes over his Republican opponent, President Gerald R. Ford. Despite early predictions from political analysts that the election would "hardly be a contest," the electoral vote was quite close, 297 to 241 votes. In at least thirteen states, including Ohio, New York, Pennsylvania, Alabama and Texas, the black vote proved to be the most decisive factor in providing Carter's margin of victory. In Mississippi for example, Carter received 147,540 votes from blacks, enough support to create a slim statewide majority of 11,537 votes over Ford. The largest number of black voters in history came to the polls. Had the black vote been excluded or as divided as the white electorate, Carter would have been soundly defeated. The political message was clear: Jimmy Carter became president largely on the votes of the most oppressed sector of the U.S. population. Black elected officials, intellectuals and religious leaders had convinced blacks the Carter's election was essential for their salvation.

This essay was written during the autumn months of 1977. A version of this article was given at the Militant Labor Forum in West Atlanta, September, 1977. "An Anatomy of Black Politics" was published in the Summer, 1978, issue of the *Review of Black Political Economy.*

25

Most black leaders had not anticipated that Carter would receive the Democratic Party's nomination for president, and were the last part of the old Franklin D. Roosevelt coalition to fully accept him. Many were suspicious of his record as governor of Georgia and his reluctance to commit himself to a political platform throughout the state primaries. After August, black Democratic leaders began to promote the Carter candidacy. Early supporter Andrew Young spoke of Carter in glowing tones, insisting that he "is a product of the Southern church and knows the language and culture of the black community." Atlanta's black Congressman conceded that his man had none of the graces that "came from Ivy League colleges and liberal arts education. But his heart is right, his instincts are sound and his training is very practical."[1] Former civil rights activists such as Martin Luther King, Sr., black mayors and religious leaders, realizing gradually that the Carter-Ford election would be close, stepped up their efforts. Many black leaders organized Operation Big Vote, a national effort to register black voters. In Buffalo, New York, black disc jockeys hosted dance parties to register young voters. Thousands of Baltimore blacks were registered in shopping centers and at factory gates. In Chicago's South Side, hundreds of hungry blacks registered in MacDonalds' "restaurants." Five thousand Houston blacks registered while attending an event at the Astrodome."[2]

On television and radio commercials, blacks were reminded repeatedly that their votes would be crucial in determining the outcome of the election. Black newspapers reminded blacks that Richard Nixon had received 94 percent of the Republican vote, 66 percent of the votes from independents and 42 percent of all traditionally Democratic voters. In all, the Nixon-Agnew ticket received almost 70 percent of white America's vote. In the aftermath of Watergate and Vietnam, fifteen percent black unemployment and welfare cutbacks, blacks could no longer tolerate another Republican administration in Washington. "Black Democratic leaders turned right around and sold Carter to their followers with the zeal of late converts," *The New Republican* observed one year later. "Here, they said, is not just your ordinary, run-of-the-mill Democratic liberal; here is a man who grew up poor amidst poverty, who was raised side-by-side with blacks, who understands black culture and aspirations." The descendant of slave holders was carefully packaged for black voter consumption—and about 93 percent of all black voters bought the merchandise.[4]

Black voters also provided the margin of victory in at least eleven important Congressional races. In Lousiana, Democrats Richard Tonry and Jerry Huckaby were narrowly elected to Congress over conservative Republicans, largely with black support. South Carolina blacks provided the winning margin for Congressmen Kenneth Holland and John Jenrette. In the Senate, black votes amounted to more than the candidate's margin of victory in three races in Ohio, Tennessee and Michigan. In Missouri, blacks cast 119,956 votes for Democratic underdog Joseph Teasdale, providing him with a 12,209 vote margin over the incumbent Republican Governor, Christopher Bond. Black support for all Democratic candidates seldom fell below eighty percent.[5]

A second reason for the importance of November 2, 1976 was the nearly unanimous vote of confidence the black public voiced in their elected federal officials. Four of the seventeen members of the Congressional black caucus received over 90 percent of the vote in their district races. Twelve of the black representatives garnered over 80 percent majorities. Only four Congressmen, Ronald V. Dellums (Berkeley), Andrew Young, William Clay (St. Louis) and Harold Ford (Memphis) were seriously challenged, but none of their opponents received more than 39 percent of the district's vote. Black elected officials, black labor union officials, civil rights workers and community leaders had registered 9.5 million blacks: an increase of one million above 1972. 64 percent of all registered blacks went to the polls compared to 58 percent only four years before.[6]

Perhaps most importantly, the alternative of black Republicanism, which had quietly gained respectability within black suburbs and within the black business community in recent years, suffered a major defeat. The percentage of blacks who consistently identified themselves with the interests of the Republican Party increased from a low 2 to 3 percent in 1968 to roughly 8 to 11 percent in 1972. Large numbers of black petty bourgeois who had been attracted to Nixon's version of "black capitalism" in the early seventies and who had been turned off by the rhetoric of black revolutionaries in the sixties pulled the voting booth levers for Jimmy Carter. Those few black Republican leaders who publicly assessed the 1976 campaign were disillusioned about their party's prospective chances to gain black supporters. Robert Keyes, a black organizer for President Ford's California campaign, complained in the *Sacramento Observer* that Ford "ran a traditional white-oriented campaign, with virtually no minority or female input." Republicans feared "that any overt actions or appeals by President Ford to the blacks would stop the trend of Southern white rednecks and right wingers who were allegedly coming on the Ford bandwagon . . ."[8] William Walker, an influential black newspaper editor and Republican, suggested that the Republican party had ceased to be a viable political organization for blacks. "Gerald Ford's defeat," he wrote, "can be directly attributed to not getting any support from Negroes."[9] The net effect of the election was the crippling of the black renaissance within Republican politics. The massive public mandate seemingly guaranteed black elected officials that they would face no real opposition from black Republican opponents in the future.

Dozens of articles appeared in numerous black newspapers and journals, predicting that the Carter administration would appoint many blacks to positions of authority within the federal bureaucracy. Typical of most remarks were the comments of Eddie N. Williams, President of the Joint Center for Political Studies. Williams argued that since blacks had "played a major role" in electing Carter, it was now reasonable to assume that the new President would swiftly "make blacks full partners in the nation's policy making franchise. If Jimmy Carter wants to show Black America that he is aware of the role they played in his election and of their high expectations," Williams suggested, "he could start by integrating" all influential positions within the governmental "apparatus."[10] Black politicians, journalists and intellectuals were sure that Carter would gradually proceed with the desegregation of the state. "Black Americans, like all other citizens, have a non-negotiable right to participate in government at all levels," J.K. Obatala argued in *The Nation*. The new President had "a moral obligation to do whatever is necessary to protect everyone's right to earn a living.... The right to work is not politically negotiable." The Democratic Party and Carter were expected to "develop people who can go out into the marketplace and fend for themselves."[11]

Few black intellectuals, politicans and civil rights leaders fully realized that Carter would not, nor had any intention, of initiating a second New Deal for the ghetto, or at least revive the concept of full employment within the HumphreyHawkins bill. Robert S. Browne, publisher of *The Review of Black Political Economy,* warned that "the gravest danger in President-elect Carter's victory is that too much will be expected of the new Administration, with the inevitable disappoinment which will set in when he fails to work miracles." Browne added that the Carter administration might impose "a flurry of new 'programs' upon our existing economic structure, but the results fall short of what is desired."[12] Carter appointed relatively few blacks to major administrative positions, and for several months remained silent about the creation of federal jobs for minorities. Yet black Democrats remained hopeful— Andrew Young was appointed Ambassador to the United Nations. Throughout the winter and early months of spring they decided to wait for the President to act.

By May 1977, the Carter administration announced an end to "new programs" for social welfare and education in an attempt to balance the federal budget by 1981. With the approval of Arthur Burns, Federal Reserve Board chairman, Carter announced that his new priorities were to cut inflation and to stimulate the business sector. Bert Lance, head of the Office of Management and Budget, and chief economist Charles Schultze criticized liberal Democratic economic proposals which emphasized the creation of public jobs for the chronically unemployed. Although Carter had campaigned the previous autumn that he would cut the defense department budget by 5 to 7 billion dollars, defense spending increased to 111.8 billion dollars. In June and July many liberal Democrats raised sharp criticisms from the left of the Carter Presidency. Senator George McGovern declared that "the corporations have cried the wolf of 'business confidence' and the administration has run scared." The *New Republic,* which had announced itself to be "Cautiously For Carter" on election eve, criticized Carter's foreign policies and attacked his "moral" opposition to the use of Medicaid funds for abortions.[13] Liberal intellectuals like Arthur Schlesinger, Jr., Barry Commoner and Michael Harrington joined the growing chorus of trade unionist and progressive oppositon to Carter's entire domestic policies. Gradually, black leaders like Urban League's Vernon Jordan voiced cautious criticisms of Carter.

One year after Carter's electoral victory, the political and economic climate within the black community was the worst since the severe recession of the late fifties. Official unemployment figures for blacks ranged from 14.5 percent for men to 40.4 percent for teenagers. Unofficial unemployment figures of the Urban

League were considerably higher-up to 25 percent of black men, 45 percent for youths. Thousands of blacks in virtually every major industrial city in the Northeast were waiting in line for jobs. The so-called economic "recovery" of 1976-1978 never reached the ghetto. Black middle class voters who had anticipated a flood of social legislation similar to Lyndon Johnson's Great Society were disgusted with Carter's budget balancing and the small number of federal appointments made available to them. In late summer, 1977, fifteen black leaders summitted at the Urban League headquarters in New York City to propose a counter political strategy to meet the steadily deteriorating conditions of the black urban poor and working classes. Many of the black leaders who attended the conference—Parren Mitchell, Bayard Rustin, Benjamin Hooks and Jesse Jackson—had been major supporters of Carter only months before. Declaring that they had been betrayed, Jackson charged Carter with "callous neglect." Gary, Indiana mayor Richard Hatcher explained, "Now it's difficult for any black leader who pushed the election of Jimmy Carter to face the people he campaigned with."[14]

What went wrong? Neither Carter nor the Democratic Party can be accused of "betraying" the interests of blacks and the poor, since they never committed themselves to the transformation of the U.S. political economy which is essential in destroying the inequities which black leaders complain about so vociferously. While the black petty bourgeoisie and the leaders of black civil society almost unanimously believe that the Democratic Party can solve the continuing problems of black people in the United States, the majority of blacks either do not vote or do not support the Democratic Party at all.[15] Black leaders failed to understand that "there is no bargaining leverage in a situation where a black vote for the Democratic Party is *expected* and *delivered*," wrote political scientist Ronald Walters. "Further, and more importantly, there is no structure through which commitments may be obtained if leverage cannot be exercised...."[16] Black Democrats had sparked false expectations of prosperity within their own constituencies after Carter's election, and were now attempting to divorce themselves from their own campaign slogans and promises of twelve months before.

As black civil rights leaders and politicians' criticisms of the Carter administration become increasingly bitter, it becomes necessary to separate the political rhetoric from political reality. A critique of black politics and the class formations in which black people occupy relative to the entire U.S. political economy explain the origins of the current black political crisis. The failure of black politicians and most intellectuals to clearly understand their tenuous relationship with the capitalist state and the rapidly developing class conflicts between the black elite and black working class and poor people is at the heart of this crisis.

Growth of a Black Middle Strata

One principle contradiction within black society is between the politically advanced but economically oppressed black majority, and the politically backward, economically privileged black elite. The black petty bourgeoisie, represented in business and financial institutions, the churches and colleges in the media and fraternal organizations, express tendencies toward political accommodation and individual advancement within the government. The black elite influence the politics of millions of less affluent, less educated blacks to vote for the Democratic Party against their best, long run interests.

The base of the conservativism within black electoral politics is the newly emerged black middle class. According to U.S. Bureau of the Census statistics, between 1969 to 1973 the income of black families in which both the husband and wife worked and the husband was under 35 years of age rose from 84 percent to 92 percent of the median white family income. In 1969, black families (using the above criteria) earned $8,423 per year, compared $9,926 for whites. Four years later, these black families were earning $11,873, compared to $12,962 per year for whites. Outside of the Southern states, black and white family incomes in which both partners work and where the husband is under 35 years of age are roughly equal. In 1970 these black families earned a median income of $11,045 per year, slightly more than the median white family income of $10,578 per year. Even during the recession year 1973, black family incomes in the North and West amounted to $13,235 per year, compared to $13,332 for whites. Political economist Alfred E. Osborne suggests that it is no longer possible to employ the standard black/white income ratio in many comparison cases, because it fails to measure the important income distinctions within the black community.[17]

A review of census statistics reveals not a general elevation of black income levels during the seventies, but a polarization of many blacks at extremely low income levels and the development of an affluent upper income strata. In 1971, for example, the median family income for blacks was only $6,440. Almost forty percent of all black families earned less than $5,000 per year, yet 10.6 percent of all black families earned $15,000 or more per year. Black families in which both the husband and wife worked and the husband was under 35 years of age accounted for about 16 percent of all black husband/wife families and only 10 percent of all black families. These young affluent families, plus the well established black doctors, lawyers, ministers, businessmen, educators and others, constitute at least 15 percent of the total black population.[18] This economically privileged group of blacks have been the recipients of new business and professional positions, due to affirmative action, political pressures from government and civil rights groups. Thousands of blacks attend formerly segregated graduate and medical schools; thousands more were hired into middle management positions by corporations and large foundations. The pursuit of class collaborationist politics by this new petty bourgeois strata has, during the past decade, paid economic dividends.

The single most influential element within this new black petty bourgeoisie is the black entrepreneur. Although there are fewer than 230,000 black businesses in the United States, black businessmen have always wielded significantly more political power and economic influence than their numbers would indicate. Thousands of black grocery store owners, gasoline station proprietors, bankers, black insurance executives and record company distributors have for generations advocated "a segregated economic system" controlled by black businessmen, "which exists along side of or within the larger United States capitalist system." Historian Arthur Tolson observed recently that once Richard Nixon became President, many "black Americans clamored for a realistic application of black capitalism." Tolson noted that large numbers of blacks "have been and are still trying to get into the mainstream of the. . . . capitalist system."[19] Several black intellectuals, notably Theodore Cross in *Black Capitalism*, preached that black Americans should buy stock in corporations, purchase property in ghetto areas, open black banks and assume a more active role within the expansion of private enterprise in black communities. Simultaneously, black politicians like the former head of C.O.R.E. and black power advocate, Floyd McKissick, argued that both private foundations and major corporations could play a vital role in the creation of a black business sector, inside the traditional capitalist system. McKissick, Roy Innis of C.O.R.E. and other black power leaders advocated that "existing white-controlled economic enterprises be transferred to black ownership," while maintaining the concept of private enterpise.[20]

Within the marginal confines of black business, black economic institutions have grown substantially since 1969. The number of all black firms rose from 163,073 in 1969 to 194,986 in 1972. Black-owned businesses recorded gross receipts amounting $4.5 billion in 1969; three years later, total gross receipts were $7.2 billion. Overall, however, black gross receipts accounted for less than 0.29 percent of the national total.[21] During 1974, black businesses increased sales by a scant one percent over 1973, while the top *Fortune 500* industrial corporations reported gains averaging 25 percent in the same period. Motown Industries ($45 million), Johnson Publishing Company ($34 million) and Johnson Products ($33 million), the three leading black controlled corporations for 1974, generated $112 million in sales-in contrast to Exxon corporation, the leading white controlled corporation, which earned $42 *billion* in sales during the same period.[22] Despite the minimal growth of black owned businesses in relation to the total economy, the illusion of the viability of black capitalism is promoted through the media, cultural propaganda and even by the small black entrepreneurs themselves.

Unlike the white petty bourgeoisie, the black middle class has never maintained a substantial economic base. Because black capitalism has consistently failed to produce any surplus capital, black political, business and civic leaders place great emphasis upon obtaining federal subsidies and private foundation grants as a means of providing the base for cultural and political activities. At virtually every black college, medical and graduate school, the highest educational priority is placed on "grantsmanship," the writing of proposals for outside money. Black fraternities and sororities play an important economic as well as cultural role within the life of black communities by raising money for social activities. Fraternal organizations have rebounded from near obscurity during the sixties to provide the political and economic leadership on many campuses and college communities. Almost every significant structure of black middle class civil society—the churches, cultural centers, colleges and community welfare groups—have become partially or completely dependent upon the government or private foundations for a portion of its fiscal support. Increasingly these groups have come to view "desegregation" as greater economic dependence upon the state, and the creation of more job opportunities within the government bureaucracy and economic institutions.

The black petty bourgeoisie generally reject the cultural images of the traditional South and the blues for images which reflect its upwardly mobile aspiration to merge within white civil society. The black petty bourgeois demand for a "respectable" black presence in the media is a logical outgrowth of their rejection of traditional black culture. In increasing numbers the black petty bourgeois is cast in situation comedies, or reads the six o'clock news, or is illustrated in commercials. The standard Negro middle class magazine, *Ebony*, and dozens of conservative, black-owned and operated local news weeklies across the country, set the assimilationist aesthetic standards of black America.[23]

The hegemonic political influence of the black petty bourgeois strata over black working class and poor people is perhaps best translated in the continued control of the Democratic Party of the black community. Roughly 80 percent of all people in the United States, black and white, who earn in excess of $10,000 or more per year vote in the Presidential elections. People who have attended college or who have at least a college degree also participate in Presidential elections at a rate of 80 percent. Only 47 percent of all eligible U.S. voters with an eighth grade education or less voted in 1972, and only 37 percent of all people who earn under $3,000 yearly go to the polls. Since the percentage of blacks beneath the poverty level or who do not finish high school is greater than the percentage of whites in the same category, the black voter profile has a greater bias towards upper income groups than does the white voter profile. One could argue that the typical Northern, black businessman, accountant or college professor has at least twice the voting power or electoral political influence as does a Southern, black welfare mother, since statistically the former would be far more likely to vote consistently. This means that the average black politician will be far more responsive to the interests of a group of black lawyers, ministers or technicians than a group of unemployed workers or factory laborers, even though the later would outnumber the former group by far within any black community. Black Congressmen are more sensitive to the stated class interests of the black petty bourgeoisie; therefore, while they rhetorically criticize the Carter administration's lack of concern for the poor, they collaborate with the state for political concessions which generally affect a minority of affluent blacks.

Despite the development of a black middle class strata, the realities of black life are more desperate than ever before in recent history. While the black income ratio for working, two parent families rose steadily and even surpassed white, two parent working families, the real gap between all blacks and all whites has increased. In 1971, median white family income was $10,672, compared to $6,440 for blacks, a gap of $4,232. By 1974 white families were earning a median income of $13,356, blacks were making only $7,808, a gap of $5,548. The median black family continues to earn only 58 percent of the amount earned by a similar white family.[25] The rapid inflation rate has made the old theoretical concept of "poverty" as based on a level of income obsolete.[26] When measured by all social and economic criteria, there are today more blacks in poverty, or permanently unemployed, or who are working part-time involuntarily than in any time in recent U.S. history.[27]

Class exploitation is experienced particularly by black women. There has been a tremendous increase in the number of black households headed by females—from 18 percent in 1950 to almost 33 percent in 1975. Two-thirds of all black poor families are headed by women.[28] In May 1975, black women received an average weekly income that was 75 percent of what black men earned and only 58 percent of what white men received. The unemployment rate for black teenage women was almost 40 percent several years ago, and has risen since then.[29] About 60 percent of all families receiving food stamps are headed by women, and 55 percent of the current food stamp recipients fall well below the official poverty level. Many black women who are eligible for food stamps do not participate in these programs.[30]

The polarization of the black class structure reveals the political behavior of the black elected officials. The majority of blacks who have not benefited from increased salaries during the desegregation of certain businesses and state bureaucracies in the past ten years remain outside the state. They usually do not vote because of a realistic cynicism towards the existing political order; they do not identify with the existing black leadership; when they do vote, it is a case of "the lesser of two evils" rather than a principled commitment to the Democratic Party's liberal wing. The petty bourgeoisie, conversely, defend the gains of the civil rights movement by conscientiously voting for proponents of their class interests. By supporting the reformers within the Democratic Party, the black middle class increasingly identifies their own political interests within the state.

The Failure of Independent Black Leadership

Part of the crisis in black politics involves the breakdown in black leadership. Traditionally, the black church hierarchy provided black communities with effective political leaders who were, at least theoretically, capable of challenging the white establishment without fear of economic sanctions. The civil rights movement elevated ministers like Andrew Young, Ralph Abernathy, Hosea Williams, Jesse Jackson and Martin Luther King, Jr., to national prominence. The state's response to black spontaneous uprisings in the streets was the elevation of a segment of the more conservative, civil rights leadership into state and corporate positions. Many of these black lawyers, educators and businessmen saw the new openings within business and government as a path toward personal fiscal security and political advancement, as well as a method of "legitimizing" the gains of the desegregation movement. Many hundreds of black state legislators, sheriffs, county commissioners and small town mayors believed that through their elected positions they would be able to expand the Movement through increased social services for blacks. As popular struggles in the streets, the colleges and community centers gradually died down, black elected and appointed officials discovered that they occupied a managerial position within the state: they could pacify the black constituency through increased public services and create public jobs for blacks, but they could not challenge the historical direction of the political economy. They could not, as it were, demand the economic reorganization of the basic mode of production. As growing numbers of dissatisfied blacks at all income levels express disapproval of the Carter administration, the black "leaders" are discovering that they are unable to lead their "constituencies." Somewhat opportunistically, they are reduced to complaining about a system they cannot change (and are now an integral part of): they are forced rhetorically to condemn Carter, the candidate they campaigned for with such moral fervor only months before.

There were several social forces in the early sixties which could have posed an alternative challenge to the increasingly conservative black Democratic and business leadership. Black Southern farmers and rural landowners had for decades organized effective political institutions—from the Colored Farmers Alliance of the 1880s to militant black tenant farmer organizations which were oriented toward political confrontation with the state rather than class collaboration. Also, black ministers as a group have often been the most effective moral critics of the state and white civil society. But both groups, for different reasons, failed to develop as hegemonic political forces within black politics.

The expansion of capitalism into the South during the post-World War II period effectively destroyed the prospect of an agriculturally based, Southern black middle class. Blacks who had for generations owned large homesteads were forced off the land by corporations, and were forced to migrate north or to Southern cities like Atlanta, Charlotte, Memphis and Birmingham. Alabama provides an excellent example of the economic disfranchisement which occurred throughout the South. From 1954 to 1969 black farm owners declined in number from 18,408 to 7,226, a 60.7 percent decrease. From 1959 to 1969 the number of acres owned by black Alabamians declined by 50 percent, from 1,262,583 acres to 636,859 acres. In 1969, the average black-owned farm made gross profits of only $3,226; and only 5.8 percent of all acreage in the state was owned by blacks.[31]

The sudden transformation of the Southern economy from a predominately agricultural economy in the 1940s to a capitalist base today had important political consequences. Land owning blacks provided the major force for the rural civil rights movement in the sixties. Black farmers who were active in voter registration campaigns, are more likely to run for public office than non-landowning, rural blacks, and consistently provided a solid electoral base for independent black political parties (such as Lowndes

County Freedom Organization and the Mississippi Freedom Democratic Party). Blacks owned less than 6 million acres in 1974, and were losing land at an annual rate of 300,000 acres.[32] The destruction of a black agricultural base has, in turn, led to the demise of the political influence of rural, land owning blacks and to the proletarianization of Southern urban blacks. It also helped to promote the hegemony of predominately Northern, urban, middle class blacks over the general black electorate.

Hundreds of black ministers were selected for leadership positions within white churches during the sixties, as white religious liberals placated the black community through financial donations and moral support for civil rights legislation. Gradually, most of these ministers quietly resigned their roles as advocates for progressive change. Gilbert Caldwell, professor at New York Theological Seminary, observed that many of his black colleagues give "the impression that we are the 'exceptional men,' that we were chosen because we were 'different.' In the minds of some, we are the overt manifestation of the church's readiness to embrace all God's children."[33] The major white religious denominations have pulled small but influential numbers of black members and clergy during the past two decades, circumventing their own guilt on the political issue of desegregation.[34] As most of these churches invest tens of billions of dollars each year in major American corporations such as Exxon, Gulf Oil, General Motors, IBM, Union Carbide and Coca Cola, the church leadership assumes a quasi-state character. Black church members, like their political counterparts within the federal, state and local governments, are absorbed into the conservative structures which they had intended originally to reform from within.[35]

Black politics of the seventies has assumed the modes of dependency, which Frantz Fanon spells out clearly in his essay on "The Negro and Hegel." The state, which stood before blacks as a "liberator" in the civil rights movement, subsequently imprisoned them through equal opportunity affirmative action, expanded public services and so forth.[36] Conventional black political logic assumes as given that popular, mass struggles accomplish little; violence should be avoided at all costs; real political power lies within the liberalization of state institutions in their relationship with black people. As William R. Morris, the Housing Director for the N.A.A.C.P., recently wrote, blacks should look "to their

Government to make it possible for them to secure decent housing . . . freedom from crime, and other debilitating influences of the slums." Black businessmen and petty bourgeois taxpayers had a right to expect government intervention into private enterprise to promote "a fair share of the economic benefits" for Negroes. For example, "blacks desirous of careers in the housing industry need Government help to overcome racially-exclusionary pracices in professional and trade organizations in housing."[37] The federal government must expand social welfare services to increasingly larger numbers of blacks.

The problem with this argument is that it comes precisely at a period of government wage freezes, public service lay-offs and a decrease in state support for programs within civil society. The black elite view the state as neutral or even progressive, rather than as an institution which blunts class contradictions and racial contradictions. The state undertaxes the rich and shifts the burden of taxation on the poor and working classes. Sales taxes and property taxes are largely the burden of lower class apartment dwellers, small homeowners and the working class generally. The state does not tax the interest on municipal bonds, and even provides generous tax subsidies for corporations.[38] For the majority of black people, the state exists as an institution of exploitation. Any economic or social benefits derived from the marginally progressive elements within the state, such as affirmative action programs, seldom affect the oppressed black majority. Liberal capitalist reform programs have been punitive towards the poor, or at best paternalistic.[39]

The political dependency of the black elite is manifested in its relationship toward the Democratic Party. After flirting with the National Black Political Assembly at the Gary Convention in 1972, Ronald Walters observed, "some of the major black politicians (a few of whom were intimately connected with developing N.B.P.A. strategy) conveniently "cut-and-run" from the prospect of an independent black political formation.[40] The Black Congressional Caucus, black business leaders and most black intellectuals are privately convinced that the concept of an independent black political party is unrealistic. Congressman John Conyers argued recently that "the liberal-left wing of the Party, it must be conceded, is the only viable political instrument for progressive change currently on the scene."[41] Julian Bond, perhaps further to the left than any other major national black politician, states that the only means to improve black economic and social conditions was through "seeking out coalitions" and "by increasing voter registration." Although the "Democratic Party is in great disarray," blacks could not constitute an independent political force. "We are only 12 to 13 percent at best of the entire population of this country. That percentage has never been able to do anything for itself."[42]

Unfortunately, the new "accommodationists" have no where to turn. Their political dependency upon the Democratic Party has tended to make the white status quo shift the burden of black poverty and economic oppression squarely on the shoulders of blacks themselves and then stand aside; when, in truth, the burden is caused by capitalism's inability to provide full employment, to provide the basic essentials of education, social welfare and economic improvement at every level of black society. The black elite are unable to support their patrons and continue the protest traditions of the Movement simultaneously. As poet Mari Evans writes, they are unable to "Speak the Truth to the People."[43]

Whither A Black Political Party: Notes on the National Black Political Assembly

"Pre-occupation with power," Mayor Richard Hatcher of Gary, Indiana observed,"while neglecting ideology, is the prelude to opportunism and betrayal." Prophetic words, indeed. At the National Black Political Convention in Gary, Indiana in March, 1972, Hatcher served as Co-Chairperson and delivered these words of warning at this keynote address. He encouraged Convention participants to press toward an "independent black agenda." Hatcher proclaimed his complete support for "marches and demonstrations," "sit-ins," "trade union activity," "cultural renaissance" and "all avenues to liberation." Blacks should, nevertheless, be "willing to give the two major parties one more chance in the year 1972" to redeem themselves. On this powerful yet curiously contradictory note, Hatcher committed the National Black Political Assembly to a half decade of internal growth and confusion, achievement and dissention.

By the autumn, 1972, a large number of black elected officials who had pledged allegiance to the long-term ideal of a black political party or a pre-party formation had carried out their "opportunistic betrayal" by working unconditionally for the Mc-Govern-Shriver organization and with various Democratic state and local organizations. At the second National Assembly meeting in Little Rock, Arkansas in 1974 only a minority of the elected officials and Democratic leaders appeared who had attended the Gary Convention. Yet the general tone of this second national convention was optimistic. The leadership of the Assembly had moved part of the Executive's power to the hands of Ron Daniels, a northern Ohio black nationalist and community activist who was objectively more progressive on all major issues than his predecessor, Charles Diggs. In Massachusetts, the Assembly had been active in electing a black progressive to the state legislature; in the Midwest, Assemblies were becoming embryonic centers of electoral political power.

At the Little Rock Convention, Hatcher made it clear that a break with the Democratic Party was inevitable. He observed that Senator Ted Kennedy was "in Alabama hugging Gov. Wallace," and that the only solution to the social and political oppression of black people was through "collective" struggle. He urged the absent black leaders—Roy Wilkins, Coleman Young, Tom Bradley, Ed Brooke and Vernon Jordan—to reassess their decision not to participate within the National Black Political Assembly. "If our leaders abandon us," Hatcher informed his audience, "we are lost." Nevertheless, Hatcher and other black elected officials who attended the convention conceived of such "independent" political action in *fundamentally* different terms than did others on the Executive Council, and especially the President, Ron Daniels. Black Democratic officials were in the midst of a rethinking process about their past rhetorical commitment to what was readily becoming an advanced, black political program, taken up at grassroots levels in Assemblies across the country.

Maynard Jackson told the Little Rock Convention that the Assembly should provide "even the poorest and most destitute person, especially in Black America, an alternative to agony." Black politics, just like "love," should be good jobs, the absence of racism, the absence of sexism and fair wages for all working people." By the spring of 1977, however, Jackson had moved so far to the right of the political spectrum that he brutally suppressed a strike of Atlanta sanitation workers. The striking workers, members of the American Federation of State, County and Municipal

Employees, were fired after walking off their jobs. The sanitation employees averaged salaries of only $7,500 yearly, and had not received wage increases in over three years. Jackson's strike busting actions won the acclaim of the Reverend "Daddy" King, the white business establishment and Atlantan suburbanites. Jackson, who like Hatcher did not attend the Cincinnati convention of the National Black Political Assembly in 1976, remarked casually that he did not care if his black employee's union "went out of business tomorrow."

Despite the successful ground-laying activities which local and state Assemblies, particularly in Ohio, Pennsylvania, Massachusetts and New York were accomplishing, the entire national structure was on the verge of a profound political crisis. Due to the broad appeal of the idea of a nationwide black pre-party formation, the N.B.P.A. attracted a large number of supporters who held a wide variety of political goals, hidden agendas and differing levels of commitment. On the east coast there were several opportunistic liberal Democrats who sought the support of the Assembly for their individual candidacies for public office. There were Pan-Afrikanists and black nationalists of the Marcus Garvey orientation; cultural nationalists and black writers. In general, the divisions among the participants within the Assembly could be described in three political tendencies: left, right and center.

The Left, broadly defined, was the most fragile and chaotic of all the competing factions. This included a few members of Marxist-Leninist parties, such as the Socialist Workers Party, and some college students in the Young Socialist Alliance. Few, if any members of the Communist Party or "revolutionary Marxist-Leninst" tendencies, such as the old October League and individuals in the Philadelphia Workers Organizing Committee were ever involved in the Assembly. By the Sixth Pan-African Conference held in Dar Es Salam, Tanzania, in the summer months of 1974, Baraka and a significant portion of the Congress of Afrikan People had renounced their former black nationalist views and embraced a version of Marxism-Leninism as their political *modus vivendi*. Also on the left were a small number of black intellectuals and community organizers who had been influenced by black leftist theoreticians like Earl Ofari, Robert Allen and James Boggs. They advocated a complete, immediate break from the Democratic Party, the development of totally independent electoral forces for blacks at the community level and a dialogue with white progressive forces. Many on the left were openly hostile to black nationalism, and had acquired a political practice which made it difficult for them to sustain a meaningful political dialogue with others to their right. Significantly, the left had little or no roots within the black industrial working class.

The Right within the Assembly was not always numerically dominant, but drew its authority from its hegemonic status within the broader political terrain within the black community. Its leaders included black elected officials such as Diggs, Hatcher, Tennessee State Representative Lois Deberry, California State Representative Willie Brown and Manhattan Borough President Percy Sutton. For briefer periods of time, other prominent black politicians participated in the creation of the Assembly: Coretta King, John Cashin, Jesse Jackson and Walter Fauntroy. All of these individuals recognized the potential of having an independent electoral political base outside of the Democratic Party. None of them, however, were prepared to isolate their immediate constituencies and jeopardize their own careers by splitting from the periphery of power within the state. Most had been vocal advocates of Black Power, but the majority identified with the N.A.A.C.P. on cultural issues such as school desegregation.

Also within the Right were a large number of cultural nationalists or nationalist-separatists. The group's major ideological mentor was the Chicago-based poet and publisher Haki Madhubuti (Don L. Lee). The nationalist-separatists participated in a number of important nonelectoral political organizations outside the Assembly, such as the Congress of Afrikan People and the Student Organization for Black Unity. Like Madhubuti, most of these nationalists viewed the fundamental political conflict facing blacks in the United States could be viewed solely in terms of race, black vs. white. Ideologically, they looked to Julius Nyerere's model of socialism, *ujamma*, as the kind of economic system they desired for Afro-Americans. In real political practice, however the nationalist-separatists tended to act as the informal allies of the moderate black elected officials. The nationalists within the Detroit Assembly in 1977 worked for the reelection of Mayor Coleman Young but not with black Marxist lawyer Kenneth Cockrell, who was also running for citywide election. Madhubuti and other nationalist-separatists cooperated with other black nationalists to their immediate left, however, and genuinely supported the goal of establishing an independent black political organization outside the major parties.

The Center tendency, somewhere politically between Left and Right, was from the beginning the foundation for the Assembly. Intellectually it was influenced by the works of black scholars like Ronald Walters, James Turner, Harold Cruse and William Strickland. In practical political activity, it was led primarily by Ron Daniels and Mtangulizi K. Sanyika, black nationalists who also applied a materialist analysis to the contemporary social and economic problems facing black folk. In theory, the Center desired an ultimate break with the Democratic Party, but it recognized that this process would take a considerable number of years. The Center advocated the establishment of local Assemblies within black communities throughout the country as a means of building local recognition and allegiance. It supported black candidates running for office on the Democratic Party ticket, but at the same time, understood the limits of electoral politics. Although there was a considerable degree of dissent over particular strategies and tactics for Assembly building, the core participants of the faction worked very well with one another. One of the few black elected officials to the Center was Ronald Dellums.

The period 1974-75 marked the first major splits within the Assembly's facade of unanimity, occuring both on the Left and the Right. On the Left, Assembly Secretary General Baraka had moved within two years from a position of separatism and black cultural nationalism to a position of Orthodox Marxism of the thirties variety. Perceptive black critics termed this sudden transformation "Magic Marxism." This metamorphosis fundamentally changed the N.B. P.A.'s longstanding, close relationship with the Baraka-led forces of the Congress of Afrikan People. After a series of violent confrontations, a coalition of Right and Center elements in the Assembly, then led by Daniels, increasingly isolated Baraka. In November, 1975, at an Assembly conference in Dayton, Ohio, they effectively isolated Baraka and his supporters from leadership positions within the Assembly.

Similarly during this same period many black Democrats had become frightened by the progressive political positions and implicitly socialist economic programs which the Center leadership had espoused within the Executive of the Assembly. Using the

"Baraka problem" as an excuse, they dropped away from active participation within Assembly programs and activities. Richard Hatcher, Jackson and other elected officials moved to the right of their stated principles of 1972, and gradually renounced the concept of the Assembly itself.

The net effect of these departures from the Right to support Carter and the purge of the Baraka-led Left almost combined to destroy the Assembly as a viable, national political idea. The leadership by early 1976 was concentrated in the hands of a small number of capable men and women who, at great personal sacrifice, continued to pursue the mandate of the Gary Convention. Ideologically in the middle between the moderate black Democrats and Baraka, they represented agendas which could accurately be described as "left nationalist": black nationalistic in culture and implicitly socialist in economics. Daniels, the national leadership and the Ohio Assembly in particular were able to bring off another major Convention in Cincinnati in March, 1976. They succeeded in attracting new members into the existing local and state Assemblies, and achieved, solidarity around the " '76 Strategy" of running an Independent Black political candidate for President under the Assembly banner.

Yet the stream of departures and new additions, the bitter dissention and power plays within the national organization, were problems which even the most dedicated members of the Executive could not overcome. The primary choice of the leadership for an Independent Presidential candidate, California Congressperson Ronald V. Dellums, had personal and political reasons for not committing himself to a rigorous national campaign. Selecting Julian Bond, State Senator from Georgia, as a second choice, the state Assemblies were informed through the Executive that Bond had expressed an eagerness and a commitment to run. Suddenly, as many delegates from 26 states were enroute to Cincinnati, Bond announced his support of liberal Arizona Congressperson Mo Udall for the Democratic nomination and openly rejected the N.B.P.A. candidacy. Bond's decisions completely surprised the leadership, brought havoc to the entire proceedings surrounding the convention and alienated large sections of the delegates. By Friday night of the gathering no one knew whether Dellums would reconsider becoming a candidate, or whether a candidate could even be found to represent the Assembly's body of politics in a national election.

A number of participants from Virginia, Illinois and several other states openly questioned the procedures established for the Convention. An important and numerically significant element at the gathering consisted of a motley assortment of individuals—black academicians and professors, agent provocateurs, fraternity men looking for a good time, Black Democrats and the politically naive who were ignorant of the crucial struggles which had taken place between Baraka and the Executive—in short, people who added either nothing or precious little to the content of the Convention. Other participants, better informed on the issues, charged that the Center leaders (i.e., Ron Daniels, Mashariki Kurudisha, Co-chairperson of the Assembly and delegate from Pennsylvania, and Mtanguliza Sanyika, Chairperson of Political and Organizational Development) were collectively structuring the Convention program in such a manner that individual needs or perspectives were being ignored or slighted. The Illinois delegates termed the three central leaders of the Executive the "Triumvirate." The state chairperson for the Virginia Assembly confronted the leadership on the final day of the gathering, calling the activities of Daniels and others "Barakaism." Most of these political misunderstandings and confrontations could have been avoided in advance, with concerted planning on the part of the leadership and a coherent program anticipated by all members. Yet with the central question of the candidacy out of focus and in the aftermath of the struggles and purges of the previous year, no one could possibly settle grievances within the span of a single weekend.

The legacy of the bittersweet Cincinnati meeting throughout the remainder of 1976 almost caused the final breakdown of the Assembly. The Right—Black Democrats, elected and appointed official ministers, many cultural nationalists, Muslims and many people without permanent political commitments—had lost its leadership within the Executive with the voluntary departure of Hatcher, Diggs, Jackson, et. al. Conservatives were still evident within the leadership ranks of several major state and local chapters of the Assembly in the Midwest. The Center which now comprised the majority of the leadership was politically further to the left than the typical rank and file member of a local Assembly. The Reverend Frederick Douglass Kirkpatrick had agreed to head a symbolic campaign for the N.B.P.A.; but without news coverage, ample support from the local Assemblies and devoid of funds the campaign was unsuccessful. The leadership called reassessment meetings at Pittsburgh and Louisville late in the year, attempting to reorganize discouraged elements of the organization by pressing forward toward conferences of concrete issues affecting the Black community; nevertheless, it remained clear that despite Centrists leadership, the entire organization was in deep trouble.

The Right, and especially the nationalist-separatists, believe that the Assembly can accommodate virtually all tendencies within the black community; the Centrists believe now that certain sections of the black community, such as committed black bureaucrats and politicians and elements of the black elite cannot be won over to the organization's 1972 Statement of Principles. The present political climate throughout the country tends to prove that the Centrists' analysis is basically correct, and if anything, too modest in its reservations and criticisms concerning the black elite. Grassroots interest still remains for an independent black political party, an alternative to status quo politics, among black workers, students and radicalized sections of the academic elite.

This division of political analysis still divides the elements of the Right and the Center within Assembly meetings, as a regional conference held in Pittsburgh in October, 1976 illustrated. The Western Pennsylvania Assembly drafted a proposed United Front charter uniting all major elements of the local black community around several basic political problems. At an evening ceremony on October 9, black Democrats and Republicans, representatives from the N.A.A.C.P., influential ministers and local organizers met at the Y.W.C.A. to affirm their United Front. The regional activities of the Assembly centered around registering blacks for voting and in making overtures to established black political institutions to promote progressive change through electoral avenues. This strategy conflicts with the activities of other Assemblies, where emphasis has been placed on nonelectoral, political struggle moreso than establishment politics. With reservations, the Center leadership endorsed the Western Pennsylvania Assembly's activities and coalition, but continued to stress the importance of using electoral politics as a tool for mass education rather than the primary means of political trans-formatior

The critical theoretical failure of the Assembly since 1976 has been the inability to establish a prospective timetable within its own internal development toward the establishment of a viable political organization which can compete with the Democratic and Republican parties on the electoral level. One of the Assembly's leading theoreticians, Harold Cruse, broke sharply with the Center/Right leadership over this central question in early 1979. In an essay published by the Afroamerican Research Consortium at the University of Michigan, Cruse condemned the Assembly's lack of an official position on the transition from a pre-party formation to an autonomous political party. "One cannot escape the conclusion that, despite all the rhetorical criticisms of Carter . . . that Daniels and the N.B.P.A. are still formally committed to the politics of the Democratic Party," Cruse declared. "This is demonstrated by the fact that Daniels and the N.B.P.A. are still committed to black Democrats—John Conyers, Charles Diggs, Julian Bond, Ron Dellums and others."

Cruse's accusations against the leadership were based on two different charges. First, since the Cincinnati meeting the Assembly had only sponsored a series of local or regional meetings which did not conclude with a formal commitment "to declare a clean break with the Democratic Party." One of the conferences in question, originally planned for the spring of 1979, showed "a graphic display of ingrained amateurishness, organizational incompetence, strategical and tactical callowness, black sentimentality . . . and a lack of political imagination," according to Cruse. Second, because of the influence of Cornell University's Africana Studies Center and its director, James Turner, the Assembly had a "strong and persistent tendency to substitute the African reality for the Afro-American reality, and to make the latter subordinate to the former." Cruse believed that the Assembly "under the leadership of Daniels" was "a lost cause," because of its "serious flaw" in "black political philosophy"—the practice of "distorting" black America's unique social conditions and problems through the prism of African politics and culture.

Cruse's critical statements were distributed widely during the summer months of 1979 and generated heated debate. Many activists working within the Assembly disagreed with the manner of Cruse's critique, the lack of respect shown to the leadership, and clearly said as much. Others thought that Cruse's statements against Turner were gross distortions, because neither the Cornell faculty nor the Center leadership under Daniels had ever displayed a narrow, cultural nationalism or stricly "Africanist perspective" within the organization. Nevertheless, the major issue raised by Cruse, "Whither a Black Political Party?" went largely un-answered.

What is to be done to resurrect the ideal of a black political party in the United States? An effective, mass black party could come into existence, filling the ever widening vacuum created by the rightward transition of many black elected politicians. A mass independent party for the future could grow from the ranks of black labor, students and the unemployed—but only if this party bases its agenda on the historical debates and internal growth of the Assembly over the past decade. Despite its advances and achievements, the N.B.P.A. will not survive as a growing political force within the black community unless it learns from its own turbulent history. The basic lesson from its rich and contradictory legacy of struggle can be summed up in a single observation: there is no capitalist road to black liberation in this country.

The entire history of the nineteen seventies was a history of a retreat from confrontation and principled, political struggle toward self-serving coalitions with the very forces which serve to destroy us as a people. Further trust and coalitions around political superstars could only be viewed as a basic betrayal of the Assembly's commitment to build a black political party in the United States. Moreover, there will undoubtedly be future confrontations between the reformist, Right forces within the Assembly and the progressive Center leadership and cadres over the nature of political coalitions which the Assembly promotes. Out of this struggle will eventually evolve the nucleus for the organization necessary for a final break with both capitalist parties.

Toward an Understanding of
Martin Luther King Jr.

More than any other American, Martin Luther King, Jr. symbolizes the triumphs and the disillusionments of the Civil Rights Movement. The long campaign to desegregate Southern schools, businesses and ballot boxes was an effort to assert humanity within the context of racial hatred and violence. From the marches of small black school children facing the police dogs of Bull Connor's Birmingham to the voter education efforts in sharecroppers' houses, the movement radically transformed Southern society. Like Frederick Douglass and W.E.B. DuBois before him, King personified the aspirations of an entire group of people. In the aftermath of his murder in Memphis and in the light of his achievements, it is relatively easy to forget the shortcomings of this man. Of such stuff heroes are made, and legends for future generations.

In 1957, King helped to create the Southern Christian Leadership Conference. From this black religious base he led numerous assaults against the segregationist state and civil society, waging popular campaigns in Birmingham, St. Augustine and Selma. He was jailed over one hundred times, spat upon and beaten by white racists. He was nearly murdered in 1958 when he was

51

stabbed in the chest by a black woman. However, he continued to search for new Montgomerys, situations where white America would be forced to look at itself in the mirror of world opinion. By the late 1950s, King had become a household word for religious activism within the conservation black church hierarchy, a representative of the social gospel.

One quarter century has gone since the bus boycott, and King's assassination was over a decade ago. The majority of black youth under 18 know of King as an historical personality, but not as a living, creative human being with both strengths and weaknesses. The malaise of the 1970s has provided sufficient distance psychologically and politically for former white and black opponents of King to make a sudden *mea culpa* and embrace the deceased hero. The controversial and embattled civil rights organizer is thus transformed into a potential media superstar.

Abby Mann's 1978 production of *King*, a well publicized six hour television production which aired on three consecutive evenings on NBC, perpetuated the myth of Martin Luther King. In a sequence of well acted and at times moving scenes, Paul Winfield portrayed the Civil Rights leader from his peaceful graduate school days at Boston University to his death in Memphis. Winfield and Cicely Tyson, who played Coretta Scott King, did their utmost to emerge unscathed from Mann's pseudo-documentary style of direction and from an overly simplistic, good-versus-evil script. But in the end *King* told us only a little more about the personal dimensions of Martin Luther King than we already knew. The contemporary public figure was beseiged by nagging doubts and directed like a puppet by a paternalistic white lawyer and an elitist Negro intellectual, according to the television script. The real legacy of Martin Luther King was completely missing.

King attempted to capture both the public and private man, and failed to do justice to either. In Boston at the beginning, we are shown a dapper graduate student who loved to rap to young black women. "Mike" had earned the nickname "Tweed" because of his love for stylish and expensive suits. At a later period we observed a socially-conscious King who rejects the opulent house selected by his wife in favor of a modest flat in the northwest side ghetto of Atlanta. Nothing is made, though, of King's two early suicide attempts. His love affair with a young white woman while he was a senior at Crozer Theological Seminary was also not mentioned.

King gave the public a myth with human failures, not a human being who struggles against his own weakness and contradictions.

Part of the problem came from the film's "view at the top" perspective. Mann deliberately focused on relatively insignificant issues, like the singing of Tony Bennett or the peculiar, personal preoccupation of J. Edgar Hoover with sex and racism. Certainly it is impossible to understand the movement without reviewing personalities, but the emphasis on individuals sacrifices a larger review of the pressing economic, social, and cultural issues which sparked black rebellion in the late fifties.

In Montgomery on the eve of the bus boycott the median annual income for a black urban worker was $970. Two out of three families had outdoor toilets. Barely two thousand blacks were registered to vote in the city. Black children were cursed and black women were routinely abused by armed drivers on city buses. The bus boycott, and the hundreds of other desegregation demonstrations that followed, were not primarily concerned with King's "soul force," satyagraha, or with saving white men's consciences. Black folks marched, were brutally beaten, raped and sometimes killed because they desired a better existence for themselves and their children. By concentrating on Martin's ambiguous relationships with the Kennedy family and with Lyndon Johnson the central issues which created the Movement were obscured.

The highpoint of King's influence both in the white world and within the state hierarchy was 1964. Martin's influence increased with the death of John Kennedy. Kennedy had never been a strong proponent of civil rights activism and King believed privately that Kennedy's strong emphasis upon maintaining Southern influence within the leadership of the Democratic Party was a central cause for the administration's lukewarm desegregationist position. Nevertheless after learning of the President's assassination, King was pragmatic enough to respond to the inquiry of why Kennedy was killed by drawing upon the larger social conditions of the United States. His death was caused by "a morally inclement climate," Martin stated. "It is a climate where men cannot disagree without being disagreeable, and where they express their disagreement through violence and murder. It is the same climate that murdered Medgar Evers in Mississippi and six innocent children in Birmingham, Alabama. So in a sense we are all participants in that horrible act that tarnished the image of our nation . . ."

This was, of course, precisely what the Johnson administration wanted to hear. King met with Johnson for a fifty minute meeting on December 3, 1963, and was extremely impressed. Although Johnson had voted against bills which supported the Negro's rights to political equality until 1957, King was already predisposed to favor Johnson. Like many Southern whites Johnson could truly understand the social conditions which constituted the essence of the Jim Crow system of race relations. Only through a pragmatic coalition with Southern moderates like Johnson, King thought, could the desegregation of the South be achieved.

In his book *Why We Can't Wait* published in July 1964, King openly endorsed Lyndon Johnson's public commitment to black rights. "Johnson's emotional and intellectual involvement" are both "genuine and devoid of adornment," King gushed approvingly. Johnson seemed "to know that poverty and unemployment are grave and growing catastrophes, and he is aware that those caught most fiercely in the grip of the economic holocaust are Negroes." King still thought of politics as, essentially, decisions made within the electoral structure. Johnson and the liberal Vice-President, Hubert Humphrey, would initiate massive federal programs which could implement his social goals of integration and domestic human rights. King's erroneous judgment was shared to a greater extent throughout the Civil Rights elite, especially within the conservative wing of the N.A.A.C.P. and the Urban League. With the nomination of conservative Republican Barry Goldwater running against Johnson's Great Society, King's public and enthusiastic support for the Texas racist ensured a massive vote by blacks for the Democratic Party. In retrospect, it also allowed Johnson to have a free hand in the development of his escalation of U.S. troops in the Vietnam conflict, a debacle which ultimately took the lives of thousands of young black men.

As early as 1958 there were substantial criticisms of King's posture on economics and culture. The most revealing article of the period was written by Harold Cruse in an edition of *Presence Africaine*. Cruse noted that King had written that recent political events in Egypt were indicative of a movement "toward the promised land of cultural integration" that was a part of the colonial struggle. Cruse observed critically, "this reference to cultural integration has a familiar ring to those who know the workings of the mind of the Afro-American bourgeois intellectual on questions such as culture. Only an Afro-American racial integrationist could make such a statement, revealing such fundamental misconceptions on the nature of colonial revolutions." Cruse pointed out that King's understanding of the dimensions of colonial revolution was warped by his acceptance of integration within the confines of the United States. "If such were the true state of affairs in Egypt," Cruse commented, "I would say 'God help the Egyptians!' For it is not the Egyptians who are out of step with their own revolution: it is we Afro-Americans who are out of step with the rest of the colonial world."

Many activists within S.N.C.C. began to refer to King as "De Lawd" about this time, a sort of Southern black preacher who was elevated into prominence by his association with the white power elite. King was no revolutionary, and never in his life approached the stage of political development achieved by Malcolm X. He did not advocate the ultimate necessity of transforming the U.S. economic system; he sought the Negro's full and unqualified participation within it. King did not argue for the building of cooperative or socialist institutions within the black community; instead, he argued for equal opportunity within bourgeois cultural institutions and the private market economy. And it was because of his moderation, rather than any unique personal characteristics which set him apart from his contemporaries, that elevated him into superstardom. *Time* named King as "the man of the year" for 1963. *Time*'s editorial writers admitted that King had none of James Baldwin's "bristling wit," none of S.N.C.C.'s John Lewis' "raw militancy." But of course, if he had been a Lewis, he would not have received the so-called honor from capitalist America's leading newsweekly. King subsequently received the 1964 Nobel Peace Prize amid similar accolades from the capitalist press of Western Europe.

The political antithesis of King during the period was, of course, Malcolm X. Long before King declared that "the promises of the Great Society have been shot down on the battlefields of Vietnam" he praised the former segregationist to the skies. More on target was Malcolm X's evaluation of Johnson as "a fox who duped the Civil Rights leadership." While King was elevating the concept of integration to the pinnacle of Civil Rights objectives, Malcolm X explained that it was "a Northern liberal smokescreen that confuses the true wants of the American black man." When Martin wept for John Kennedy, Malcolm X understood correrctly that his assassination was "like the chickens coming home to roost."

In some respects, Malcolm was the ideological descendant of Martin Delany and Henry Highland Garnet, the leading black nationalists of the 1850s and 1860s. Both Malcolm and Delany had little faith in peaceful demonstrations to counter white racism. Both believed that violence was an essential part of political struggle and should not be arbitrarily dismissed on philosophical grounds. Malcolm was projected by the white-owned media as the ideological opponent of King; just as in many respects Delany had been the black nationalist alternative to the integrationist abolitionist leader Frederick Douglass. The white power elite attempted to show Malcolm as a madman, a lunatic and advocate of terrorism. Negro Civil Rights leaders repeated the bogus charges which are perpetuated with the televised version of King. Instead of appearing as the representative of black nationalism, the film projects Malcolm as a distorted, frustrated nihilist, a fraud who preyed upon the emotions of black people—an image which is a basic distortion of black history.

The racial confrontations in Watts, Hough and Detroit confirmed Malcolm's analysis over King's nonviolent approach. Martin rejected the phrase "Black Power" because he believed that it would anger the Movement's white supporters. "Beneath all the satisfaction of a gratifying slogan," he insisted, "Black Power is a nihilistic philosophy born out of the conviction that the Negro can't win." Here again, King was simply out of touch with history and the realities of the post-Watts era. Young black students in S.N.C.C. and even some of King's oldest followers were tired of going to jail, being abused and shot. "Nonviolence might do something," black writer Julius Lester reflected at the time, "but a bullet didn't have morals and it was beginning to occur to more and more organizers that white folks had plenty more bullets than they did conscience." Writing in 1965, historian August Meier observed, "In a movement in which successful leaders are those who share in the hardships of their followers, in the risks they take, in the beatings they receive, in the length of time they spend in jail, King tends to leave prison for other engagements."

As Martin Luther King failed to obtain civil rights victories in Chicago and other cities, white and black liberal intellectuals began to publicly question King's future as a viable "Negro Leader." The

Urban League and especially its director, Whitney Young, was jealous of King's worldwide prestige and growing influence within the ranks of the Negro elite. Bayard Rustin voiced the opinion in December 1963, that "the civil rights movement not only reached an impasse within its current tactics but also had retrogressed in many cities to conditions that existed before this year's upsurge." King lacked "an overall social reform program," Rustin insisted without adding that he had nothing to offer in the way of meaningful suggestions. Historian C. Vann Woodward attacked King's increasingly progressive posture in *Harper*'s Magazine. Whitney Young and Edward Brooke visited Vietnam in 1967 and pleaded that the conduct of the war should be left to the White House and the Department of Defense and not to black spokemen like King. Carl Rowan and Rustin wrote several essays in national journals which lamented Martin's "tragic decision on Vietnam."

A combination of events—the riots of the mid-sixties, King's introduction into the world community through his Nobel Peace Prize, pressures from the conservative and activist wings of the Civil Rights Movement, and an increasing awareness that Malcolm X was correct on Johnson and Vietnam—culminated to move King toward a more progressive political posture. King did not become a black nationalist, but he did become much more active in critiquing white racism and class oppression both domestically and in an international context. In April 1967, King led a march of 125,000 demonstrators through New York's Central Park to the United Nations building to denounce the U.S. position in Vietnam. During the parade a group of seventy white youths burned their draft cards and Floyd McKissick and Stokely Carmichael protested against the U.S. program of genocide in Southeast Asia. By the end of May 1967, King articulated a five point peace proposal which included an end to the bombing of the North, a total cease fire and the recognition of the National Liberation Front as a legitimate representative of the Vietnamese people. As he moved against Johnson on the war, King became aware of the necessity for a fundamental economic and social transformation to transcend his more parochial concerns for integration. "For years I labored with the idea of reforming the existing institutions of society, a little change here, a little change there," he admitted. "Now I feel quite differently." A more profound revolution had to take place, King declared. "I think you've got to have a reconstruction of the entire society, a revolution of values."

King's central character in the televised presentation did not grow in political awareness as the real Martin Luther King did after the Watts riot and his break with the Johnson administration over the issue of Vietnam. In the end, the film *King* failed to do justice to this monumental figure. The Poor People's Campaign is treated as a mere extension of King's Civil Rights activities rather than a new departure more in the mold of Malcolm X during the 1964-1965 period. By creating an idealized character the movie misinterpreted the essential man and our movement. A lasting understanding of King can come about only through analyzing his transformation from a petty bourgeois, socially activist black minister to an anti-war, increasingly anti-capitalist black activist. King's courage to transform himself, to follow the path of struggle that Malcolm X so brilliantly established for all of us is his real legacy for our own time.

A. Philip Randolph and the Foundations of Black American Socialism

The Negro intellectuals and radical theorists of the 1920s and 1930s did not, themselves, fight for intellectual clarity. They were unable to create a new black revolutionary synthesis of what was applicable from Garveyism...and Marxism. Yet with such a theoretical synthesis, Negroes would not really have needed the Communist Party. They could have laid down the foundation for a new school of revolutionary ideas...

> Harold Cruse
> *The Crisis of the*
> *Negro Intellectual*
> New York, 1967

Radicalism is a relative term and three decades hence may pronounce the radicals of today as the reactionaries of tomorrow.

> A. Philip Randolph
> *Messenger*
> March, 1919

Asa Philip Randolph was the most influential black trade unionist in U.S. history. Most social historians would argue that Randolph was, perhaps next to W.E.B. Dubois, the most important Afro-American socialist of the twentieth century. His accomplishments in the fields of black union organizing, militant journalism and political protest were unequaled for decades. His controversial newspaper, the *Messenger,* was the first socialist journal to receive a widespread hearing among black working and middle class people. In 1941 he led the first Negro March on Washington Movement to protest racial discrimination in federal hiring policies, establishing a precedent which was to be revived over two decades later at the high point of the Civil Rights Movement. Early in his productive career, Randolph had earned the hatred and fear of the capitalist elite and federal government officials. Not for nothing did President Woodrow Wilson refer to the black socialist leader as "the most dangerous Negro in America."

Later in life, Randolph's contributions to the Afro-American freedom struggle came under severe criticism from many quarters. Young black industrial workers in the late 1960s condemned Randolph and other trade union leaders for not representing their problems and vital interests. To the black activists in the League of Revolutionary Black Workers, he came to represent a modern Booker T. Washington without the Tuskegee educator's acumen for political compromise and power. In 1968 when blacks demanded greater decision-making authority in New York's Public School system and charged the United Federation of Teachers (U.F.T.) with racism, Randolph heartily defended the U.F.T. and its leader, Albert Shanker. In 1976 he lent his support to Daniel Patrick Moynihan, a conservative, racist Democrat, when the latter was running for the U.S. Senate in New York. Randolph's image as a radical socialist and militant trade unionist had been utterly erased. Upon his death in May, 1979, Vice President Walter Mondale glorified the black leader, declaring that "America can speak out for human rights around the world, without hypocrisy, because of the faith A. Philip Randolph . . . showed in our country."

Thus, we approach the great legacy of Randolph with some sadness and uncertainty. So many questions are left unanswered by the path of his brilliant and yet contradictory career. Some Marxists suggest that the "decisive break" in Randolph's career occurred in 1919, when he parted company with other black socialists like Grace Campbell, Cyril V. Briggs and Frank Crosswaith, who joined the fledgling Communist Party. "The issue was clear cut," argued Irwin Silber of the New York *Guardian,* "not support for socialism in general or in the abstract, but support for and defense of the Bolshevik revolution." Randolph's decision to choose "the path of social democracy" was "the decisive turning point in a political life devoted to preventing revolutionary forces from winning leadership of the black liberation struggle."[1] As we shall observe, this split was nowhere nearly as decisive as Silber or others suggest. Randolph's admiration and support for the Russian Revolution continued for many years. Throughout his early career, especially between the years 1919-22 and 1935-40, he welcomed the support of Marxist-Leninists, while reserving the right to differ with them politically. In general, there is actually much greater continuity within the political thought and practice between the younger and older Randolph than is usually thought.

This essay does not attempt to present Randolph's entire political life in any comprehensive manner. There are numerous books and articles which document his long and productive career, usually in a very positive light.[2] Instead, this essay will examine Randolph's early career as a militant journalist, Socialist Party candidate and trade unionist; from his arrival in New York in 1911 until the late 1920s. Many of Randolph's major accomplishments, such as the founding of the National Negro Congress during the Great Depression, his March on Washington Movement of 1941 and the civil disobedience campaign against military conscription in 1948 are either discussed briefly, or not at all. This is because the fundamental outlines of Randolph's socialism and political activism were firmly established during this early period. The roots of his thought are developed during the chaotic experiences of World War I and its aftermath. Secondly, the foundations for subsequent black working class activism and modern black nationalism are established in the twenties. The competing political forces in Harlem of that period—Garveyism, left black nationalism, militant integrationism, Marxism-Leninism—are themes which constantly reoccur within the black movement today. The political decisions which Randolph made during the twenties, for better or worse, set much of the pattern for socialism and trade union work within the black commuity. The attempt here is to critique Randolph's emergent theory of social transformation during his formative decade of political activism and to develop an understanding for the consequences of his sometimes eclectic political practice. The legacy of Randolph's politics and trade unionism which is carried on by his protege Bayard Rustin will also be considered in this light.

Background to Harlem Radicalism

The historical period of World War I and the immediate postwar years brought substantial changes both to blacks in the U.S. in general and for blacks in industrial labor in particular. For the first time in history, a substantial number of Southern, rural blacks were moving to the industrial urban North. Against the paternalistic advice of Booker T. Washington, between 1900 and 1910, the percentage of blacks living in New York City increased by 51 per cent, while in Chicago and Philadelphia blacks increased by over 30 per cent. Almost one half million black men, women and children left the South before and during World War I. Simultaneously, writes Philip Foner, "the first black industrial working class in the United States came into existence." The number of blacks employed in U.S. industry between 1910 to 1920 rose from 551,825 to 901,181. By 1920 about one third of all Afro-American workers were employed in U.S. industry. However, only about 15 per cent of these workers held skilled or semiskilled jobs. The great majority of black workers earned a living in the very lowest paying and physically difficult jobs.[3]

As the political economy of black America took a decisive shift toward the industrial North, a number of competing political interests became involved in organizing, leading and interacting with the new black labor force. Broadly conceived, there were at least four potential political forces which presented alternative agendas to black industrial workers during this period. They consisted of (1) the old Booker T. Washington-capitalist alliance, which included conservative local black ministers, businessmen and journalists who preached cooperation with the capitalist class; (2) the American Federation of Labor, which in theory called for black support, but in practice upheld a strict Jim Crow bar; (3) the Marxist trade unionists in the Workers Party, later the Communist Party and many members of the Socialist Party, which advocated black-white labor unity; (4) independent all-black labor organizations, which operated outside of the "House of Labor," including black nationalist groups influenced by Marcus Garvey. Randolph was simply one of a number of voices, competing for the allegiance and leadership of the new black working class.

The very success of Booker T. Washington in attracting white capital to his many enterprises, from the National Negro Business League to Tuskegee Institute, spelled ultimate disaster to the new black working class in the North. Washington's Northern constituency, the aggressive but fragile black entrepreneurial elite, firmly supported the idea of a capitalist-Negro alliance against white labor. Washington had argued that blacks should appeal to white employers to hire black workers, since they were "not inclined to trade unionism" and not in favor of strikes. Tuskegee scientist and inventor George Washington Carver was an intimate friend of auto industrialist Henry Ford. Thus, major black newspapers such as the Chicago *Defender* supported Washington's strategy of alliance with the capitalist class. Many prominent black ministers, Republican politicians and businessmen counseled black workers to reject unionism. Despite this influence, the overwhelming majority of new immigrants from the rural South quickly saw through this strategy for what it was, a "dead end" Jim Crow policy which only perpetuated the lower level economic status for the black working class.

On paper, the American Federation of Labor (A.F.L.) sought to recruit the budding black proletariat to its cause; in actual practice it was scarcely less reactionary than the Ku Klux Klan. Between 1919 to 1927 the number of black locals in the A.F.L. dropped from 161 to 21. Many unions had a long established policy of Jim Crow. Sometimes blacks were admitted to separate lodges, and then forced under the authority of a white local. The new president of the A.F.L., the United Mine Workers (U.M.W.) former secretary-treasurer William Green, was no friend of black workers. Green had tolerated Ku Klux Klan influence within the U.M.W., and had never taken a strong stand against racial segregation. Green's concern for black labor was only stimulated in the 1920s when it appeared that many Afro-American workers were moving toward Marxism and/or independent trade union activism.[4]

The only white groups which defended black worker's rights during this period were on the left. Growing out of the militant tradition of the Industrial Workers of the World (I.W.W.), thousands of socialist organizers of both races campaigned for worker unity against the issue of white racism. When the "Wobblies" split over the question of the Soviet revolution, many joined the Communist Party (C.P.), such as William Z. Foster. In 1920 Foster brought together a biracial coalition of Marxists and reformist trade union activists to create the Trade Union Educational League. The T.U.E.L. advocated the building of a worker and farmers' political party, greater racial egalitarianism inside the A.F.L. and the creation of militant unions for noncraft workers.

C.P. leader Earl Browder edited the T.U.E.L.'s publication, the *Labor Herald*. In 1925 the C.P. was also active in the formation of the American Negro Labor Congress, an all-black labor group which advocated the building of "inter-racial labor committees" to promote the introduction of black workers into previously segregated crafts. As the Communists grew more influential in organizing black workers, the fears of A.F.L. leaders mounted.[5]

Related to these developments in the labor left was the rapid growth of independent black workers' organizations. As thousands of black laborers came to the North, the base for all-black, militant activism in labor increased dramatically. In 1915 a national organization of black railroad workers was created, the Railway Men's Benevolent Association. Within five years it had 15,000 members. In 1917 the Colored Employees of America was founded, one of the first of many groups which attempted to organize all black laborers. Two years later the National Brotherhood Workers of America was established, a coalition of black workers from almost every occupation, including blacksmiths, electricians, dock workers, porters, riveters and waiters. Until its demise in 1921, it represented a potential alternative to the racist policies of the A.F.L. To the left of these organizations, black radicals and Marxists urged the development of independent socialist strategies for black labor.[6] Randolph's entire life must be viewed against this initial period of his activism, a time of tremendous growth and opportunities for black labor in the industrial North.

Randolph's personal background conformed in most respects with that of other first-generation black immigrants from the South. Born in Crescent City, Florida, on April 15, 1889, Randolph grew up in Jacksonville during the "nadir period" of black-white anti-racial relations. Inspired by the DuBois's *Souls of Black Folk* as a teenager, young Asa decided to leave the South and settle in New York City. Arriving in Harlem in the spring of 1911, Randolph first desired to make his career as an actor. Failing at this, he drifted from one job to another. It is at this point, however, that Randolph's development became exceptional. From 1912-1917 he attended courses at the City College of New York. One leftist philosophy professor, J. Salwyn Shapiro, acquainted Randolph with Marx's writings and other socialist literature. His discovery of socialism was so "exciting," he later reflected, that he studied "Marx as children read *Alice in Wonderland.*"[7] He formed a group of radical "free thinkers," called the Independent Political Council, and began to follow closely the activities of the Industrial Workers of the World. He began to identify himself with Harlem's premier black socialist and "leading street-corner orator," Hubert Harrison. He joined the Socialist Party in the end of 1916, and began to lecture on black history and political economy at the Socialist Party's Rand School. By the beginning of World War I, Randolph and his new black friend, Chandler Owen, a fellow socialist, had become "the most notorious street-corner radicals in Harlem, exceeding even Harrison in the boldness of their assault upon political and racial conditions in the country."[8]

Randolph and Owen became involved in a series of efforts to organize black workers in their community. After several weeks' work they had succeeded in gaining the support of 600 black elevator operators in the city to start the United Brotherhood of Elevator and Switchboard Operators. The new union's demands included a minimum wage of $13 and an eight hour day. Receiving a federal charter from the A.F.L., the short-lived organization tried, and failed, to organize a strike to force recognition. Randolph and Owen were also actively involved in the Headwaiters and Sidewaiters Society as editors of the union's journal, the *Hotel Messenger.* After a dispute with the Society's president, William White, the young Socialists were fired. Within two months, they organized their own monthly magazine, the *Messenger,* with the critical financial support provided by Randolph's wife, Lucille, who earned a living as a popular and successful Harlem hairdresser. Over the next months, the new publication acquired the enthusiastic support of older radicals like Harrison and younger militants like Jamaican socialist W.A. Domingo.[9] Between 1917 until 1928, the journal received the support of a wide variety of Harlem radicals and liberal black intellectuals of various shades: William Pickens, a field secretary of the N.A.A.C.P.; Robert W. Bagnall, N.A.A.C.P. director of branches; Wallace Thurman, Harlem Renaissance author; esssayist George S. Schuyler, a socialist who evolved into a right-wing Goldwater Republican. The theoretical basis for Randolph's socialism in his early years, between 1914 and 1920, was an uneven combination of traditional religious reformism, economic determinism, a fervent internationalism, and Karl Marx. His father, the Reverend James Randolph, was a pastor in the

African Methodist Episcopal Church. Upon his move to Harlem, the first organization he joined was the Epworth League, a social club whose principle activity was Bible study and prayer. Later friends recalled that "Randolph was the outstanding" participant in all "Epworth forums." Throughout Randolph's youth, his father regarded him "as a fine prospect for the A.M.E. ministry."[10] Randolph rejected the orthodoxy of the cloth, but not the meaning of black spirituality in his politics. The language of the Old Testament would inform many of his speeches, as he deliberately used religious principles of brotherhood and humanism in organizing black workers. Even at the high point of their radicalism, Randolph and Owen spoke at black churches and worked closely with progressive clergy. "There are some Negro ministers," the *Messenger* declared in March, 1920, "who have vision, intelligence and courage. There [are] some upon whose souls the Republican Party has no mortgage."[11] Randolph continued to believe that the black church was "the most powerful and cohesive institution in Negro life." Like his friend Norman Thomas, Randolph's socialism was never rooted in an atheistic outlook on life.[12]

Like many other socialists of the day, especially those influenced by the intellectual debates between Eduard Bernstein and Karl Kautsky of the German Social Democratic Party, Randolph believed that socialism was a series of economic reforms taking place between management and labor. Through the vehicle of the trade union, the working class seized an increasingly greater share of the decision-making power within the workplace. The expression of working class politics was, of course, the Socialist Party. The revolution against capital would be a revolt of the majority against the selfish interests of a tiny, isolated elite. Randolph's definition of socialism placed deterministic limitations on all of his subsequent life's work. If the Socialist Party was, as Randolph believed, the highest expression of working class consciousness, and if blacks were overwhelmingly working class, then no other political formation could address blacks' interests as well as the party. Race and ethnicity played no role in the "scientific evolution" of class contradictions; class was an economic category without cultural or social limits. Randolph increasingly viewed any form of black nationalism as a major obstacle between white and black workers in the struggle toward socialist democracy.

The outbreak of World War I deepened Randolph's commitment to militant pacifism and "revolutionary socialism." Like Debs, Randolph and Owen opposed World War I on the principle that "wars of contending national groups of capitalists are not the concern of the workers." The *Messenger's* first issues denounced the "capitalist origins" of the conflict in a fiery essay, "Who Shall Pay for the War?" The editors told black men that they should not serve when drafted, and charged that the Wilson Administration was "making the world safe for democracy a sham, a mockery, a rape on decency and a travesty on common justice."[13] In 1918 Randolph and Owen participated in a Socialist Party antiwar speaking tour. On August 4, 1918, the two were arrested by federal agents after a mass rally in Cleveland, charged with violating the Espionage act, and held in $1,000 bail. Defended by Socialist Party lawyer Seymour Stedman, the judge warned Randolph and Owen to "return to their parents' homes" and register for the draft. Despite the warning, the young men continued their lecture tour, visiting Chicago, Milwaukee, Washington, D.C., and Boston, where black radical Monroe Trotter joined their mass antiwar rally. In Mid-August, Postmaster General Albert Burleson denied second-class mailing privileges to the *Messenger*. Within days, Owen was drafted and sent to a Jim Crow army base in the South. Only the armistice prevented Randolph from the November draft.[14]

Similarly, the Bolshevik Revolution inspired Harlem's radicals, seemingly vindicating their faith in revolutionary socialism. "Lenin and Trotsky . . . are sagacious, statesmanlike and courageous leaders," the *Messenger* proclaimed in January, 1918. "They are calling upon the people of every country to follow the lead of Russia; to throw off their exploiting rulers, to administer public utilities for the public welfare, to disgorge the exploiters and the profiteers."[15] For several years to come, Randolph argued that the Communist revolution meant the "triumph of democracy in Russia." He praised the Soviet Army's defeat of the White Russians in 1920, stating that the capitalist opponents of socialism "had not reckoned with the indomitable courage and the cold resolution born of the unconquerable love for liberty."[61] Randolph boldly predicted that Bela Kun's Hungarian Communists would eventually defeat the Social Democrats and send the aristocracy "to that oblivion and obscurity to which they ought never to emerge;"[17] he also believed that British capitalism was at the brink of "an impending financial revolution."[18] Domestically, Randolph participated eagerly in the Socialist Party's activities. In 1917, the *Messenger* campaigned for Morris Hillquit, the Socialist Party's candidate for mayor. In 1920 Randolph ran as the Party's candidate for state comptroller and polled 202,361 votes, only 1,000 less than Socialist presidential candidate Eugene V. Debs in the state. In 1921 he ran another unsuccessful campaign for secretary of state. Despite these limited failures, Randolph's belief in a democratic socialist revolution remained uncompromised—up to a point.[19]

Randolph's decisive break from DuBois—the major black leader of the N.A.A.C.P. and Randolph's intellectual mentor—did not occur until 1918, when the editor of the *Crisis* urged black Americans to support the war effort.[20] Up to this point, the *Messenger* had praised DuBois' "full merit and worth" as a race leader and opponent of "disenfranchisement," condemning only his attitude on labor. "One has not seen where the doctor ever recognized the necessity of the Negro as a scab," Owen wrote, "allaying thereby the ill feeling against him by the working white man."[21] DuBois' advocacy of the war crystallized Randolph and Owen's opposition to his entire political line—from the "Talented Tenth" theory to his worth as a critic of segregation. By July, 1918, Randolph condemned almost every major essay or book that DuBois had ever written: his landmark sociological survey, *The Philadelphia Negro,* was criticized as "a heavily padded work, filled with superfluous matter"; *The Souls of Black Folk* was dismissed as "a mass of labored alliterations. . . . " DuBois was a "political opportunist," simply representing "a good transition from Booker Washington's compromise methods to the era of the new Negro."[22]

Never one to avoid a fight, DuBois defended his anti-Socialist Party, antitrade unionist, anti-Bolshevik and pro-war positions head on. As early as January, 1912, when he was a member of the Socialist Party, DuBois complained about racism within the organization. He left the party to endorse the election of Woodrow Wilson later that year.[23] His opposition to trade unionism was well established and was reinforced by his essay, "The Black Man and the Unions," published in March, 1918.[24] DuBois' position on the war evolved from a remarkable May, 1915 essay, "The African Roots of the War," which examined the colonial and racist origins of the conflict. From the destruction of the German empire, DuBois may have reasoned, the possibility for greater African self-determination may be a result.[25] As a result, he took the position that black Americans would receive a "reward" for their loyalty to the United States' war effort against Germany.[26] On the matter of Russian radicalism DuBois was profoundly skeptical. After the "February Revolution" in early 1917, DuBois suggested to his *Crisis* readers that the event "makes us wonder whether the German menace is to be followed by a Russian menace or not."[27] Although he criticized Alexander Kerensky's "blood and iron methods" in governing Russia, he said nothing about the Bolsheviks rise to power.[28] When radical Harlem Renaissance writer Claude McKay questioned why DuBois "seemed to neglect or sneer at the Russian Revolution," he replied curtly that he had "heard things which [were] frighten[ing]" about the upheaval. I am "not prepared to dogmatize with Marx or Lenin."[29]

For the New Negro generation, these opinions relegated "the Doctor" to the status of "the old, me-too-Boss, hat-in-hand Negro generally represented by Robert Russa Moton of Tuskegee."[30] Hubert Harrison exonerated the *Crisis* editor in his journal, *The Voice.* Randolph declared that DuBois was "comparatively ignorant of the world problems of sociological and economic significance," and that his publication was filled with "errors and misstatements."[31] In 1920., the *Messenger* charged that the *Crisis* had an editorial policy of "viciousness, petty meanness" and "suppression[of] facts pertaining to the N.A.A.C.P." It attacked DuBois' associates, especially field secretary William Pickens, as advocates of "sheer 'claptrap.' "[32] It proclaimed that its God was "the toiling masses of the world," and laughed at DuBois' provincial liberalism and staid social conformity. By the end of Wilson's administration, the Justice Department reported that the *Messenger* was "by long odds the most dangerous of all the Negro publications." Throughout Harlem, Randolph and Owen became known as "Lenin and Trotsky," the most revolutionary black Bolsheviks on the scene. Their political break from DuBois seemed complete.[33]

From Class Struggle to Class Compromise

Having declared war against DuBois and the N.A.A.C.P. leadership, Randolph and Owen sought the support of other black activists within Harlem. By their own admission, DuBois remained "the most distinguished Negro in the United States today."[34] Marcus Garvey seemed a likely addition to their struggle against the *Crisis'* editor. Born in Jamaica, Garvey had established his Universal Negro Improvement Association in 1914. Inspired by the racial "self-help" slogans of Booker T. Washington, the young black nationalist eventually settled in New York City in 1916. Randolph claimed the distinction of having been the first prominent black radical to invite Garvey to make an address in Harlem. He recalled years later that "when he finished speaking . . . I could tell from watching him then that he was one of the greatest propagandists of his time."[35] Garvey was attracted to Harrison, who by June, 1917 had left the Socialist Party to form his own left black nationalist movement, the AfroAmerican Liberty League. Although Garvey was one of the main speakers at the League's first rally on June 12, 1917, he quickly established his own separate U.N.I.A. offices near the *Messenger* on 135th Street. Randolph and Garvey worked together in the International League of Darker Peoples, an organization which demanded that the African territories and colonized nations to be represented at the Versailles peace conference. Some Garveyites began to assist Randolph's efforts. Domingo, who was editor of Garvey's *Negro World,* actively worked as a contributing editor on the *Messenger.* Randolph certainly welcomed Garvey's public attacks on DuBois as an "anti-bellum Negro."[37]

The first major disagreement between the black nationalists and Randolph probably occurred over the creation of the Liberty Party, an all-black political coalition of former Socialists, Republicans and Democrats, in late 1920. The state slogan of the party was "Race First"; it advocated running a black presidential candidate and independent candidates at local levels. Randolph went to great lengths to condemn the notion on all conceivable grounds. First, the Negro party was criticized because he had no prospects for support from white workers. "A party that has no hope of becoming a majority has no justification for independent action; for it can never hope to be of positive benefit to its supporters." Secondly, the party had no economic platform. Thirdly, the proposition of a Negro President was "tragically inane, senselesss, foolish, absurd and preposterous. It is inconceivable that alleged intelligent, young colored men could take such obvious, stupendous political folly seriously." Last, the Liberty Party consisted of "opportunists, discredited political failures who are now trying to capitalize race prejudice of the Negro." The basis for this vituperative attack rested with Randolph's basic proposition that it was in the interests of "Negro workers to join and vote for the Socialist Party."[38] Although it is not clear, it is probable that Harrison's Liberty League supported the new party. Another more menacing factor, of course, was Garvey, who had long been a proponent of an all black political party.[39] J.W.H. Easton, the U.N.I.A. leader for U.S. blacks, was the party's nominee for President.[40] The idea of a separate, race-conscious, political organization, rather than the Liberty Party per se, was the real issue. Randolph and Owen had begun to view militant black nationalism as being even more dangerous than the threat presented by DuBois and his *Crisis.*

The *Messenger* began to challenge the Garvey Movement for hegemony within Harlem's black working class population. In December, 1920, Randolph issued an editorial, "The Garvey Movement: A Promise or a Menace," which took the position that "the class-struggle nature of the Negro problem" was missing from the U.N.I.A.'s work. Revolutionary black nationalism "invites an unspeakably violent revulsion of hostile opposition from whites against blacks." In Randolph's view, any all-black organization could "only misdirect the political power of the Negro. All party platforms are chiefly concerned with economic questions" and not with race. Therefore, the *Messenger* concluded, Garvey's entire program "deserves the condemnation and repudiation of all Negroes."[41] Relations with Garveyites swiftly worsened. Randolph insisted that Garvey's advocacy of an independent Africa for the Africans was unrealistic, because the Africans do not possess "the ability . . . to assume the responsibilities and duties of a sovereign nation."[42] By mid-1922 the *Messenger's* editorials literally shouted its total opposition to Garvey. "Here's notice that the *Messenger* is firing the opening gun in a campaign to drive Garvey and Garveyism in all its sinister viciousness from the American soil."[43]

Nowhere in the black press of the time was the anti-Garvey campaign expressed so bluntly and with such anti-West Indian sentiments as in the *Messenger*. The most comprehensive statement on this theme was Randolph's essay, "The Only Way To Redeem Africa," published in two parts in the January and February, 1923 issues. Every significant aspect of Garvey's program was denounced as either "foolish," "vicious," "without brains" or "sheer folly." The U.N.I.A.'s Black Star steamship line had "no hope" in succeeding; its proposal for a Booker T. Washington University will have "neither students nor teachers" since the former "will not trust it to give out knowledge" and the latter will not "trust it to give out pay." Garvey's wildest claim, that the U.N.I.A. had 4.5 million dues paying members, proved that he was "a consummate liar or a notorious crook." Randolph failed to explain the reasons for Garvey's massive popularity among black workers in Harlem, and ignored the hard evidence of the U.N.I.A.'s progressive positions on African and international affairs. Nevertheless, he concluded that "the Garvey Movement is a social-racial disease germ to the Negro which must be destroyed in order that he may proceed to build up a powerful organization to protect his interests."[44]

As the Bolshevik Revolution forced the creation of a Third International, Randolph felt himself pulled gradually toward the right. For the first time in several years he was no longer "the first voice of radical, revolutionary, economic and political action among Negroes in America."[45] Revolutionary black activists outside both the U.N.I.A. and the *Messenger* faction were making political waves across Harlem. In the fall of 1917 Cyril V. Briggs founded the African Blood Brotherhood (A.B.B.), a leftist and black nationalist group. A native of the Dutch West Indies and a former editorial writer for the New York *Amsterdam News*, Briggs began to edit his own militantly nationalist journal, the *Crusader*. The members of the A.B.B., which included Lovett Fort-Whiteman, Richard B. Moore, and Otto Huiswood, quickly were recruited into the newly formed Workers, or Communist Party. Harrison did not "go over to the Communists," according to Harold Cruse, but he did "assist them" in certain situations.[46] By 1922, the Communists had begun "to assail Garvey's program as reactionary, escapist and utopian" while simultaneously trying "to influence, collaborate with, or undermine his movement."[47] As

Marxist-Leninists, the A.B.B. also attacked Randolph's firm ties with the Socialist Party, his reformist and quasi religious theories for social transformation, his bitter hostility towards black nationalism and growing tendency toward political and economic conservatism.[48]

The *Messenger* turned on its former leftist friends almost as viciously as it had turned against Garvey. Declaring all black Communists "a menace to the workers, themselves and the race," Randolph judged their policies "utterly senseless, unsound, unscientific, dangerous and ridiculous." Black Marxist "extremists" were hopelessly out of touch with the mentality of Negro laborers, since the latter had not "even grasped the fundamentals and necessity of simple trade and industrial unionism!" As further proof that "Communism can be of no earthly benefit to either white or Negro workers," Randolph pointed out that the Soviet Union's New Economic Policy of "State Capitalism" had replaced the radical socialist economics of the War Communist years. Soviet Communists [recognize] its impracticability at the present stage of economic development of Russia." In short, he wrote, the black Communists' "statements have revealed that they are utterly devoid of any respect for fact, truth, or honesty."[49]

With some desperation, the *Messenger* turned to the N.A.A.C.P. in its campaign against Garvey. There was no indication that DuBois had changed on any of the major points that had separated him from Randolph during the war. If anything, DuBois' opposition to "State Socialism," the "class struggle," and his advocacy of black "capital accumulation to effectively fight racism" placed him to the economic right of many Garveyites, and perhaps even Garvey himself at this time.[50] What had separated Randolph and DuBois was now disintegrated by the very success of Garvey and his gospel of militant black nationalism. There was a remarkable degree of concurrence between the *Crisis* and the *Messenger,* from a principled opposition to all forms of racial separatism to a distrust of Garvey's business methods and even honesty. Both were also concerned about growing danger, as DuBois put it, of "Communists boring into Negro labor."[51]

Working closely with the N.A.A.C.P.'s assistant secretary, Walter White, Randolph coordinated an elaborate campaign against Garvey, which included the distribution of anti-Garvey handbills throughout Harlem. In January, 1923, Randolph, Owen,

Pickens and several other black leaders drafted a memorandum to Attorney General Harry M. Daugherty asking for the conviction of Marcus Garvey on charges of mail fraud, various criminal activities and "racial bigotry." Garvey was eventually convicted of mail fraud, and was sent to a federal penitentiary in Atlanta in February, 1925. By the late 1920s the U.N.I.A. had virtually collapsed, partially due to Randolph's anti-Garvey activities. The irony of this entire episode was that Randolph, a would-be leader of the black working class, had participated in the destruction of the largest black worker and peasants organization in U.S. history.

Compared to Garvey, Randolph's efforts to organize black workers met with little real success. Randolph and Owen created the Friends of Negro Freedom in 1920, a bi-racial group which promoted black entrance into trade unions and held lectures on economic and political issues. Friends of Negro Freedom included the participation of Domingo, Baltimore *Afro-American* newspaper editor Carl Murphy and black intellectual Archibald Grimke. In 1923 Randolph attempted unsuccessfully to establish a United Negro Trades organization to bring black workers into independent trade unions. Finally, in August, 1925, a few Pullman porters asked Randolph to help them establish the Brotherhood of Sleeping Car Porters. Despite the fact that several black Pullman employees had been more instrumental in organizing rank-and-file support for the Brotherhood, such as W.H. Des Verney and Ashley Totten, Randoph was named the group's president. The initial prospects for this union's success looked just as dim as all the other groups that Randolph had led. The eleven thousand black porters working on Pullman cars faced the united opposition of the federal government, the Pullman Company and its black conservative allies.

Given Randolph's early inability to build a successful and popular mass organization of black workers, it is not surprising that he began to reassess his overall theoretical outlook and political practice. Gradually socialism was given less emphasis in his writings. By 1923 the *Messenger* had succeeded in attracting several black businessmen and merchant to advertise in its pages. Colleges and Negro industrial schools followed suit. Articles by Emmett J. Scott, the former secretary of Booker T. Washington, and even Robert Russa Moton of Tuskegee began appearing in the journal.[52] Quietly editorial policies began to change. In January,

1925, Randolph declared that "Negro businessmen are rapidly rising to the high mark of responsibility." Many black entrepreneurs were "splendid, courteous" and a *"delight* to deal with."[53] Randolph's blanket condemnation of the A.F.L. and his critical description of Gompers—a "conservative, reactionary and chief strikebreaker"—mellowed into fawning and even syncophantic praise. The A.F.L. was no longer "a machine for the propagation of race prejudice," but by 1925, it was a progressive and democratic force. Randolph banned any articles critical of William Green, newly elected A.F.L. leader.[54]

The editors endorsed Hampton and Tuskegee Institutes' five million dollar fund drive by defending Washington's classical position of industrial education against Dubois' Talented Tenth ideal. "Dr. DuBois has probably been responsible for a great deal of misunderstanding about industrial education in America," they argued. "We need more brick masons, carpenters, plasterers, plumbers, than we do physicians; more cooks than lawyers; more tailors and dressmakers than pupils."[55] Given that there were approximately 40,000 black secondary and elementary teachers, 3,200 black physicians and only 900 black lawyers in the United States at this time, it is utterly remarkable that Randolph's statement could be taken seriously. The percentage of black children between the ages of 5 to 20 who were enrolled in school was about 50 percent; 25 percent of all adult blacks in the South were illiterate.[56] These remarks indicate that Randolph had moved toward a defense of private property and acknowledged the legitimacy of capitalism for blacks—a posture which he would never relinquish.

After several years as an independent, all-black union, Randolph persuaded the Brotherhood to apply for an international charter from the A.F.L. in 1928. Green was reassured by Randolph that the union would present no special problems to the A.F.L. The A.F.L. rejected the application for equal membership, and instead proposed a "compromise" of "federal union" status inside the organization. Despite criticism from leftists, black workers and some journalists, Randolph agreed to these terms. Both parties got something in the deal: Green and the A.F.L. acquired a major black union, silencing their Marxist and black critics like DuBois; Randolph received the promise of assistance from organized white labor in his growing struggle with the Pullman Company.

With characteristic enthusiasm, Randolph devoted his total energies toward building the Brotherhood. Appeals to porters to join the union were acquired on "a racialistic and religious basis." Randolph recognized that socialist dogma would not find a receptive audience among most black workers, and used Biblical passages and paraphrases through his writings. "Ye shall know the truth, and the truth shall set you free" was the standard slogan on most Brotherhood stationery. In language reminiscent of some Garveyites, the Brotherhood's literature declared its faith in God and the Negro Race: "Fight on brave souls! Long live the Brotherhood! Stand upon thy feet and the God of Truth and Justice and Victory will speak unto thee!"[57] Randolph's efforts to organize the porters received a boost in 1926, when the Garland Fund, administered by the American Civil Liberties Union, donated $10,000 to the Brotherhood. The money allowed Randolph to hire Frank W. Crosswaith, a West Indian Socialist and graduate of the Party's Rand School in New York City, as a professional organizer and executive secretary of the Brotherhood.[58] Randolph was also encouraged by the wealth of intelligent and creative leaders among the ranks of the porters: Morris "Dad" Moore and C.L. Dellums of Oakland; T.T. Patterson of New York City; Des Verney and Totten. Chief among them was Milton Webster. Two years Randolph's senior, Webster had been fired by Pullman because of his militancy. In the twenties he became a bailiff and was one of Chicago's influential black Republican leaders. Webster was appointed assistant general organizer of the Brotherhood and chief organizer for the Chicago area. Next only to Randolph, the aggressive yet politically conservative Webster soon became the major spokesperson for many of the porters.[59]

Randolph's leadership was soon put to the test against the Pullman Company. On October 15, 1926, he informed the Board of Mediation, established by the Railway Labor Act of that same year, that a dispute existed between the Brotherhood and Pullman. The Board assigned a conservative Democrat and former governor of Kentucky, Edward P. Morrow, to investigate the case. Covertly working with Pullman executives, Morrow concluded with the company that the Brotherhood should not be recognized as the official bargaining agent of the porters. In August, 1927, the Board declared that the parties could not reach an agreement and it recommended voluntary arbitration. Pullman refused to discuss the issue any further, and was blunt in its reasons for rejecting Randolph and his union.[60] Randolph had no other alternative at this point but to announce that he would call a strike to force Pullman Company into collective bargaining. The tentative date for the strike was June 8, 1928, at noon.[61]

Across the country, porters were excited at the prospect for a final confrontation between themselves and the Pullman Company. Despite red-baiting against Randolph's militant past, random firings and veiled threats, the porters almost unanimously backed the Brotherhood leadership. The strike vote, which was approved by a margin of 6,053 to 17, astonished even Randolph. Some porters made plans for a long seige, even blocking the use of strikebreakers. Ashley Totten and his associates in Kansas City began collecting "sawed-off shotguns, railroad iron taps, boxes of matches, knives and billy clubs" and storing them in a local black-owned building. Facing the prospect of an extensive and probably violent strike which would disrupt Pullman railroad service nation-wide, Randolph began to have doubts. Could an all-black workers strike succeed without some measure of white trade union and working class support? On June 8, three hours before the scheduled strike, Green sent Randolph a telegram stating that "conditions were not favorable" for a strike. He suggested that the Brotherhood engage in "a campaign of education and public enlightenment regarding the justice of your cause." Randolph quickly ordered the strike off.[62]

It is difficult to determine whether the strike would have been successful. Throughout the remainder of his life, Randolph insisted that the possibilities were nil. The historical evidence points in the opposite direction. William H. Harris' research on Brotherhooid correspondence suggests that Webster had a great deal of difficulty in convincing his local members not to strike by themselves. "Aside from disruption of peak travel, what could be more damaging to interstate commerce than to tie up the rails during the time when both national political parties were holding conventons in such remote cities as Houston and Kansas City?" Harris asked. "Even the Pullman Company recognized this as a potential danger."[63] The union was "in shambles after the abortive strike." The *Messenger* was forced to halt publication; porters lost confidence in the Brotherhood and stopped paying their regular dues. Black news-papers like the New York *Argus* attacked the leadership of "A.

Philip Randolph."[64] The Communists accused him of betraying Negro workers in the interest of labor fakers."[65] The American Negro Labor Congress charged that Randolph had "forsaken the policy of militant struggle in the interest of the workers for the policy of class collaboration with the bosses and bluffing with the strike." Within four years the brotherhoods membership declined from almost 7,000 to only 771 in 1932.[66]

It was only in April, 1937 that the Pullman Company agreed to bargain seriously with the Brotherhood. On August 25 of that same year Pullman agreed to reduce the porters' monthly work load from 400 to 240 hours, and provide a substantial pay increase. But many of his critics, black and white, suggested that these and other accomplishments would have been achieved much sooner if A. Philip Randolph had a little less faith in the system and a little more confidence in the militancy of the black working class.

Beyond Civil Rights and Trade Unionism

In the Great Depression, Randolph again exhibited real courage and some of his former political independence. Contrary to DuBois, Randolph charged that "the New Deal is no remedy" to black peoples' problems. It did not "change the profit system," nor "place human rights above property rights." Assisted by Alain Locke, Ralph Bunche and other left-oriented black intellectuals, Randolph initiated the National Negro Congress in February, 1936. Hundreds of black trade unionists, radical civic reformers and communists participated in a black united front in blunt opposition both to Roosevelt's "welfare capitalism" and to the do-nothing acquiescence of the N.A.A.C.P. Despite the breakup of the Congress in the early 1940s over the issue of "Communist control," the organization represented one of the most advanced coalition of black activists ever assembled.[67]

With the onset of World War II in Europe, the Roosevelt administration began a policy of expanding production in defense industries. Thousands of new jobs were created in industrial, clerical and technical fields related to wartime production prior to the U.S.'s direct involvement in the war. Generally, black workers were largely kept out of these positions because of a tacit policy of Jim Crow followed by white labor, big business and the federal government. Although Congress had forbidden racial discrimination in the appropriation of funds for defense training, the law was essentially a dead letter. With the Randolph's resignation from the National Negro Congress in 1940, he turned his energies toward the issue of black employment in defense industries with federal contracts. Working again with Walter White, who by this time was Secretary and dictatorial leader of the N.A.A.C.P., Randolph sought to influence Roosevelt to initiate action against white racism.

By January, 1941, Randolph was prepared to take what was, for that time, radical action. Randolph urged blacks to organize a militant march in Washington D.C. on July 1, to protest the discrimination against black workers. The idea of a "March on Washington Movement" seized the imagination of the black working class, the unemployed and even the petty bourgeoisie. The Brotherhood of Sleeping Car Porters was the central force behind the campaign. Hundreds of March on Washington Movement meetings were held in black churches, union halls and community centers. With the able assistance of Crosswaith and Howard University history professor Rayford Logan, Randolph succeeded in committing over 100,000 black people to the march. Foner observes that the "March on Washington Movement represented the first occasion in American history when a black labor organization assumed leadership of the struggle of the Negro masses on a national scale and became the spokesman for all black Americans, conservative and radical alike." Neither Garvey, Washington nor DuBois had ever succeeded in forging a popular coalition of the black business and professional elites, the working class and rural blacks toward a single, progressive cause.

The driving force behind the 1941 March on Washington was black nationalism. Taking another page from Garvey's book, Randolph insisted that only blacks participate in the march. It was important for blacks to show white America that they were able to build an effective, militant, national organization without white assistance. C.L. Dellums explained that the Brotherhood informed its "white friends over the country why this had to be a Negro march. It had to be for the inspiration of Negroes yet unborn." White progressives and trade unionists were asked to offer "moral support, to stand on the sidelines and cheer us on."[68] The demand for an end to discrimination in defense plants appealed to the typical black industrial worker who, like porters in the twenties, was on the verge of militant class consciousness. But its expression among blacks was nationalism, a force involving religious, cultural and ethnic qualities which Randolph was forced to deal with in a concrete manner. Randolph's biographer emphasizes that "a certain strain of black nationalism . . . ran through his social and religious heritage." Not surprisingly, "when the chips were down," Randolph had to return to his own origins to find the means to understand his own constituency and to articulate their aspirations. His biographer writes, "It is a wonder that black nationalism did not become the central activating force and principle of Randolph's political life."[69]

The Roosevelt administration began to take the black march seriously only in May, 1941. Roosevelt used his considerable powers of political influence to force the organizers to stop the march. As black workers in Harlem, Washington, D.C., Chicago and every major city prepared for the confrontation, Roosevelt finally agreed to sign an executive order prohibiting the "discrimination in the employment of workers in defense industries because of race, creed, color or national origin." The Democratic administration promised to create the Fair Employment Practices Committee (F.E.P.C.), a commission which would supervise the compliance of federal contractors to the executive order. Although this was not everything that the March on Washington Movement had asked for, Randolph and other leaders agreed to call off the demonstration on June 24.[70]

Historians August Meier and Elliott Rudwick point to the March on Washington Movement as the real foundation for the Civil Rights Movement of the 1950s and 1960s. "Though its career was brief the former organization prefigured things to come in three ways," they note. It was first "an avowedly all-Negro movement;" second, it involved the direct "action of the black masses;" third, "it concerned itself with the economic problems of the urban slum-dwellers."[71] Two additional points can be made as well. The F.E.P.C. was the beginning of today's Federal Office of Contracts Compliance Programs, the Department of Labor's affirmative action watchdog. The principle of equal opportunity for black people in employment was, for the first time, considered a civil right. Randolph's ideology behind the march also "prefigures" the 1950-1960s because of the impact of Mohandas K. Gandhi in his approach to social change. In an address before March on Washington associates given in Detroit in September, 1942, Randolph called attention to "the strategy and maneuver of the people of India with mass civil disobediance and non-cooperation." Huge, nonviolent demonstrations "in theatres, hotels, restaurants, and amusement places" could be a potential means to gain full equality. Years before Martin Luther King, Jr., Randolph envisioned the basic principles of *satyagraha* applied to the fight against Jim Crow.

Yet for all his foresight and commitment to the ideals of black struggle, Randolph's subsequent political behavior did little to promote the creation of a permanent, black protest organization. The March on Washington Movement's last major conference was in October, 1946, and it lapsed completely the next year. Randolph's ongoing fights with A.F.L. officials still produced meager results. As in the past, Randolph's failure to carry out the threat of militant action compromised the pursuit of his long range goals. Even at the peak of his influence, during the March on Washington Movement of 1940-41, Randolph failed to establish a mass-based, permanent force which promoted his rhetorical commitment to democratic socialism and black economic equality. Again and again, especially later in his career, he failed to trust the deep militancy of the black working class masses, relying instead upon tactical agreements with white presidents, corporate executives and labor bureaucrats. Curiously like Booker T. Washington, Randolph always preferred class compromise to class struggle.

With the end of World War II and the beginning of the Cold War, Randolph's creative contributions to the struggle for black freedom had largely ended. Like other labor leaders and socialists such as Norman Thomas, Randolph capitulated to the posture of extreme anti-Communism. Randolph and Thomas travelled to the Far East lecturing against the evils of radical trade unionism, for instance, under what later was revealed to be money from the C.I.A. He became an acknowledged "elder statesman" during the Civil Rights Movement of the 1950s. Making his peace with those black leaders he had formerly opposed in the N.A.A.C.P. and Urban League, Randolph had little to offer in the way of guidance or political theory to the newest generation of black radicals, the rebels of S.N.C.C., C.O.R.E. and S.C.L.C. Ironically, it was during this period that DuBois, now in his eighties, moved toward a more thoroughly radical condemnation of the U.S.'s political economy than Randolph ever had. The old so-called "political opportunist" had become the active proponent for world peace and international liberation, while his "Young Turk" critic had become a defender of the conservative status quo.

Since the 1960s, Randolph's role in the A.F.L.-C.I.O. hierarchy has been filled by his trusted assistant Bayard Rustin. Like his mentor, Rustin is a socialist and pacifist with a long history of principled and at times even courageous struggle. As a participant in the Congress of Racial Equality's "Journey of Reconciliation" campaign of 1947, he tested local Jim Crow laws by sitting in white sections on interstate buses in the South. With other early "freedom riders" he received a thirty-day jail term on a North Carolina chain gang. Rustin was one of the major organizers of the 1963 March on Washington, and inspired a generation of younger black activists like S.N.C.C.'s Stokely Carmichael and Phil Hutchings. But as he became head of the A. Philip Randolph Institute, founded by George Meany and the A.F.L.-C.I.O. in 1965, he acquired the language and outlook of white labor's elites. Rustin bitterly denounced Malcom X as a "racist,"[72] and condemned the Black Power movement as "anti-white" and "inconsistent." Rustin and Randolph defended the Vietnam War and criticized King for linking domestic civil rights with the U.S. involvement in Southeast Asia.

In the 1970s Rustin's position within the black movement has drifted increasingly toward the right. At the September, 1972 convention of the International Association of Machinists, he attacked black rank-and-file activists and defended the A.F.L.-C.I.O.'s shabby record on integration. The next year he was critical of the creation of the Coalition of Black Trade Unionists, arguing that the Randolph Institute should be viewed as the "catalyst" for black advancement in union leadership positions. On the international front at the time of Randolph's death, Rustin was a participant in a "Freedom House" delegation to Zimbabwe declaring that the white minority regime's fraudulent elections were democratic. Cruse analyzed him best in 1968, observing that "Rustin's problem is that in thirty years he has learned nothing new. He has done nothing new. He has done nothing creative in radical theory in American terms . . ."[73] Put another way, Rustin is a victim of what Marx postulated in "The Eighteenth Brumaire of Louis

Bonaparte;" that "all great personages occur, as it were, twice—the first time as tragedy, the second as farce." Randolph's life is tragic, because of his greatness and yet untapped potential. Rustin's is a caricature, in another historical period, of that lost greatness.

Despite the remarkable changes and shifting images we may have of Randolph, certain fundamentals for future black workers' organization and political activism become imminently clear. Throughout his career, Randolph consistently perceived the problem of union organizing from a "top-down" rather than grassroots, mass-based approach. Although he was not a porter he asked for, and received, the presidency of the Brotherhood in 1925; he left the National Negro Congress' presidency after he realized that he could no longer exercise decisive authority over the leftists within the coalition. Another characteristic was his preference for compromise. Ending the 1941 March on Washington, was the most outstanding instance but not the only ones. Another compromise of a kind occurred in December, 1965, after the establishment of the Randolph Institute. After years of criticizing the racial policies of the A.F.L.-C.I.O., Randolph reversed himself at the San Francisco national convention by announcing that racism had virtually disappeared from organized labor.

Another central feature of Randolph was his dire inability to appreciate the relationship between black nationalism, black culture and the struggle for socialism. Randolph and Owen's editorials in the *Messenger* declared that "unions are not based upon race lines, but upon class lines," and that "the history of the labor movement in America proves that the employing class recognize no race lines." This crude and historically false oversimplification led Randolph into pragmatic alliances with the white Marxists, with the A.F.L. after 1923, and later with the Kennedy and Johnson administrations. His successes in establishing the Brotherhood's rights to higher wages and shorter working hours were achieved at the expense of building any autonomous, all-black protest movement which was critical of both racism and capitalism. The *Messenger*'s vicious attacks against Garvey did not stop hundreds of thousands of rural and urban black workers from defending black nationalism. Randolph was ill equipped to understand the rank-and-file revolt of black industrial workers in the past two decades who were influenced by Malcolm X, Frantz Fanon and their Black Power disciples.

Cruse's comments on the entire generation of Harlem radicals, both in politics and the arts, are an appropriate critique of Randolph as well. Because "the Negro intellectuals of the Harlem Renaissance could not see the implications of cultural revolution as a political demand," Cruse notes, "they failed to grasp the radical potential of their own movement." Like Renaissance poets and novelists, Randolph was hesitant to place black culture, ethnicity and nationalism on the same agenda with other social and political concerns. "Having no cultural philosophy of their own, they remained under the tutelage of irrelevant white radical ideas."[74] This same assessment is also made by DuBois in a speech, *The Field and Function of the Negro College,* presented at Fisk Universtiy in 1933. DuBois criticized the literary Renaissance as "literature written for the benefit of white readers, and starting primarily from the white point of view. It never had a real Negro constituency and it did not grow out of the inmost heart and frank experience of Negroes . . ."[75] Similarly, Randolph's economic determinism, his political pattern of compromise and reconciliation, his narrow definitions of class and culture proved harmful throughout his entire career. When he did turn to the black workers with an avowedly nationalistic style and program for political confrontation of the segregationist status quo, the first Negro March on Washington, he was dramatically successful. When he overcame his Socialist Party training and used some of the language of the black church and Southern black political protest traditions to appeal to his Brotherhood's rank-and-file, he had a potentially revolutionary force. Yet his ambiguous hostility toward the Negro's nationalism negated the full potential of his efforts.

Randolph's contribution to the ongoing struggle for black self-determination was unique and profoundly important. His activities in creating the Brotherhood of Sleeping Car Porters, the National Negro Congress and the March on Washington Movement of 1940-41 were necessary preconditions to the black activism of the 1950s and 1960s. For all its faults, as Cruse suggests in *The Crisis of the Negro Intellectual,* "not a single Negro publication in existence today matches the depth of the old *Messenger.*" Randolph was the first truly great leader of the black urban working class. But unlike DuBois, he was unable to reevaluate himself and his movement dialectically; ultimately he became a prisoner of his own limited vision for black America.

In the next stage of history, black working people and activists must transcend Randolph's contradictions. If they succeed, as they must, they will begin to realize the full meaning of socialism as it applies to all aspects of black social existence. In doing so, they will carry out the legacy of Randolph, that he was unable to achieve for himself and his own generation.

PART TWO: CULTURE AND CONSCIOUSNESS

PROLOGUE TO PART II

In the West, there was a proper relation between State and civil society, and when the State trembled a sturdy structure of civil society was at once revealed. The State was only an outer ditch, behind which there stood a powerful system of fortresses and earthworks: more or less numerous from one State to the next.

Antonio Gramsci
Prison Notebooks

"Yessuh," he said, handing over the yams, "I can see you one of these old-fashioned yam eaters."
"They're my birthmark," I said. "I yam what I am!"

Ralph Ellison
Invisible Man

We have attempted to illustrate that black politics should not be viewed narrowly as electoral activity, or struggles to influence the behavior of elected officials and the federal or state bureaucracies. Political work cannot be separated easily from activities in the cultural sphere. For instance, a film on the brutal oppression of black people in South Africa provides the vehicle for discussing the ways in which black Americans' money is invested to support apartheid. What becomes somewhat more difficult is to provide an adequate definition for culture and especially its relationship to black political activity.

Most black people never really contemplate if there is a black culture, and whether it has anything to do with political work. Some people still use the word culture as an adjective to describe individuals who exhibit tastes and aesthetics which are Western European in origin. These individuals would say that art exists "for art's sake;" that aesthetics deal with personal sensibilities and creativity, while politics is simply the process of governmental decision-making. Since the Black Power movement, many black people have broken from the old tradition of dividing culture between "high culture" (e.g., Da Vinci, Mozart, ballet, opera) and "popular culture" (e.g., blues, jazz, Ralph Ellison). Still, there remains an unwritten assumption among many black activists that culture is something you do at black churches or at visits to a museum.

Orthodox Marxism adds to the confusion of black intellectuals and activists by the division of culture from economics and political activity. Many Marxists, especially those who formed the Second International in the late nineteenth century, viewed economic changes as the decisive force within all human relations. The "base" or economics evolved, bringing along with it the "super-structure," consisting of culture and politics. The Bolshevik Revolution of 1917 challenged this interpretation of social development by proving that a socialist revolution could occur within an "unripe" society which was partially feudal and partially capitalist. But although Lenin understood the necessity for cultural struggle within the transformation of the total society, most of his disciples simply replaced politics for economics in their formulas to promote socialism. They approached cultural work as being secondary, at best, to the issue of seizing the state apparatus or government. Questions of culture, which include ethnic and racial relations, family structure, the relations between men and women, raising children, education and the arts, would be settled *after* the revolution. This approach negates any realistic understanding of culture.

The essays in part two are not a comprehensive critique of Afro-American and American cultural institutions. Two articles discuss the role of the media in establishing certain norms and expectations in racial relations. One essay explores the psychological dimensions of political work. A fourth considers the theme of violence within modern American culture. All of the essays consider culture to be not merely influential, but as the most important political forum for the coming decade. Struggling for clarity in relations between black men and women is a major political goal of the black movement for black self-determination. Creating a positive, constructive image of blackness within the media must be viewed as a political effort, to be waged against the white owners of newspapers, television and radio networks. The battle to halt the use of racist language and ideology brings us closer towards a society in which all aspects of racist thought will be banned.

Cultural revolution is a necessary and preliminary step toward a complete social transformation within any modern technological society. Black people must break from the aesthetics, patterns of human relations and thought of their own conservative black elites, as well as from white leaders in dominant cultural institutions. Struggle for state power must connote the battle of blacks as a group to control critical elements of their own consciousness and civil society. The battle for autonomous black cultural forms and institutions will promote the broader struggle for control in the sphere of economics. However, we must also understand that cultural integrity and autonomy does not by itself provide the complete basis for all social change.

The struggle for black cultural clarity and aesthetic self determination will be decisive within this historic period in determining the outcome of the Black Movement as a whole. This means, in short, that black people must reestablish who they are culturally and what they wish to become as human beings within the continuum of our cultural heritage. "It is the Negro himself who must be transformed," Cruse wrote in 1968, "before his self-projection can transform a racist society into something else."

The Cultural Dialectics of Violence

Media, Popular Culture and Violence

The vacuous, contradictory character of the 1970s were expressed best within the institutions of U.S. civil society, or culture. If the 1960s were upsetting to the traditional criteria of aesthetic values, the 1970s have done more than enough to move Americans backward to the McCarthy era. As it is today, the United States has experienced a blinding retreat from critical thinking and creativity on the cultural front.

Paul Fromm, the director of the Fromm Music Foundation at Harvard, wrote about this cultural crisis in the *New York Times* in late 1978. "Our arts today are weary, stale and flat—but not unprofitable," he admitted. "The daring innovations" of the previous decade such as electronic music and multi-media works "have gone stale or vanished." U.S. culture has ceased to be innovative and now almost imitates televised commercials. Instead of cultural creativity, Fromm wrote, "we get mass entertainments tailored for the largest possible audiences." U.S. art has become the forum for big business.

93

Fromm's lament for reviving cultural creativity was commendable, but it missed the point entirely. U.S. culture, beginning at its popular foundations, is generated by its mass institutions of thought—its secondary schools, colleges and universities; its media, theatre and athletics; its museums and literature. The quality of cultural creativity is determined largely by the relative economic support these institutions receive, and by the democratic access of ethnic minorities, women and various oppressed groups have in influencing their direction. Using this criteria, the 1970s experienced a reaction of major proportions.

U.S. popular culture often attempts to restore its permanently sagging credibility by repeating cultural patterns of previous generations. In recent years the public was accosted by "Grease", "American Hot Wax", and "The Buddy Holly Story", films of uneven quality that glorify the excitement of the 1950s youth culture. Disco dancing restored some of the ballroom music of the 1940s period, although mutilated to conform to the pulsating beat of the current "crossover" aesthetic rock standards.

Most popular movies dealing with cultural and social problems, like "Saturday Night Fever", were musical morality plays. Behind the explicit language and blatant sexuality was actually a cleaned-up version of "making it" within the cultural confines of U.S. American capitalism. The social anger of the 1960s that had helped to create genuinely new creative forms was turned inward and neutralized. Even the bland, liberal social critics from *Newsweek* reluctantly agree that the 1970s were "the era of cultural homogenization, mellow sounds, nostalgia and reruns, in which revolt has been supplanted by self-realization."

When one turns to commercial television as an indicator of the status of U.S. culture, one finds an even more chaotic and antihumanist undercurrent. As each new television season approaches, a number of shows are dropped—because they do not reach a sufficient number of consumers to justify the fiscal support of the corporations in the form of commercial revenues—and a host of other programs replace them. ABC, NBC and CBS all proclaim a new season of innovative and unique shows, to be followed subsequently by other newer, and more innovative offerings for the next fall. What many of these new series and reruns have in common is an excessive use and even glorification of violence.

The large amount of violence which we view on commercial

television is fundamentally political in essence. The bloody beatings, the murders and assassinations which are portrayed repeatedly for home audiences during prime time serve a political purpose. They represent a larger, more violently political process within the country to suppress the cultures and traditional patterns of ethnicity, progressive ideas and aesthetics which form the basis for the lives of millions of black, poor, and politically oppressed groups.

Perhaps the best example of violence within the media is the widespread popularity of police shows on television. During the early 1960s during the Great Frontier administration of John F. Kennedy, it was not surprising that Westerns, rather than cops-and-robbers, were the most widely praised and promoted television shows. Bonanza, Gunsmoke, and Wyatt Earp spoke to a simpler time in white U.S. history, when there were supposedly good guys and bad guys and no one was in the middle. The heroes were white, wore white hats, rode powerful white stallions and were paternalistically kind toward women and children; they were bitterly opposed to Indians' rights, civil liberties for suspected lawbreakers, and nonviolence.

Gradually, this sort of violence became an even greater force within the public mind; violence became a part of the popular culture's basis for pleasure and entertainment. Anne Taylor Fleming describes the relationship between eros, the media and public brutality in a moving essay entitled "The Dark Roots of Violence." In the 1960s, the assassinations of the Kennedys and Martin Luther King were turned into televised pageants. "On television, people seem to die for only a moment," she observed. "There is only the now, what is on the screen." The passage of time, or more fundamentally, the processes of human history, is negated into a melodramatic production without meaning. There is no culmination of the patterns of human life; people are killed, but the finality of death is missing. States Fleming, "we watched the war in Vietnam. We began to accept violence as a natural part of our public lives." Americans adopted the public message they viewed on their televisions and grafted it onto their private, personal lives. "We grew meaner with each other than we imagined," she says, "we stopped hearing our own voices. Sex became a battleground, pleasure a bone between dogs."[1]

Violence thus assumed many new cultural and social forms.

Growing bored with their suburbs, souring on the "American Dream," the middle-class, middle-aged white elite began to practice "wife swapping." The very notion implies ownership; the woman as a form of a husband's private property is exchanged or bartered for another. Human beings became objects, just as products on television or in other commercial media can be exchanged at suburban supermarkets. Voyeurism became hip; sadomasochism became an accepted sexual/public activity. Fleming is correct in her assertion that "in voyeurism there is the seed of violence." The distance between the subject and object of recognition expands, as violence and an abstract roughness replace sensibility and real emotions. Aesthetics succumb to whatever television executives find it is profitable to promote at the moment. Violence becomes not only acceptable, but is a form of sensual pleasure, an expression of popular culture. The violence in the marketplace and media is replicated in the life of the individual.[2]

With the Vietnam War, the ghetto riots and the explosion of Black Power, white people in the United States experienced a series of psychological shocks. After the defeat of U.S. troops in Southeast Asia and after the collapse of the Johnson Administration's credibility, sections of the white public could not be fooled: the good guys in government were actually the real villains; the man with the white hat was the murderer of this country's youth. The Lone Ranger's mask had become, as it were, a black badge of oppression.

Politically, the media and the state attempted to rectify this situation; their solution was a drive toward more violence. The Nixon administration charged commercial television for being too soft on crime, too liberal and too permissive. A number of stations which did attempt to report objectively and responsibly on the massacre at My Lai, or on the Pentagon's cost overruns, were warned point blank that they could lose their licenses to broadcast. As in the Red Scare of the 1950s, when Hollywood movie studios fired many of their best and most gifted writers because of their progressive political views, television corporations were more than eager to capitulate to Nixon's demands along the cultural front.

Suddenly a rash of "good cops" appeared on home television screens. Jack Webb was retrieved from mothballs to star in a remake of the Dragnet series. Action, sophomoric dialogue and politically-sanctioned violence were basic elements of the new cop shows of the 1970s. Rockford, Baretta, Starsky and Hutch seldom chased after white collar criminals, political hacks and Watergate conspirators. Increasing numbers of illegal police acts were committed on television. Has Steve McGarrett of Hawaii Five-O ever gone to the county court house to pick up a search warrant? According to studies at Drexel University in 1969, completed at the beginning of the Nixon administration, the percentage of television police who regularly failed to advise suspects of their constitutional rights was 21 percent. By 1971, the figure was over 50 percent.

According to another survey, the average child in the United States will witness about 18,000 murders on television by the time she or he finishes high school. It is not surprising, then, that all our children have become gradually and seductively accustomed to both private and public violence. Rape and murder no longer matter. They are no longer surprised at the massive destruction of entire populations through the pursuit of genocide. They acknowledge the infallibility of businessmen, politicians and government bureaucrats. They accept without remorse the inhumanity of humankind. Their ability to think critically and independently apart from the media recedes before the grey reflections of the television tube.

Consciousness and Violence

The supreme paradox of U.S. civil society resides in the extreme poverty of ideas displayed within the context of the world's most economically productive society. The U.S. Appalachian population may be starved by capitalist standards, but in the world community of the hungry and dispossessed, they are quite well off indeed. Many labor union bureaucrats fight not so much for cost of living incentives but for the right *not* to accept overtime. In the aesthetic institutions of the United States, in literary and artistic circles, cultural originality and ethnic creativity is largely a thing of the past. The media, the arts, the communications systems and educational structures perform a single task with quiet efficiency: the masking of the violence which has become the central creative force in capitalist America. "The cultural mainstream of this nation is an empty street," Harold Cruse suggested, "full of bright lights that try to glamorize the cultural wreckage and flotsams of our times. Over this deranged, tormented cultural wasteland reigns a social stratum—a white cultural elite of America, the soured cream of our creative and aesthetic intelligentsia, that dominates nevertheless the roar of prestigious acclaim."[3] U.S. civil society acts as an educational force which translates the will of larger material forces into specific cultural terms. Intellectuals, artists and educators perform the function of ministers of state, rational defenders of the corruption and violence which intrinsically becomes part of the system.

This poverty of ideas among U.S. society's paramount cultural forces indicates the level of profound social contradictions within the society. One finds a recent desire to return to the past, to recapture in cultural terms a less complex, socially vigorous era. Thus the media projects "Westerns" which glorify the rugged individualist, a "Roaring Twenties" Prohibition period piece or a 1950s satire. These changes in the arts represent "a social nostalgia for the past (which) has become almost obsessive," British historian J.H. Plumb writes. "Does it spring from a growing sense of anxiety, of unease, of dislocation?" Plumb asks whether it is "true the world man has created for himself can only be lived at an immense emotional cost to himself?"[4] Plumb misses the point here, for this preoccupation with the cultural past implies that bourgeois intellectuals are increasingly less able to mask the terror of the cultural and social marketplace. It also represents an attempt by the capitalist class to stop history—that is, to reverse the evolution of society through the manipulation of the popular consciousness. Small wonder that the "law and order" administration of Richard Nixon employed police tactics against leftists and blacks which were rationalized as "vigilante" justice. In similar ways the film industry harmonizes the cowboy-like murder of ethnic minorities to Herbie Hancock's so-called progressive jazz in *Death Wish,* while disco replaced the sensitive cultural creativity of Charlie Parker and Bessie Smith.

The issue of violence as a cultural attitude has political and economic significance, particularly to the Afro-American. As the civil society glorifies violence and personal anarchism in the aesthetics, blacks have imitated these irrational cultural patterns of the larger society and have crystalized them in their own politics. During the Sixties many black radicals seized the politics of chaos and violence for its own sake, devoid of the theoretical frame which was crucial in critiquing society. From the Black Panthers and H. Rap Brown to the Northern ghetto followers of Robert Williams, would-be revolutionaries quoted Mao on the character of the struggle: "Political power comes out of the barrel of the gun."[5] Lacking a developed sense of their own history and their cultural origins many black radicals seized upon Frantz Fanon's concept of therapeutic violence without ever really comprehending the existential and Marxian roots of his theory.[6] At times black historians and social critics used a colonial analogy to describe our present social conditions, without appreciating fully the truly dynamic character of U.S. civil society. More often than not, black radicals who glorified the hatred of all whites did so to fill the vacuum left by the lack of an ideology to adequately describe modern society's complex cultural forces and inherent contradictions. As the New Left ultimately glorified the politics of absurdity, some of Black Power's most articulate spokespersons soon retreated to a variant of neo-Booker T. Washington conservatism or irrational, neo-anarchist rhetoric.[7]

Black historian Vincent Harding, among others, has been particularly disturbed by this reflexive trait of nihilism so evident within contemporary radical black politics and cultural institutions. "We have imbibed so much of this society's love for instant success without struggle or suffering that we may not bring anything truly different out of our bag of blackness. It may be that we have been so nurtured on the romance of the gun that we will let it become a substitute for winning the minds and hearts of our people—just like America." In their rush to jubilee, the former Civil Rights advocates lost their cultural bearings; in their desire for political self-determination, ultra-leftists like Imamu Baraka and revolutionary opportunists like Eldridge Cleaver substituted the use of violence for a critical understanding of culture and its relevancy to social transformations. Harding continues, "Here again the gun, this time the gun of blackness, may stop students and others from doing the hard work: winning our brothers to the struggle."[8]

The tragedy of modern Afro-American protest thought in culture, politics and violence is a general crisis in social theory and originality. This crisis is shared by U.S. society as a whole. The deeper the economic contradictions of capitalism, the more violent the character of the bourgeoisie and its agents, the politicians, become. At this point, the role of civil society becomes crucial, for it is in the best interests of bourgeois intellectuals, artists media personnel and advertisement managers to promote massive consumerism, tasteless fads and fashions. For blacks, a social revolution must begin first at a philosophically liberating and cultural level. Blacks, as society's most wretched, oppressed caste and class, must say "No" to the culture and politics of the oppressor. Psychologically, this connotes turning one's back to the Other, demanding of oneself a higher ethical consciousness. More importantly, in the context of civil society this connotes a general rejection of popular U.S. cultural norms and expectations and the beginning of a cultural and ultimately economic struggle for all of society. The cultural struggle projects ethics as politics, and places theory in command of violence and force.

The consciousness derived from one's culture may be at once both conservative and liberating. The terrain of traditional aesthetics, approached from the cultural habits of a people, may be the starting point from which the radical social critic turns away from contemporary culture. Gramsci often implied that culture's vehicle, civil society, expresses both who a people are or were and also where history is taking them. The U.S. South provided blacks with a dual consciousness. In a climate of servile labor production and paternal racism, the faith and spirituality of blacks became in many ways quite conservative. Yet Afro-American religion, the social institutions and aesthetic character of black slave stories and folklore, defended the humanity of the oppressed. The cultural norms of the blacks attempted to subvert the peculiar institution by consciously posing an alternative sense of values, a black sense of being, a different and independent ethical behavior. As conservative as this cultural structure was, its ultimate aim was quite revolutionary: an end to the world as it was, and the establishment of an ethical existence under radically different economic rules and procedures. This alternative sense of being provide us with a starting point, the cultural consciousness to reject unethical politics and violent economic structures for a higher form of life.

Critical and ethical aesthetic attitudes which transcend the culture of violence are not solely and uniquely Afro-American. Nguyen Khac Vien also speaks of moral consciousness as being a central tool for the emancipation of the Vietnamese people. "The Vietnamese and Chinese have particularly exhibited more of a moralistic tone than Communist Parties elsewhere, where the bourgeoisie has exercised ideological leadership over a long period of time," writes Vien.[9] In Italy, Gramsci also insisted that revolutionary politics could only challenge the "particular cultural and moral level...which corresponds to the needs of the productive forces for development, and hence to the interests of the ruling class," when their social theories posed an alternative cultural consciousness.[10] Like the Vietnamese, Afro-Americans have historically posed moral alternatives to the cultural and social traditions of the underdeveloped white Southern bourgeoisie. Their sense of culture conserved for black people a spirit of humanity and dignity from which struggle for new definitions in economics can be waged.

Rape and Race

Only a decade ago, Eldridge Cleaver was perhaps one of the most prominent of all the advocates of Black Power. A devoted, self-proclaimed follower of Malcolm X, a former member of the Nation of Islam, Cleaver had served "hard time" in the California prison system. His work first appeared in *Ramparts* magazine, a countercultural antiwar publication. Once released from Folsom Prison, he gravitated into the newly formed Black Panther Party and was subsequently Minister of Information. His 1968 candidacy for President on the Peace and Freedom Party ticket and his seven year exile made Cleaver a *cause celebre* among large numbers of black and white activists.

His major theoretical work, *Soul On Ice,* was published in early 1968. Instantly it struck a responsive cord among black and white liberals and certain New Left intellectuals. Julian Mayfield, who should have known better, exalted the semi-autobiographical, semi-polemical essay. *Soul On Ice,* he declared in *The Nation,* is "beautifully written by a man with a formidably analytical mind. (He) makes you twist and flinch because he is no damned gentleman. He throws light on the dark areas we wish he would leave alone." Author Max Geismar read the volume and concluded that Cleaver was "simply one of the best cultural critics now writing, and I include in this statement both the formal sociologists and those contemporary fictionists who have mainly abandoned this

province of literature for the cultivation of the cult of sensibility."
Comparisons were made which contrasted Cleaver favorably with
Frantz Fanon. Black Studies and Literature departments assigned
the paperback as required reading. Cleaver's prestige as an author
and cultural theorist was critically important when, in 1969, he and
a section of the Panthers publicly attacked Stokely Carmichael and
other Black Powerites on the grounds of narrow nationalism and
racial provincialism.

Throughout this earlier period of Cleaver's prominence, few
critics seriously examined the content of his exegesis for the
necessity of violence or force in political life, and especially, its
relationship to women. In his initial chapter "On Becoming," he
describes himself as a kind of angry, eclectic anarchist, hungrily
drawing his own emerging political worldview from Milhail Ba-
kunin. "I began to look at white America through new eyes," he
explained. "Somehow I arrived at the conclusion that, as a matter
of principle, it was of paramount importance for me to have an
antagonistic ruthless attitude toward white women.[11] Curiously,
the real object of antagonism, the white male, is not confronted in
Cleaver's outlook or political practice. Cleaver concluded that he
could best "step outside of the white man's law" by violating the
single-most, prized "property" of the white male—"his" woman.
An act of violence against her would indirectly serve to diminish the
white man's authority over his own mind.[12]

This conviction was reinforced by Cleaver's subconscious
acquisition of white aesthetic and cultural standards. Despite his
violent rhetoric to the contrary, Cleaver never came to terms with
his own self-hatred and deeply felt passion for what the image of the
white woman represented. He states, "At the moment I walked out
of the prison gate, my feelings toward white women in general could
be summed up in the following:

> "To A White Girl"
> I love you
> Because you're white
> Not because you're charming
> Or bright.
> Your whiteness
> Is a silky thread
> Snarling through my thoughts
> In redhot patterns

Of lust and desire.
I hate you
Because you're white.
Your white meat
Is nightmare food.
The skin of Evil.
You're my Moby Dick,
White Witch,
Symbol of the rope and hanging tree,
of the burning cross.
Loving you thus
And hating you so,
My heart is torn in two.
Crucified.[13]

Cleaver concluded that the only way that he could resolve this dilemma was to become a rapist. "Rape was an insurrectionary act. It delighted me that I was defying and trampling upon the white man's law, upon his system of values, and that I was defiling his women—and this point, I believe," he added, "was the most satisfying to me because I was very resentful over the historical fact of how the white man has used the black woman." Again here, Cleaver selects a method which does not confront his supposed enemy, the white man, but simply relives the brutal sexual pattern of master-slave relations—what in some slave colonies in the Americas was termed the *droit de seignior.* "I felt," he confides in *Soul On Ice,* "I was getting revenge."[14]

Whose revenge? For earlier in his narrative, Cleaver reveals: "To refine my technique and modus operandi, I started out by practicing on black girls in the ghetto—in the black ghetto where dark and vicious deeds appear not as aberrations or deviations from the norm, but as part of the sufficiency of the Evil of the day—and when I considered myself smooth enough, I crossed the tracks and sought out white prey. I did this consciously, deliberately, willfully, methodically...." One wonders whether Cleaver, in wrestling young black women to the ground and physically assaulting them, was actually "practicing" for the real thing—white women—or in reality projecting his own self-hatred of blackness and his hatred and fear of all women into the very act of rape. The confession that he did indeed rape black women negates his own justification—that he was acting out his antagonism against white males, or capitalism, or the system of white power. Later, Cleaver denounces his past rapes, and in his words he began writing "to save myself." Interestingly he adds that he had acquired "some insight into my own motivations."

We can condemn Cleaver's logic as twisted, antihuman and demented—for it is all that and more. Certainly any political theories based upon the act of force or violence that violates the human essence or being of any individual or persons are bankrupt. But in a real way, Cleaver's sudden rise to prominence as a cultural guru of the late sixties and his statements about women—black or white—tell us something important about the essential nature of rape within modern cultures or society.

First, Cleaver admits that rape is an act devoid of sexual connotations. In effect, Cleaver does not discuss the inherent sexual attractiveness of his victims. He does not disclose their approximate ages, height, weight, skin color or clothing. In a blunt and rather matter of fact way he tells his readers that he began to rape white women because he opposed the white man's laws and value systems. He began to rape sisters because he had to gain technique and knowledge in the act of physical violence against any women, and besides, black women were readily available in his natural environment. In both cases, the act of rape has nothing to do with sexuality *per se:* it has everything to do with violence and the uses of power. He used violence to exert the power of his "manhood" against black women "for the cause;" violence is aimed against white women because they are surrogates for the historic injustices committed by white males.

Second, the victims of rape are viewed as property. In this way Cleaver accepts the dominant view in U.S. capitalist society that all women belong to someone other than themselves. Black women belong to black men. White women belong to white men. White men can be attacked by attacking white women. Black women can be physically attacked because they belong to black men. The circle of violence thus remains unbroken; males' property rights precede all other rights.

If Cleaver was an isolated case, we might be willing to dismiss his work as a product of self-hatred and sexist illogic. What makes these passages in *Soul on Ice* so important is that its second observation—women viewed as common property—forms the foundations of much of U.S. law; ironically, its first observation—

that rape is an act of political terrorism, not sexual pleasure—is denied by much of U.S. law. Cleaver's commentary reveals the basic, violent truth about rape without challenging capitalist property relations; U.S. jurisprudence denies the truth of rape as violence as a means to oppress all women and simultaneously to perpetuate capitalist property rights.

Consider the example of Archie Simonson, former judge of Dane County, Wisconsin. In the spring of 1977, three boys attacked a sixteen year old girl under a stairwell in a Madison, Wisconsin, high school. Judge Simonson declared that one fifteen year old boy was only reacting normally, because the provocative clothing of the high school girls and the general sexually permissive climate had provoked his act. The girl he helped rape was wearing blue jeans and a flannel shirt. The rapist was ordered to stay at home for a time under court supervision, rather than being sentenced to serve time in jail or a rehabilitation institution. When feminists protested his decision, Judge Simonson lashed back. "There should be a restoration of modesty in dress and the elimination from the community of the sexual gratification business," he stated. On his decision not to punish an admitted juvenile rapist, the judge declared, "I'm trying to say to women, 'stop teasing'."

As a campaign to oust Simonson from his position was mounted, the judge continued to justify his decision in the most provocative terms. Even in court, he explained, "women (appear) without bras and with the nipples fully exposed, and they think it is smart and they sit here on the witness stand with their dresses up over the cheeks of their butts, and we have this type of thing in the schools." On the theory that women are the cause of rape, Simonson asserted that "it sure raises a lot of interest in my mind from time to time." By September, 1977, Simonson lost the judgeship in a special recall election to lawyer Moria Krueger. But the election was an anticlimax for Simonson. Throughout 1978 and 1979 he was on the lecture circuit and talk shows, getting paid as a celebrity.[15]

The pattern of violence against women grows geometrically with the political surge of feminism. F.B.I. statistics note that *reported* rapes doubled in less than a decade, from 27,620 in 1967 to 56,730 in 1976. Cases of battered women have reached an all-time high. And according to all observers, the number of unreported rapes and beatings of black and white women dwarf the amount of reported incidents. For example, statistics of the Los Angeles Ad Hoc Committee on Rape, one out of every three women over the age of fourteen living in Los Angeles County will be a victim of rape during their lifetimes.[16] According to a study by the Law enforcement Assistance Administration, black and other minority women are more than 1.7 times as likely to be rape victims than white women. Only a small proportion of minority women are raped by white males.[17]

Throughout the 1970's, black and white women fought back. Against the twisted polemics of Cleaver, against the blatant sexism of Simonson, against the weight of U.S. law enforcement officials, the court system and the sexist fabric of U.S. civil society—they declared a resounding "No" to violence. This is especially true for black women. When Dessie Woods, a twenty-two year old black Georgia woman, shot an attempted white rapist with his own unlicensed handgun, she became the criminal in the opinion of the law. She was drugged, beaten and forced into solitary confinement by the Georgia police; on February 2, 1976, she was sentenced to serve twenty-two years in a women's penitentiary. In North Carolina several years before, Joanne Little killed her attacker, a white jailer, and was forced to flee to New York to obtain freedom. In both instances black women asserted their rights as black people, as human beings and as women in their rejection of physical assault.

The patterns of violence against women are political and assume international dimensions. Turning to Simone de Beauvoir in *The Second Sex,* we find that:

> Women as a rule are unfamiliar with violence, they have not been through the tussles of childhood and youth as have men; and now the girl is laid hold of, swept away in a bodily struggle in which the man is the stronger. She is no longer free to dream, to delay, to maneuver: She is in his power, at his disposal....It is not uncommon for the young girl's first experience to be a real rape and for the man to act in an odiously brutal manner; in the country and wherever manners are rough, it often happens that—half consenting, half revolted—the young peasant girl loses her virginity in some ditch, in shame and fear.[18]

These patterns begin at childhood, and end at the grave. The overwhelming majority of sexually abused children are female, and the great preponderance of sexual offenders are men. The patterns are immune to race and class distinctions; white and black men beat and mutilate their wives and lovers, sisters and daughters, while the state and civil society perpetuate reasons for the violence.

And what of race, and its relationship to violence against women? Racial differences or distinctions reinforce and in many instances initiate the act of violence against women, accentuating the traditional rights of men over women into an overtly political statement. When Ronnie Horne, a white insurance salesman, attempted to rape Dessie Woods, he was motivated by his racist contempt for her blackness as much as by his sexist hatred of her womanhood. Racism reinforced the normal pattern of relations between all men and women by preconditioning Horne to assert both his whiteness and his masculine right to own any woman he desired. Thus, the slaying of Horne by Dessie Woods was a three-fold rejection of the dialectic of violence against blacks, against women, and against the capitalist concept of private ownership. Horne's attempted rape can be viewed as a statement in favor of the old plantation-style master-slave relationship; Wood's act was both revolt against that slavery and simultaneously an act of personal and collective self-assertion.

The destruction of capitalism will not, contrary to the opinions of many white and black leftists, obliterate sexism and the traditional pattern of physical violence against women. Rape is only one important chapter of this violence—forced sterilization, the political attack against lesbians, the inability to receive abortions on demand, and the lack of birth control information are other aspects of this anti-woman assault. Socialist countries on the whole have made some significant, qualitative steps toward the abolition of this kind of violence, but the battle cannot be won simply by transferring the ownership of the basic means of production from the capitalists to the working class.

The struggle against violence must be waged within all progressive social movements if there is any possibility that any fundamental changes are to take place. Male theoreticians, black or white, who do not place the struggle for democratic and human rights for women at the center of their postulates for social transformation are simply replicating the hegemonic practices and the thoughts of the older, racist and capitalist civil society. Through a process of self-criticism and extensive reeducation men must make a break from the logic of what it has meant to be male, in order to redefine themselves and their relationships with women.

The entire history of black people in the Americas has been underscored by the habitual violence of white men against black women. In the great majority of nineteenth century slave revolts in the United States, there is scant evidence that black rebels were the least bit interested in retaliating against slave owners by raping their former plantation masters' wives. Certainly after the Civil War there is virtually no real evidence to the old claim that black men were sexually attacking white women in the South. Virtually all of the racist literature which warned white women against black men's sexual intentions published between 1877 and the Civil Rights Movement was pure polemical trash; phony situations were certainly contrived to lynch young black men, such as the Scottsboro Boys case in 1931. Constantly on the defensive, most black men have been too busy defending their loved ones and their communities to project their hatred of the system into a political demand to "punish" white women. Therefore, when Cleaver accepts the old plantation mythologies and builds a political theory upon them, he has not only inverted the reality of black history, but deliberately accepts the sexist reasoning of the old master himself. By the act of rape and by extension any systematic pattern of violence against women, Cleaver negates his human potential and "surrenders" to the white, male world.

The End of Bourgeois Violence

While imprisoned in Mussolini's fascist prisons Gramsci observed that there was an integral, dynamic relationship between the culture of a society and its central mode of production. The evolution of organized religious institutions, schools, political and cultural organizations creates fundamental changes within the material world and the relations of business and exchange between individuals. Those cultural institutions which economic determinists relegated to "superstructure" Gramsci saw as being vitally linked to the broader economic tendencies in society. Political and economic contradictions could not be understood outside of the culture and the ethics of a particular historical *block*. Thus "the claim, presented as an essential postulate of historical materialism, that every fluctuation of politics and ideology can be presented and expounded as an immediate expression of the structure, must be contested in theory as primitive infantilism..."[19] The violence and force so evident within U.S. popular culture has initiated even more social contradictions within the economic structures of society. As history progresses dialectically, the violent tendencies and antihuman attitudes which express contemporary aesthetics and ethics initiate similar destructive social tendencies within the marketplace.

As U.S. capitalist culture matures the importance of violence has matured, developing into the fundamental cultural value for our time. The roots of the violence and the direction of capitalist cultural relations initiate patterns and behavior affecting the material world, civil society and economic forces violently and unevenly, lurching through periods of collapse and boom.

As Marxist cultural writer Christopher Caudwell observed, "the bourgeois state becomes a theatre of the violent and coercive subjection of man to man for the purposes of economic production." Violence and the alienation from reality form an exploitation of the spirit and mind, the cultural manifestations of bourgeois hegemony. "Bourgeois culture has discovered that what pays is bourgeois violence."[20]

From the perspective of an oppressed culture, the radical rejects those aesthetic images which reflect the vulgar consciousness of the bourgeoisie. Herbert Marcuse noted in 1969 that the forces of "the market" attempt to minimize the "music, literature (and) art" of the rebellion, particularly those cultural traditions of blacks. An ethical and revolutionary cultural consciousness must "abandon the direct appeal, the raw immediacy of their presentation, which involves, in the protest, the familiar universe of politics and business, and with it the helpless familiarity of frustration and temporary release from frustration." Artists who turn their backs to Western forms become political figures in the struggle for the liberation of all humanity; political theorists who understand the necessity for constructing a revolutionary culture outside of violent capitalist dogma become artists. "Today's rebels against the established culture also rebel against the beautiful in this culture, against its all too sublimated, segregated, orderly, harmonizing forms."[21]

U.S. capitalist culture perpetuates itself through its promulgation of false consciousness and the projection of popular force and violence, which in turn justifies the inequities of the material world. With Hobsbawn we might argue that violence itself has become the central creative factor in all social relations. As bourgeois culture slowly disintegrates, the social products of capital have and will project a vulgar individualism and aggressive antihumanism. Our major cultural task is to pose an alternative set of ethics and aesthetic values in challenging the hegemony within society of the white, largely male, capitalist class.

Roots Reconsidered

Over one hundred years ago, my great-grandfather, newly freed after the Civil War, left the black belt plantation where he had been a slave. Travelling with his wife and small children, Morris Marable settled in the rocky, upcountry hills in northeastern Alabama. He cut down pine trees and prepared the virgin red soil for cultivation. Eventually he became a prosperous farmer on a small scale, the leader of a struggling black community near Wedowee, Alabama.

Whenever he was asked about his life and its meaning, Morris Marable would respond that all he tried to do was to keep his children "out from under the white man's thumb." In other words, he and thousands of black farmers like him were struggling for self determination and economic autonomy apart from the white South's Jim Crow system. He was *not* attempting to integrate within a system that viewed him as a social or genetic inferior. Nor did he try to pattern his family's behavior after that of his white oppressors. He was primarily concerned with pursuing the political goal of black self sufficiency and black self respect.

This background of generational struggle, human dignity and suffering is common to almost every Afro-American. This heritage, which begins with our roots in traditional African civilizations, provides the basis for all black identity. Black scholars of history and sociology like W.E.B. DuBois, E. Franklin Frazier and John Hope Franklin have discussed in broad terms the impact of enslavement upon a race of people, and the brutality involved over a period of generations. More recently, white and black historians have depicted the institution of slavery in various ways, from an enterprising although racist capitalist business to a complex struggle for human survival and dignity. What most of these historical studies have not accomplished was the portrayal of the enslavement experience in individual terms. How did an individual Black family survive the experience of systematic exploitation? What can we learn from the pursuit of our roots into slavery and beyond?

The quest for understanding one's identity through the sojourn through the past, was the basis for the novel *Roots,* perhaps the most important cultural achievement of the 1970s. After nine years of research, Alex Haley, a self-educated writer and the author of the best-selling biography, *The Autobiography of Malcolm X,* has reconstructed the cultural beginning of his family and its transition from the West coast of Africa in 1767 to the present. Haley's sweeping historical novel was in a sense the culmination of an historical movement beginning with the influential works of Kenneth Stampp, Herbert Gutman, Eugene D. Genovese and John Blassingame. Upon its release, *Roots* immediately became a national best seller. Achieving the number one position on the *New York Times'* Best Seller List for hardback books, *Roots* editions sold over 900,000 copies in one single month. The publishing industry claimed that final sales figures for *Roots* will reach into the millions.

At Tuskegee Institute, Miami-Dade Community College and over 270 other colleges, courses in African and Afro-American history were initiated based on the reading of Haley's work. *Roots* was acknowledged as a classic in American history, and thousands of college students, housewives and grassroots people lined up whenever Alex Haley appeared to autograph books throughout the country. The popularity of the novel and its broad appeal illustrated the successes of the Civil Rights and Black Power movements for creating the social and intellectual climate to provide legitimacy for Afro-American history and the truths it contained.

As successful as the novel became, *Roots'* most enduring fame arose from its initial serialization in 1977 by the American Broadcasting Company. Allocating six million dollars for production, spending millions more for promotion and in the recruitment of an "all star" white and Black cast from television and the motion pictures, ABC's media interpretation of *Roots* was an instant success. *Variety* reported that "the miniseries established a standard by which program productivity must be measured, set in motion changes in programming concepts and patterns that will profoundly alter traditional methods" of television entertainment. Over 130,000,000 viewers saw some segments of the series, with a nightly average of about 70,000,000 people. The first telecast of *Roots I* on January 23, 1977, captured 40.5 percent of all American television sets, the thirteenth highest rating in media history. Remarkably, the popularity of the program continued to grow the longer the miniseries was on television. The last program on Sunday, January 30, became the highest rated television show of all time, rating in at 51.1 percent. Seven of the eight shows ranked in the top ten in terms of all-time television ratings. The *Roots I* series enabled ABC to become the most popular commercial network for the first time.

From the beginning, much of the criticism of *Roots I* was superficial. White television critics centered on minor historical flaws and shortcomings in acting rather than on the central message of the miniseries. Richard Schickel, a critic for *Time* magazine, called *Roots I* a "*Mandingo* for middlebrows." He complained that *Roots I* was just another simple melodrama in blackface, offering "almost no new insights, factual or emotional" about slavery. Chicago *Sun Times* critic William Granger deplored the series as being so "bad at times that I was filled with embarrassment." Alex Haley's novel was "reduced to a plodding pseudo-Hollywood pop-historical B-movie," argued the *Village Voice.* Historians remarked pointedly that Kunta Kinte's first home in America, a large cotton plantation in Spotsylvania County, Virginia, should have been growing tobacco at that time. There was no wire fencing in the Tidewater South during the 1760s as depicted in the 1977 film, and the date of Nat Turner's 1831 rebellion is pushed back ten years. The white author of the controversial, best selling novel, *The Confessions of Nat Turner,* William Styron, blasted Haley and called *Roots I* "crude" and "dishonest tripe." More racist whites manifested their outrage against *Roots I*'s message by resorting to violent rhetoric. In Greenville, Mississippi, white teenagers verbally assaulted black youths, jeering, "You ol' slave, my granddaddy owned you once upon a time." One white woman interviewed by *Time* magazine in Atlanta believed that "*Roots* was awful. The Blacks were just getting settled down, and this will make them angry again."

Most Black critics applauded *Roots I* without reservations, both the novel and the televised version, at least initially. But Black reflections on the subject of enslavement raised substantial questions of Haley's books and, more pointedly, of the ABC interpretation. Harold Cruse recognized the "contrived, commercialized and romanticized" aspects of the televised *Roots I*. "For one thing," he noted, "under those conditions (during Reconstruction), you don't just tie up a plantation owner to a tree and then get into a wagon and casually drive away as if there weren't bloodhounds and night riders who would track you down," as depicted in the last episode. Yosef ben-Jochannan, African historian and writer, was critical of *Roots'* emphasis on American history at the expense of the African culture of Black people. "I was not stimulated by *Roots* at all" because the presentation "did not show my roots, just an aspect of myself." Interviewed in *CORE* magazine, ben-Jochannan suspected that the entire miniseries "was done in a manner to placate the powers that be in American society." Black pschologist Nathan Hare agreed with ben-Jochannan's assessment. "We have to be skeptical from the standpoint of where it comes from—it comes from the oppressor, the master," he noted. "The agenda and the timing of it were also wrong."

There were a number of problems with the serialization of *Roots* by commercial television. Excellent Black actors and actresses were selected for certain roles, such as Cicile Tyson as the mother of Kunta Kinte, the show's major figure, and versatile Ben Vereen as Kinte's grandson "Chicken George." Otherwise, ABC did Haley and its Black audience no favors; the entire production schedule took on twenty one days per segment: it spiced up the story with plenty of interracial sex and some soft core sadism to generate viewer interest. Left unsaid by most critics, Black and white, was the fact that ABC released and promoted *Roots* for one reason only: to make money. ABC's basic interest in Black history was how it could increase its profit margins, particularly within the Black community.

Perhaps the major distortion in the transition of the novel into the first television series involved the role of the Black woman as the bearer of culture and racial identity. Characters who never make an appearance in the novel are created especially for the popular television audience. The proud Mandinka maiden, Fanta, for instance, becomes an early victim to the vicious sexual advances of white slave traders. After a series of rapes by whites and life on the plantation, Fanta accepted her situation and makes of it the best she can. She deliberately purged her rich African heritage from her memory—its history, lifestyle, values and people. She became, like so many other slaves on Kunta Kinte's plantation, an American. But Haley never created Fanta, or any female character like her. The televised version of *Roots I* treated Bell, Kunta Kinte's wife (portrayed by Madge Sinclair) as a cunning yet long suffering Black female who accepts slavery as being superior to the chance of being free. Gone was Bell's sensitivity and warmth she exhibited for her man inside Haley's novel. Kunta's daughter, Kizzy, is sold and raped at age sixteen by Tom Lea, a vicious Southern cracker, and she bears his mulatto child. In the novel, Kizzy detests her young son for several years, and burns with rage at the thought of her master. In *Roots I* Leslie Uggams does her best to convey the anger and desire for revenge against Lea after being raped, but comes up short with conveying the full meaning of enslavement upon Black women. Harold Cruse said it best: "When you see Leslie Uggams and her long polished nails, you just have to laugh." Repeatedly the televised version of *Roots I* failed to question the ambiguous and complex sexual relationships between Black men and white men, Black men and Black women, and Black men and white women. We obtain a glorified glimpse at Mister Charlie exerting his *droit de seigneur* over his servile concubines, but whether Miss Ann was partaking similar sexual pleasures from Chicken George was anybody's guess.

Another basic criticism of the televised version of *Roots* is that of emphasis. To Haley, the central question of his research was, "Where did I come from?" Haley's study explored in detail the meaning of Black Africa to his personal heritage. Only one serial in eight reveals the rich history of Black West Africa, and even then the televised version said precious little about the African extended family system, the celebrated kingdoms of Mali and Songhai, the influence of Islam on Black life and the general social and cultural traditions of the region. Haley's book originally devoted a lion's share of his narrative to this central historical consideration.

Some Black critics asked the question, "Why has it taken so long for commercial television to produce a series or even a single program with the creative and emotional power of *Roots*?" Historically, white-dominated, capitalist-controlled television has never given the American public even a vaguely accurate retelling of slavery, the Reconstruction and Jim Crow periods. Today, there has not yet been one serious, regular dramatic series with Black people as the central characters, even of the quality of the *Waltons*. More often than not, Blacks are still the subjects of Norman Lear-type comedies. They are portrayed as dancing, joking children, at best partially aware of the full vicissitudes of racism, unemployment and exploitation. Race as the central element of drama still raises monumental questions about whiteness in America, something that neither directors, producers and owners in the television media cannot answer.

Roots: The Next Generations, or *Roots II,* based on the turbulent period of American history spanning four generations of black families, was subsequently shown in 1979. Alex Haley's more recent story moved from the post-Reconstruction period of the 1880s, through the Great Depression and two World Wars. The 14-hour television dramatization was largely historically accurate and the acting was superior in quality to *Roots I.* At times, the scenes were genuinely moving and succeeded on an artistic level. On balance, however, *Roots: The Next Generations* must be judged a failure on political rather than purely aesthetic grounds. The second movie was largely lacking in a single-minded expression of the political attempt of blacks for self determination and racial autonomy.

During the first two segments of the dramatization, we observe the relationship between Sister Carrie (Fay Hauser), a black school teacher, and Jim Warner (Richard Thomas), a member of the town's influential, aristocratic family. Warner is attracted to the black school instructor not because of the unique qualities of her black femininity, but primarily because she is "educated", has "read and understood the poetry of Emerson" and is a "lady" in Victorian terms. In essence, Carrie is fundamentally a white woman with a black skin, a cultural casualty of the white educational system. Whether Carrie has ever had a relationship with a black man is anyone's guess. After their marriage, Colonel Warner (Henry Fonda) disowns his son, and the pair eventually settle down in the black community. Beyond the cultural confusion of the couple resides a socio-political issue—the relationship between black men and women, and the survival of black families in a period of reaction. The relationship between Carrie and Jim set the tone for much of the remainder of the film.

Alex Haley's great-grandfather, Tom Harvey, is confronted with the love affair between his eldest daughter Elizabeth (Debbi Morgan) and a mulatto, John Dolan (Brian Mitchell). Harvey (Georg Stanford Brown) rejects his daughter's suitor on the grounds that he is "too light," too reminiscent of white people. Yet, curiously enough, his "best friend" during slavery was white (ironically his former slave driver) and his friend Carrie is "carrying on" with Colonel Warner's son. None of this makes much aesthetic sense, and none of the participants seemed to understand the political meaning of it all.

Throughout the narrative of *Roots II,* we were treated to the image of the black man who acquiesces to Jim Crow, to filthy conditions and lower wages. There was no room for the black nationalists militants of the era—John Bruce, T. Thomas Fortune, Marcus Garvey, Henry X. Turner. When editor Chandler Owens was mentioned, he is denounced by Will Palmer (Stan Shaw), Alex Haley's grandfather, as a "dangerous and unpatriotic radical". The DuBois-Washington controversy was presented as a fundamental conflict between an "Uncle Tom" educator and a black civil rights activist, rather than a disagreement over strategies and tactics to pursue the goal of black self determination. The N.A.A.C.P. was presented as a respectable organization, but there was little discussion of the important political contributions of the Nation of Islam, S.N.C.C., S.C.L.C. and other activist organizations. The viewer was left with the impression that Malcolm X was assassinated by Elijah Muhammad's followers, without exploring the question of C.I.A.-F.B.I. complicity.

Finally, at the end of our journey toward the rediscovery of our black heritage, the viewer was confronted with Haley himself. The youthful peccadilloes of Haley with a black prostitute were shown in glorious detail, giving the direct impression that either: a). Haley has a great deal of contempt for black women, or b). black women enjoy giving up sex and getting paid for it. What would old Kizzie say about her great-great-great-grandson? Haley's own family disintegrates during his years as a Coast Guard public relations officer. Finally, when Alex met and eventually bedded a middle-class, "assimilated" black woman, we were presented with the most astonishing sight of all—Haley (James Earl Jones) allows his white agent to walk into his bedroom while both he and his black amour are nude. Certainly, we have to ask the question, what does this mean within the context of building meaningful black male-female relationships? Evidently Haley was seeking not the approval of the ghost of Kunta Kinte, but that of the white man himself, in his own bedroom.

However, *Roots II* was not a total failure as art. Dorian Harewood, playing Haley's father, was a brilliant choice. The young actor showed skill and sensitivity portraying a young university professor, attempting to challenge the dominacy of the white plantation owners in rural Alabama. Similarly, Fonda and Marlon Brando (playing George Lincoln Rockwell) excelled in projecting both the complex paternal and psychotic roots of white racism. The weakest segments tended to be on Alex Haley himself.

The central question that must be raised is why *Roots I* and *Roots II* were able to have such a profound impact on the consciousness of Black and white America when other series such as the *Adams Chronicles,* the *American Issues Forums* and the plethora of Black television shows failed to evoke similar outbursts of popularity. Some critics attributed this to the promotional campaign for *Roots*, which began as early as 1975. Others claimed that its real media power was derived from the fact that it was broadcast on eight consecutive nights, a first for commercial television. Some critics noted that the novel was already a bestseller, and that this was a prime reason that so many people tuned their television sets to *Roots I* and *II*. Haley himself attributed the successes of his television series and his novel to the fact that his story was that of "Everyman—that race had little to do with his narrative, and that his odyssey was speaking to the broader human condition. But something more fundamental in the content and centrality of the issues treated was, in the last analysis, more responsible than these or other reasons.

For Black people, both *Roots* presentations confronted those of us who refuse to struggle toward a newer level of social reality and consciousness. *Roots* was a call to struggle, based upon a clear understanding of our history in America. It was a summons to prepare ourselves through reconsidering our past. We must understand where we have come from, and in what ways other Black people demanded an end to their own oppression under the most brutal of circumstances. Through the eyes of a Kunta Kinte, we see ourselves being whipped against a barnyard door; we lose a portion of our foot when we attempt to escape the degradations of the slavery system; we protest in vain when our daughter is taken from us and raped by a white man. If under these kinds of conditions, Black people were able to struggle for a higher level of humanity and in a real extent able to achieve it, what is keeping us at this particular point in history from entering into this historical struggle? *Roots* pressures contemporary Blacks against the wall of historical responsibility, forcing us to reevaluate our temporal commitment to material objects and wealth instead of the more lasting values of freedom and liberation.

Roots asked the question, What is the capacity of an oppressed people to struggle against amazing odds to assert their humanity? In *Roots I*, we observed that the Afro-American experience within slavery was not one of constant opposition, but one which represented both opportunism on the part of some as well as outright and unqualified protest on the part of others. There is a real tendency among the oppressed to succumb to the will of the master class or race; there is also a countervailing tendency to resist and certain characters manifested both tendencies within the novel. Kizzy, the daughter, retained Kunta's pride in Africa, a land she has never seen, while the well-dressed Black driver portrayed by Richard Roundtree had virtually no sense of himself as a Black man, outside that of the consciousness of the master. These are real problems which confront contemporary Black American society today, questions which each individual must face. All Black slaves were not Nat Turner, but the potential for a Nat Turner existed within each slave who carried within himself or herself a deeper sense of culture and racial identity. If we do not admit this to ourselves, we cannot hope to struggle against our own weaknesses today.

Roots was probably, since the Movement of the 1960s, the most significant example of "living history" experienced by American audiences. As in the Civi Rights Movement and in the antiwar demonstrations, television became the forum for a piece of human history that white America would rather forget or even pretend that it did not exist. *Roots* reminded white America once more how the country was founded, and that its cultural and legal institutions rested upon the basic contradictions of human inequality and exploitation. More fundamentally, *Roots* isolated the centrality of race within the making of the American character: racism gives America many of its most unique characteristics.

Both *Roots* episodes since 1977 have allowed White America to understand the reasons for black anger and rage when confronted by white racism. The series has also given whites a list of "token liberals" with whom they can identify—from the ship captain of Kunta Kinte's vessel, to Jim Harvey, to Simon Haley's patron at the *Saturday Evening Post*. When television finally dismisses even these benevolent characters as victims of racism, and restores to primacy the question of black self determination in both family and political relations, we shall begin the construction of a truly nonracist society.

The Psychopolitics of the Movement

About two miles from my home in Tuskegee, Alabama, down a narrow country road, stands an old country church. Every Sunday morning, a handful of old Black men, dressed in ageless dark suits walk slowly past my front porch towards the chapel. Their wives and daughters, wearing colorful print dresses, walk a few feet behind them. Arriving an hour or two after dawn, they assume their regular seats on the church's rugged pine benches. After several opening hymns, they listen to their minister, a stern looking, heavy-set man, delivering a lesson from the Old Testament. He pounds his sweating palms against the withered pages of the Bible, deliberately making his point, searching the faces of his congregation. Finally, he sits down slowly and listens to his choir, a collection of old, ebony ladies from the community, chanting songs that Sojourner Truth and Frederick Douglass probably sang as slaves more than one hundred years ago.

The thesis of this article was first developed in a lecture at a conference in March, 1977, sponsored jointly by the Frantz Fanon Center and the Institute of the Black World, held in Atlanta. I expanded the scope of the paper and it was subsequently published in the Spring, 1978 issue of *State and Mind: People Look At Psychiatry.*

Writing about the Black religious experience, James Baldwin in *Go Tell It On The Mountain* captures the mood of the church and its people:

They sang with all the strength that was in them, and clapped their hands for joy. It was, for them, the very bread of life. Something happened to their faces and their voices, the rhythm of their bodies, and to the air they breathed; it was as though wherever they might be became the upper room, and the Holy Ghost was riding on air. On Sunday mornings the women all seemed patient, all the men seemed mighty.

The church provided the setting for escapism and transcendence from white racism. The Black sharecropper who worked sixteen hours a day could, through the practice o his faith, "seem mighty" in his own eyes. The Black woman raped by the white landlord could transcend her exploitation through the strength of her emotional gospel.

The traditional Black church before the Civil Rights Movement created the cathartic release so essential for Blacks to survive the degradation of Southern life and labor. During periods of mental stress, Black families found strength and solace within the tenets of Black religion. Social welfare services which provided psychiatric counseling for Blacks were virtually nonexistent before 1950, and such services which have been made "available are not viewed as sympathetic" toward Blacks, observes Howard University professor Harriette McAdoo. "Rather than seek aid from an alien, unfriendly community agency, the Black family often turned to their minister." In this way, Southern Blacks found the ability to reject the logic of racial segregation and the racist, personality stereotypes of the proverbial "Uncle Tom," which Southern whites perpetuated since slavery.

The campaigns for desegregation of Southern politics, economics and culture—termed the Movement by its participants—was built largely upon the Black church, and in turn upon the important psychological images created within the context of Black religion. Many Black ministers inspired their congregations to break the local Jim Crow laws in favor of a "higher" moral law, which promoted the transformation of oppressed men and women into social activists. Through church-inspired nonviolent, direct action, rural and working class blacks were given an opportunity to act out their deep anxieties and hostilities against the entire system of white racism.

Since the massive campaigns of the sixties, we have become accustomed thinking of the Movement for the desegregation of Southern society as being totally healthy in a psychological sense and progressive in its political momentum. The sight of young school children, pregnant women and the elderly being arrested for a moral and political cause still sparks the imagination. What we have not done accurately since the sixties is to assess the problems created within and by the Movement, the psychological contradictions within the very successes of desegregation. We have not yet linked Black consciousness, Black culture and what one could call Black mental health to transformations in contemporary politics and culture within Southern society. We have not yet isolated the psychological failures of the Movement, nor analyzed why the struggles for desegregation stopped far short of achieving a genuine social revolution.

The Civil Rights Movement was, foremost, a cultural rejection of a total way of life and thinking, the existence of racial segregation. It involved politics, of course—the N.A.A.C.P.'s legal battles to question the constitutionality of segregationist laws, student and youth organizations to fill Southern jails and to confront the racist police in the streets, and the ministers of the Southern Christian Leadership Conference to provide moral support. Jim Crow was more than a series of antiquated laws, but a complex cultural and psychological reality of exploitation, based upon the ongoing economic exploitation of Black labor. The Movement appealed to Southern Black people to transform themselves, to reject the psychological fetters of racism, to revolt against the old ways and to assert their own humanity. Not unlike the traditional Black church, the Movement urged Southern Blacks to renew themselves through faith, to liberate themselves from the anxieties and depression that segregation created.

Why did the Movement gradually stop, and in the end, fail to transform society? A basic reason is that many Civil Rights workers, especially the committed activists of the Student Non-Violent Coordinating Committee, were prisoners of their own psychological illusions—racism, sexism, elitism. Exceptional Black women like Fannie Lou Hamer and Cynthia Washington destroyed many myths about female inferiority by spearheading desegregation projects, registering Black voters and by organizing "Freedom Houses." Many white Northern women who participated in the Movement "taught in freedom schools, ran libraries, canvassed for voter registration, and endured constant harassment from the local whites," writes Civil Rights veteran Sara Evans. Despite these and many other contributions, most white and Black males in S.N.C.C. treated women co-workers condescendingly, at best. In 1964, Ruby Doris Smith Robinson, one of the most influential S.N.C.C. leaders, helped to organize a sit-in in the S.N.C.C. office "protesting the relegation of women to typing and clerical work." By 1965, Evans recalls, "the positions of white women in S.N.C.C. (were) in steep decline." Commitment to the newly emergent Antiwar Movement caused a number of white males to leave the South; feminism gave white women new insights into the social dynamics of the Movement, pointing out the distinctions between S.N.C.C.'s egalitarian theory and sexist practice.

The intense and often ambiguous working relationships between Black men and white women produced major divisions within the daily functions of the Movement. The psychological image of the white woman in the South was still the chaste, virginal child-bride, the standard for purity throughout Southern popular literature and culture. Southern Black men had learned at an early age that sexual intercourse with a white woman was the most serious *political* crime a Negro could commit against segregation and society. Responding to the old models of segregated sexual relations rather than the new models generated by the Movement itself, many Black males routinely slept with white women co-workers. Historian Staughton Lynd, the director of the Freedom Schools, recalls that "every black S.N.C.C. worker with perhaps a few exceptions counted it a notch on his gun to have slept with a white woman—as many as possible." Conversely, many white women found that their "sexuality was confirmed by Black men" moreso than by white lovers, as one woman wrote. Some white women, raised in traditional, petty bourgeois homes in the North, used Black lovers as a rejection of their bourgeois class origins or their parents' social status.

By 1964 many young Black women accused white women of doing only "shit work", one declared, "while Black women are out in the streets battling with the cops." Black men often viewed Black sisters as "amazons" while thinking of white women inside the Movement as highly-prized, sex objects. Some Black women reacted to these sexual stereotypes by creating newer ones, which were actually rooted within the historical legacies of slavery. These sisters rejected feminism as being "white-oriented," deplored the political principle of abortion-on-demand, and attempted to bear as many children as possible—"to produce Black children for the black nation." Some accepted and even glorified the traditional Southern stereotype of the strong, silent but sexual Black earth-mother. Cynthia Washington, a director of a freedom project in Mississippi in the mid-sixties, writes that "our single-minded focus on the issues of racial discrimination and the Black struggle for equality blinded us to other issues...."

The sexual-racial antagonisms which divided S.N.C.C. seriously hindered attempts of hundreds of young, idealistic people to challenge racism and segregation. For many, the struggle against their own weaknesses, longstanding prejudices and illusions was far more difficult than the political struggle against Jim Crow. Civil Rights activist Debbie Louis wrote, "this kind of interrelating meant each learning to be open and honest, and to accept the honesty of others. For people who had been raised in a culture based on the denial of personal honesty," she notes, "involvement on this level required a painful self-examination." The prevailing popular culture of racism, the sexist stereotypes held by both men and women, and the psychological patterns of dependency which exploitation creates over several generations could not be uprooted easily. In the end, the Movement may have failed to create a new interracial society in the South because its advocates had first failed to transform themselves.

The basic definitions which had guided the Movement from the beginning gradually lost all meaning by the Nixon years. Originally, the enemy was identified clearly as the segregationist cop, politician, judge, businessman and minister. Everyone involved in the Movement, from children to welfare mothers, Black intellectuals and sanitation workers had a basic understanding of the problem and the methods which could be used to fight against it. But as the Movement collapsed beneath the weight of its own contradictions, the source of immediate oppression shifted from white racists and overt racism to elements within the black community. The more conservative participants within the Movement, the Black middle class—lawyers, politicians, businessmen, educators—began to identify its goals with the reformist values in the white Establishment. Within several years, the economic and political status quo in many Southern towns and cities had been joined by many of the Black Civil Rights leaders, a merger which created an entirely new political situation. How do you protest against the inherent racism of a political system, many youth asked by the middle seventies, when your city councilmen, mayor and state representative are all Black?

This merger between the Black middle class and the former segregationist politicians was made possible by the rapid expansion of Southern capitalism to include marginal Black participation within the past decade. The commercial forums of culture, the public arts, the sports industry, entertainment, music, the advertising industry, news media and all major educational institutions have moved 'to incorporate many of the best and the brightest representatives of Afro-American society. Inside banks and credit corporations, small Black businessmen have begun to merge their economic interests largely with those interests of the white managerial elites and major corporations.

The Black leadership has increasingly reflected the values of capitalist America, but the majority of Southern Blacks, who still accept the conceptual framework of desegregation that the Movement projected during the sixties, have not yet comprehended that the rules of the game have changed. Southern municipal and state governments are now willing, and in some cases quite eager to permit Black middle class representation within the system. Small numbers of the educated, mostly affluent members of the Black middle class now occupy influential positions within business, the media and government. The Movement forced Southern capitalism beyond token desegregation but did not nearly complete the task of revolution—the creation of full political and economic democracy for every income level of Black society.

Not coincidentally, this conservative reaction in politics has contributed to unique forms of mental stress and illness. Materially, Black classes have declined in their growth of real income due to continued high inflation combined with increased unemployment. The "great leap forward" which many Blacks anxiously assumed would be for all Black people in the aftermath of the Movement has not occurred, nor will it ever occur under a capitalist economic system. Economic underdevelopment has promoted among many Blacks an acute social frustration and feeling of inadequacy. The Black working classes have begun to observe the rapid elevation of certain Black elites within society but for themselves will experience no corresponding material change or cultural advancement. The sort of self hatred which the Black Power movement attempted to eradicate will return under the guise of the cultural ethos of the Black middle class, reinforced by commercials, the Black media and other institutions of popular culture. The replacement of white policemen by Black officers; the removal of white merchants from Black neighborhoods and the introduction of Black-managed but white-owned and financed businesses in the ghetto will promote the illusion of rapid social advancement for Blacks, without changing the economic reality of poverty.

The psychological illusions created by segregation still continue to dominate important aspects of Black female-black male relations. Most Black women are still far more submissive, apolitical and much more likely to define themselves in respect to their position as a mother and wife than white women. Many of the old Southern stereotypes of black female sexuality have also returned. Some Black women remain psychologically dependent upon white standards of beauty, and physically change their facial and physical appearances to conform more closely with the white aesthetic ideal. Black Southern women continue to be the most economically and sexually exploited of all American groups, yet for the most part cannot coalesce their interests within a predominately petty bourgeois, Southern feminist movement, which continues to misinterpret the needs and interests of Black women.

Few psychologists have explored the increasing anxieties of the Black middle class. Harriette McAdoo and other Black sociologists and psychologists believe that "the social class division" between Black working class people and the Black petty bourgeoisie "may be stronger than it is within white families." The Black recipients of new, higher paying jobs from affirmative action and desegregation programs in government, colleges and business are usually surprised to discover that they are unable to leave the ghetto. In most Southern cities, changes in the socioeconomic status of the Black middle class have not been accompanied by concomitant changes in residential segregation. Occupational and age factors, rather than income level, determine the patterns of Southern residency. Those upwardly mobile Blacks who leave black neighborhoods and settle in predominantly white communities face even more directly the social rejection and violence of the middle class white culture. Isolated from Black churches, schools and other cultural institutions, some Blacks experience severe personality and emotional crises. In integrated schools, Black children receive an ethnically biased curriculum. Psychiatrist John J. Hartman suggests that the black child in this setting "is taught that the language he has learned at home and in his neighborhood is 'bad' and inferior. The price to pay for adapting the speech and language pattern of a feared, hated and envied majority may be one of psychological conflict involving one's identity, self-perception and sense of worth."

"Social deviance," as defined by most psychologists and other intellectuals is a term which connotes specific patterns of behavior which are not shared by those participants within the "normal" society. As Frantz Fanon revealed, within a racist society the racist is the healthy or normal person. For the Black middle class, overt Black political struggle contains an unhealthy (or from a racist perspective, a healthy) individual and collective sense of humanity. To be "deviant" within a capitalist society is to question or to react negatively to the basic social values of the society. The new Black elite who have opted for social status and economic mobility have not yet begun to question the character of the cultural and economic system which they have assimilated into. Yet to attempt an honest analysis on this question for the Black petty bourgeoisie would mean increased psychological crisis and "class suicide."

For those Black men and women who remained outside the system, the unwillingness or the inability to question the oppressive, racist character of capitalism condemns them to a permanent world of psychological crisis. There exists an undeveloped sense of conflict, and an acute sense of alienation and "Black rage." In classical mental health terms, this angst or extreme alienation could be manifested in increased drug addiction, prostitution, suicide and other forms of social isolation. The Black church has lost thousands of members during the decade, and is unable to exert its message of transcendence upon increasingly desperate people. For critics of the theories of bourgeois behavioral science, this means that for the majority of Black people, that healthy personalities cannot be constructed without continuing the Movement beyond reforms, toward a complete restructuring of American society and capitalism.

Mental health itself has as an idea a certain materiality, an expression of decisions made and criteria established by the accepted intellectuals of capitalist society. One locates a rational order for individual behavior within the cultural models for proper character of the bourgeois himself, in such a world. As deviant behavior is isolated a norm comes into being. That norm, once located within the parameters of bourgeous behavior, assumes an oppressive character. As this conceptual framework of middle class mental health is overturned by socialist critics of psychology, more and more healthy Black people and peoples of other cultures and classes will be created. We will also establish the conditions for creating increasingly violent confrontations between the new, "healthier" individual and the corrupt society which is still in the birthpangs of creation.

The old ideas of what constitutes a healthy or diseased person live within ourselves. Like the Civil Rights workers of fifteen years ago, we are inclined to postulate a theoretical model for the struggle-oriented, humanistic individual, without reflecting critically upon our own internal contradictions. We discuss society's sexist character within study groups and at universities without first attempting to divest ourselves of our own sexism. Many women and Blacks manipulate sexual or racial illusions as a way of avoiding political contradictions within themselves.

As the individualistic and elitist cultural values of capitalism are internalized by sections of the black middle class and even by Black workers, the task of internal and external human psychoanalysis for liberation becomes increasingly more difficult. Internally, we must reorient our academic labor in favor of the class interests of Black and working people. Externally, we must put forward intellectual alternatives to psychological behavioral norms as being, first of all, political acts, a series of principled, deliberate assaults upon the values of capitalism. We must learn to place ourselves and our theoretical models in direct confrontation with behavioral science ideology as it supports the justification of society as it is.

The psychological problems of the Movement demand that mental health models cannot be divorced from the political transformation of society. In turn, there is no social science route toward real mental health for the Black community that does not include a socialist critique of the entire set of economic and cultural relations between Blacks and whites in America. But most importantly, we must begin the hardest task of reeducating ourselves and others towards a new political analysis and mental health models which promote human liberation. Let us revive the Movement beyond its initial reforms toward ever new definitions of humankind.

PART III: ON THE SOUTHERN QUESTION

PROLOGUE TO PART III

After all that has been said . . . there still remains a part
essential to a proper description of the South which it is
difficult to describe or fix in terms easily understood by
strangers. It is, in fine, the atmosphere of the land, the
thought and feeling, the thousand and one little actions
which go to make up life . . . Within and without the sombre
veil of color vast social forces have been at work,—efforts
for human betterment, movements disintegration and
despair, tragedies and comedies in social and economic
life, and a swaying and lifting and sinking of human hearts
which have made this land a land of mingled sorrow and
joy, of change and excitement and unrest.

W.E.B. DuBois
The Souls of Black Folk

The creation of a coherent economic strategy has been the will-
o'-the-wisp of black politics. Throughout U.S. social history black
activists have attempted to relate their political efforts toward
establishing a stable, economic base for the black community.
Their failure to do so speaks to their theoretical inability to
understand the nature of the U.S. economic system, and the historic
role of black people at the bottom of that system.

133

Illusions about black economics began with Booker T. Washington's theory of a separate, capitalist development. His National Negro Business League accepted the civil and political segregation of the races as an established fact, and sought to transcend Jim Crow by a policy of separate black capital accumulation. The "ghetto bourgeoisie" could control some aspects of their own limited economic sphere, especially before World War I. But with the development of monopoly capitalism, the majority of "mom-and-pop" grocery stores, black insurance companies and black merchants were increasingly driven from their own markets within the black community. Even during his lifetime, the economic nostrums of Washington's "cast down your buckets" philosophy had only a minor impact upon black political economy.

The South is the focus of discussion in Part Three. Economically, it was until recently the least developed of all regions in the United States along capitalist lines. It was also the birthplace of Afro-American nationality and culture, and since 1970 it is increasingly becoming once more the demographic and political center for the majority of black people. The South thus seems to provide hope for a variety of black efforts at economic development. At the root of these attempts at black capitalist self sufficiency, from Floyd McKissick's Soul City in North Carolina to Johnny Ford's political maneuvers in Tuskegee, Alabama, is the idea that racism is not a product of the capitalist economic system. In other words, if black people had access to sufficient amounts of capital then that racism would be diminished.

Ironically, this renaissance of neo-Booker T. Washingtonian economic thinking has occurred precisely at a time when a general Reaction has been mounted to counter the limited gains blacks achieved against the segregationist state. In the realm of electoral politics, large numbers of blacks in the South have been elevated to positions of marginal influence; however, the real seats of political power are occupied by the same social and political classes that commanded the scene twenty-five years ago. In cultural and educational institutions, the white South now permits a greater and more democratic access of blacks into the existing system, but segregation *per se* has done little to nothing in regards to transforming the essential character and limitations of Southern civil society. If anything, autonomous black cultural institutions, such as the black church and the traditional "Blues Culture" of rural blacks, has suffered more under integration than segregation; black people seemingly are acquiring the worst aspects of bourgeois culture at the expense of the very legitimate and creative aesthetic and social traditions which they once could claim.

But it is within the field of economic relations that the Reaction in the South has had its most devastating impact upon black people. Independent black rural farmers have been forced out of the market (and usually off the farm entirely) with the expansion of agri-businesses since 1960. Black urban businesses have found it increasingly difficult to exist, as black consumers increasingly buy their goods at newly integrated supermarkets and at suburban shopping malls. By late 1979, even McKissick's Soul City was suing the federal government for lack of promised support. The coming of advanced capitalism to the South should demolish, once and for all, the myth of Black Capitalism.

Political struggle in the South, and across the nation, must involve a pragmatic but visionary economic strategy, a critical program for human development that will constitute a transition between capitalism and socialism. It would be grievously incorrect to assume, as many Marxist-Leninists have, that socialism can be constructed within black America anytime in our immediate future. Socialism is not on our generation's agenda; even if it was, we have not yet constructed a critical theoretical framework, drawing upon both the traditional works of Marxism *and* the relevant theoretical studies of black American activist/writers like DuBois, Oliver Cromwell Cox and others, which could become the basis for *praxis* in the struggle toward a socialist economic order. An extensive cultural and ideological struggle, waged and led by black working people, must be a concomitant part of that attempt toward economic redefinition.

We must recognize, however, that modern capitalism cannot produce freedom and self-determination for black people. Any strategy of transition must view the public ownership of the basic means of production as the decisive and final economic goal of black activism. Our critique of Tuskegee, Alabama, and the South generally, attempts to contribute toward that process of economic redefinition. By describing the fundamental contradictions within the economics of the New South, we might observe the embryonic patterns of alternatives in economic development that must occur in the future.

Reaction: Thoughts on the Political Economy of the South Since the Civil Rights Movement

Introduction

A conservative political and cultural reaction has occurred since 1968. Despite the rhetorical triumphs of Black Power, the influx of blacks into economic and political positions of privilege and the establishment of Black Studies curricula in Southern schools, a retreat from the political logic of the sixties developed. Both before and after King's assassination, key members of S.C.L.C. and the N.A.A.C.P. who had worked closely with King for almost a decade privately refused to come to terms with his new political position. Many continued to praise the King legacy publicly but as in the case of some of Malcolm's former followers, they privately denounced the international perspective and the anti-imperialist analysis implicit within King's final speeches. The material realities of America had forced King to abandon his older reformist ideas for a higher form of social and ethical criticism; this was something which other leading integrationists could not or would not do.

A host of S.N.C.C. activists retreated under the cover of the "Black Power" slogan into local and state electoral politics, to build a political foundation. Black entrepreneurs like James Farmer and

Floyd McKissick forged a Booker T. Washington-type alliance with the Nixon administration to establish black petty bourgeois power.

Despite the successful voter education and registration drives of S.N.C.C. a decade ago and despite the successful organization of independent black political parties in Alabama and Mississippi, representative democracy between the races is actually at a standstill. Four million black Southerners are registered compared with about two million blacks in 1964, but the Civil Rights Movement fell far short of achieving equal political power for blacks. Black elected officials number 1,847 in the South, but that amounts to only 2.3 percent of the total number of elected officials in the region. Blacks constitute 20.5 percent of the South's total population and make up popular majorities in over 100 counties, yet only ten counties are effectively controlled by Blacks. Only two black Congressmen are from the South, and these persons represent the region's major metropolitan areas. This small, elected black elite represents, with few exceptions, the interests of the black petty bourgeoisie and maturing corporate interests within the New South. It tends to represent political philosophies to the right of their Northern counterparts; e.g., Barbara Jordan's staunch and sincere defense of the character of John Connally at his milk fund trial; Andrew Young's solitary black vote endorsing the 1973 appointment of Gerald Ford to the Vice Presidency.

Carter's ultimate victory—and the Southern blacks' central role within that campaign—also constituted a reemergence of another "New South" onto the center stage of that tired drama which is American politics. There have been several New Souths at different stages of the nation's history—the New South of Atlanta Henry Grady and the Redeemer Democrats during the 1880s; the New South of the "Atlanta Spirit" and the neoprogressives of the twenties; the "moderate segregationist" South of the T.V.A.— Maury Maverick—Claude Pepper mode. In each instance the black petty bourgeoisie played no major role of importance in determining the function of the state, the nature of "white democracy." C. Vann Woodward had observed correctly that integration was the basic political reform of the Progressive South. The rapid rise of Barbara Jordan, Andrew Young, Ben Brown and other Southern black moderates signifies a basic change from this tradition of whites-only politics; the Southern white ruling class has decided that it can accommodate certain representatives of the Afro-American community. Jordan's speech at the 1976 Democratic National Convention and Young's central importance to Carter's candidacy represented the black petty bourgeoisie's endorsement of the New South creed. Their successes represent a compromise of the real class interests of black people with the American political economy of exploitation.

Like a number of Black Republican politicians during the 1880s many Black Southern Democrats have renounced the political liberal-left within the national Democratic Party and have cemented an alliance with new representatives of the South's upper class, despite their rhetoric to the contrary. Blanch Bruce retained political prestige through an association with the Bourbon Democratic aristocracy, the economic conservatives and the aspiring capitalists of the first New South. Bruce, a plantation owner and well-to-do entrepreneur in his own right often had more in common with Mississippi Senator Lamar and Wade Hampton than with his own black sharecropping constituents. Despite their roots in the Desegregationist struggle, Andrew Young and other less prominent black Southern politicians have made similar compromises with white power.

Economic Foundations of Southern Reaction

The fundamental reason for these political developments is economic. Since the late 1960s, conservative economists and corporate leaders alike have commented upon the "booster" character of the South's modern economy. During the economic recessions of the Nixon-Ford administrations Southern business was the leader in stock market revival through their high profit margins, automobile sales and purchases of equities. Conservative, capitalist economist Elliot Janeway notes that "stock brokerage firms with national networks of branch offices report that the retail stampede to buy stocks began in the South. Its impact on Wall Street was to spread the word overnight: 'When in New York, do as the Southerners do.'" Consumer confidence in the South immediately after the recession remained at 70 percent, the highest level in the country. Large numbers of foreign industries have relocated in the South in recent years to take advantage of low corporate tax levels; Volvo recently opened an assembly line in Chesapeake, Virginia; Michelin of France has already invested 300 million dollars in three South Carolina factories. Since 1960, gross personal income in the South has risen from 133.6 billion dollars to 263.9 billion. Per capita personal income has increased from $1,707 to $5,198, while the industrial output of Southern factories has leaped from 25.8 billion to 54.0 billion dollars. The New South of the 1970s, like the original New South of the 1880s depends upon the finance capital and rapid commercial expansion of heavy industry. During the post-Reconstruction era the capital influx into the South came from New England and the Mid-Atlantic states; today this capital comes from the North, the West Coast, and all parts of the world. In the 1880s, new cities like Birmingham, Winston-Salem and Atlanta were being created by commerce and industry; today the newer giants are the cities of Houston, Miami, Tampa Bay and Dallas-Fort Worth, and the suburban metropolitan areas of older towns such as Atlanta.

Coinciding with the rapid expansion of commerce and industry into the New South has occurred the process of proletarianization—a decline in agriculture employment, the destruction of a vital petty bourgeois agrarian class, the loss of black land tenure and a significant increase in non-farm employment. From 1964 to 1974 twenty-nine percent of all Southern farms ceased operations, a total of 454,000 fewer farms. The general economic tendency since 1960 has been the increased isolation of the Southern agrarian petty bourgeois class in favor of agribusiness corporations. Without exception, in every region of the south the family farmer is being replaced by impersonal, profit-oriented bourgeoisie. In Florida, Tropicana, Coca-Cola and twelve other agribusinesses account for sixty percent of all citrus products grown in the state and employ a vast majority of farm laborers. Holly Farms, Inc., of North Carolina, has in less than a single decade absorbed the market of the majority of the nation's independent poultry farmers. The federal government's farm policies under Kennedy, Johnson, Nixon and Ford encouraged the destruction of the independent middle class farmer's market in the South, resulting in a real decline in agricultural output in the region, from 8.3 billion dollars worth in 1960 to only 7.4 billion dollars last year. Profits for Southern agribusiness remained high even during the recession years—for example, in 1973 Holly Farms netted 11.5 million dollars before taxes.

The South's political economy has become top heavy—corrupted at the top with the importation of heavy industry involving cheap labor, the political and cultural hegemony of a predominantly white bourgeoisie and managerial elite, the destruction of the black and poor white agricultural classes and the expansion of an impoverished urban proletariat devoid of a cultural sense of collectivity and lacking a militant labor union consciousness. The rapid expansion of textile mills into the South's piedmont sections during the past four decades illustrates the workings of the Southern political economy. By the 1970s the South employed almost seventy-five percent of all textile workers in the nation, although less than ten percent of the 589,000 workers are presently members of unions. Textile workers in the South are also ranked at the bottom of all industrial workers nation-wide, earning an average of $3.46 per hour compared to $6.43 per hour in the automobile industry.

The Southern police act, and even perceive themselves to be, an arm of coercion of the new bourgeoisie, escorting scabs through picket lines. The relative backwardness of Southern black labor provides the Carter-black elite strata with another beachhead of political support; an economic basis for reactionary politics. Yet Southern labor's relative backwardness also indicates a real potential for radical change, given an activist leadership. The labor situation provides real parallels with the condition of national labor during the early 1930s, on the eve of radical labor militancy—if, again, the laborers themselves are raised to a sufficient level of education and working class consciousness.

This aggressive process of mature, capitalistic economic development bears with it a complementary tendency toward agrarian underdevelopment. The small towns and villages of the picturesque, rural South lose their former share of the economic market to the massive metropolitan powers of Atlanta, Memphis, Birmingham, Charlotte and Nashville. The rural petty bourgeoisie become increasingly dependent upon the economic, political and cultural initiatives of the metropolis bourgeoisie. This dependency creates a lumpen development of the former sharecropper and rural working class, forging a stratum of permanently unemployable men and women with scant formal and technological education. This lumpen economic pattern of quasi-neocolonialism is characterized by the influx of outside capital into the countryside and the concentration of the best lands and other resources, such as credit, labor and capital in the hands of the few. The lumpen development of the black South isolates black religious and ethical figures and other traditional leaders from their communities, creating black bourgeois "leaders" with little popular following. In any agrarian society, the entire civil structure of the culture of the oppressed becomes contradictory and irrational, filled with the tensions and philosophies from the old ways of life and the brutal material realities of the new individualistic age. From the tensions and economic contradictions springs, ultimately, a period of revolt.

Black elected officials have largely ignored the processes of proletarianization and lumpen proletarianization which are occurring within the South's new political economy. The attention placed upon the narrow political struggle for integration and equal opportunity to participate within the bourgeois state has obscured the more fundamental social problem for blacks—the destruction of the independent black farming class throughout the region. In 1950 there were 560,000 farms under black management in the South; by 1971 there were only 98,000 farms, and since the recession there appears to have been a severe drop in the latter figures. Black farmers have virtually disappeared: in 1950 there were 3,158,000 black farmers, but two decades later only 938,000 remained. Federal government and private foundation support for black farmers has been at best insufficient. Black tenant farmers and sharecroppers have experienced a violent economic purge during the same period, and high market prices between 1964 and 1969 pushed many thousands of black tenant farmers off their lands. In 1969 there were eighty percent fewer black tenants than there had been only five years before. Many of these farmers and their families were pressed into the new factories and industries arriving in the South.

The high rate of industrialization and the underdeveloped consciousness of labor in the South directly contributed to the conservative character of Southern black politicians. Working class activism throughout the South is thwarted by universal right-to-work laws which permit all workers to refuse to become union members. Only fourteen percent of all non-farm workers have joined unions, compared with over thirty percent of non-farm workers nationally. The void of widespread, militant labor union praxis and a culture of protest and the lack of a viable black left has its intellectual origins in the middle of the nineteenth century within slavery's political economy. Impoverished whites and blacks should have been logical allies economically, but the extreme racism of local whites has traditionally pushed poor whites into the political arms of reactionary conservatives like Lester Maddox of Georgia. Because white laborers foster a backward culture of racism, the white bourgeoisie finds it easier to pay all Southern workers significantly less than the amount which laborers receive nationally. During 1974 total employment fell 2.1 percent in the South compared with less than one percent for the entire nation. The super-exploitation of Southern labor, the feeble condition of unions and the loss of black properties has combined in the historical creation of a first and second generation black proletariat whose political leaders within the electoral arena represent the cultural and social attitudes of their exploiters.

The South's recent story in economics has pressed both capitalist parties into creating viable Southern strategies. Nixon's "Sunbelt" strategies, combined with his firm grip upon the white middle and upper-middle classes, provided him with an impressive margin over George McGovern in 1972. Likewise, Carter's campaign has clearly identified new Southern moderates as being pivotal to his election chances—men like South Carolina's John West, Arkansas' Dale Bumpers and David Pryor, Mississippi's William Waller and Louisiana's Edwin Edwards. The Reagan candidacy for the Republican nomination was the recipient of much former segregationist sentiment, and without the California Governor's impressive primary victory in North Carolina and his overwhelming support among Southern conservatives like Jesse Helms he could not have mounted a serious challenge to President Ford in 1976. The South receives far more federal allocations from the government than the older industrial and agricultural regions of the North, which also accounts for the region's political power. Comparing federal taxes paid in 1975 with federal outlays, for instance, the Southeast received 9.5 billion dollars more than it paid the government while the East lost 10 billion dollars and the Midwest lost 20 billion dollars.

Occurring with the entrance of blacks into Southern politics and the emergence of the region's national prestige has also been an expansion of state institutional forms. Southern governments during previous New South periods were seldom more than petty courthouse committees of Black Belt plantation owners and the lawyers of industry. The "Atlanta Spirit" of the twenties was characterized in politics by "Neowhigs" like Virginia's Harry Flood Byrd and Arkansas Governor John E. Martineau, conservatives who reluctantly expanded state services on a pay-as-you-go basis, and then only along a whites-only policy. Contemporary politicians have reversed this dominant theme in Southern government by demanding staggering increases in the budgets of state and local government.

One unlikely advocate of big state government has been George Wallace, Governor of Alabama. During his administrations he supervised the construction of fourteen new junior colleges, fifteen trade schools and introduced the largest highway construction program in the state's history. The state bureaucracy tripled in size under his administration; the proportion of Alabama residents employed in public welfare programs, about 34 percent is the second highest in the nation. Wallace and other vocal segregationists, like Louisiana's Risley Triche and Georgia's Herman Talmadge, have openly renounced their racist rhetoric and legislation of only ten years ago and now demand that their state governments keep up with the rising expectations of black constituents. While participating with moderate white politicians like Carter, Bumpers and Pryor, the old-line racist politicians have aided the establishment of massive and poorly managed state bureaucratic structures.

The growth of state bureaucracies within the New South manifests key elements and contradictions within the region's political economy. The rapid underdevelopment of the rural petty bourgeoisie required new state sponsored welfare agencies. The rapid industrialization of the urban centers and the influx of a new first-generation working class called for state government intervention similar to the New Deal programs of the thirties.

Black and White Southern Labor

The history of the relationship between black and white laborers in the South is at best ambiguous. Since the late nineteenth century blacks acquire the reputation as strike-breakers or scabs. The Negro laborer was viewed as a temporary source of cheap labor by white managers of capitalist enterprises, and as such, seemed to pose a continuous threat to the direct economic interests of the white working class. There were numerous incidents, however, of black-white cooperation within the struggles of organized labor. During the reorganization of the United Mine Workers during the early 1930s in Alabama, white coal miners worked with black miners to establish a strong bi-racial base. In 1935 there were 23,000 UMW members in Alabama, 60 percent of whom were black. With the emergence of segregation as the central political and cultural factor within Southern society, inter-racial cooperation in the workplace steadily declined.

In the post-World War II South, bi-racial working class coalitions became virtually nonexistent. When the Chattanooga Central Labor Union passed a resolution supporting school desegregation in summer, 1955, nine individual locals issued counter-resolutions against their organization and in favor of white supremacy. Several locals left the union, declaring that the organization's resolution was "Communist-inspired." During the early 1960s Local 12 of the United Rubber Workers of America, at the Goodyear Tire and Rubber Company plant in Gadsden, Alabama, was the battleground for numerous black white labor struggles on the question of racial equality. The white-dominated local refused to process grievances of black employees who protested against segregated dining facilities and Jim Crow restrictions throughout the plant. Black workers with many years of seniority were regularly laid off without pay while white employees with less seniority were allowed to work. Few black Civil Rights workers in the South attempted to convert white trade unionists in the South to a favorable position on integration. It was usually the white petty bourgeoisie and especially the college-educated upper classes who seemed to welcome the reformist demands of the Movement. Support for George Wallace, Lester Maddox and other segregationist politicians usually came from the white working class. Union halls throughout the South were often meeting places for the Ku Klux Klan and the White Citizen's Councils. In a number of important union certification elections conducted by the National Labor Relations Board, blacks often voted against unions and provided the margin of defeat.

To some extent, the separation between Southern black and white workers was manifested nationally by the strained relations between Civil Rights leaders and trade unions. Historian Philip Foner observed that "the courageous and militant blacks faced intimidation and repression, and the movement . . . was in constant need of funds and moral support. But the AFL-CIO gave neither." Among the most influential proponents of the thesis of a Negro integrationist-white labor alliance was Martin Luther King, Jr. With the exception of A. Philip Randolph, King became the leading Civil Rights spokesman who worked closely with various unions and their leaders. Speaking before a convention of the United Packinghouse Workers Union in 1957, King insisted that "organized labor can be one of the most powerful instruments in putting an end to discrimination and segregation." Unfortunately the labor establishment refused to accept this vanguard role within the process of social transformation. Individual labor leaders like Walter Reuther gravitated toward the centrist-conservative factions within the Movement, lending their personal and limited organizational support to the politics of desegregation. The majority of union leaders still accepted the historical image of the black laborer as innately inferior or as the perpetual scab; they used neither their personal nor institutional influence to support the goals of the Movement. "Most union leaders," Foner writes, "feared repercussions and avoided adopting a stand clearly in favor of egalitarian racial principles."

In the wake of the movement, black and white worker relationships have remained relatively backward. The illusion of equal opportunity and the elevation of a limited number of black professionals into the business bureaucracy continues to dominate black and white working class consciousness. Even in the majority of the new Southern factories, blacks continue to be hired as janitors or in unskilled or low paying positions. Donald F. Roy argued in "The Southern Labor Movement" that the racial divisions within the working class South "have a depressing effect on union organizing. . . ." Certain "white jobs" have been historically "protected from the large Negro labor surplus by the color bar." As a result many white laborers recognize implicitly that the super exploitation of black labor power allows for seemingly artifically higher wages for white workers. "Not only have white workers and management found basis for consensus in their mutual rejection of the Negro," he notes, but the "threat of possible job replacement" by blacks forces the white worker increasingly to the political right.

Race becomes a driving wedge that separates and alienates workers and forces whites into the waiting arms of white management. "And by pre-empting low status jobs," Roy concludes, "the Negro has withdrawn from the white labor market the alternative jobs that might have provided employment insurance to those who would risk firing for union activity."

The area of the South with the worst record of inter-racial labor cooperation in recent decades remains the Black Belt. Despite the general growth of industrial development throughout the South since 1960, industrial employment has declined steadily in the Black Belt. In Macon County, Alabama, for example, the total number of workers employed in industry in 1950 was 9,719. By 1960 the figure had dropped to 7,833 workers and by 1970 the figure was 7,213. In the most industrialized county of the Alabama Black Belt, Dallas County, total industrial employment dropped from 20,266 employees in 1950 to 18,776 employees in 1970. As Alabama industrial employment climbed from 1,040,126 in 1950 to 1,235,287 in 1970, Black Belt totals declined from 136,059 to 105,504 during these same years. In a climate of decreasing industrial jobs and overall rising unemployment, occurring within the social context of a Movement to halt *de facto* and *de jure* segregation in employment procedures, labor solidarity across the color line dissolved. Black Belt white workers clung desperately to their jobs, swallowed their complaints about low wages and deplorable working conditions, and remained apathetic about unionization. White laborers viewed the move toward the desegregation of Southern society as being a real obstacle to their own individual and collective social and economic mobility.

The illusion of black mobility within the framework of the Southern political economy is perpetuated within the cultural apparatus, the publishing industries and the media. Blacks are suddenly given an equal billing within current events on the front pages of major newspapers; black newscasters and reporters have become a permanent fixture on the late afternoon and evening newscasts in even small Southern communities. But within the media itself, black workers have yet to achieve any substantial gains in income during the seventies. Within the publishing industry in Alabama, almost seventy percent of all blacks employed are found in service jobs, at the lowest paying levels. Roughly ten percent of all black employees hold blue collar jobs; less than one percent are classified as "professionals." In Louisiana, 90 percent of all blacks employed within the publishing industry are classified as service or blue collar workers. The percentage of black managers, executives or professionals is less than five percent of the total black work force within every Southern state. Black representation within the media industry is also far less than the percentage of black people living in Southern states.

For all of these problems and contradictions, there are indications that the "times are a-changin." The Amalgamated Clothing and Textile Workers Union is currently organizing the 450 industrial workers of the J.P. Stevens and Company plant in Montgomery, Alabama. Despite Stevens' promise that union organizers would not be harassed, pro-union employees were fired in 1976 and 1977. Other employees were harassed and coerced into resigning. Stevens employees in Montgomery have no health insurance or pension programs; no parking facilities; no lunchroom or medical facilities. Sixty percent of all workers are black but there is not a single black superviser in the plant. These conditions in Montgomery are not unusual; they are typical of the conditions for Stevens employees in any of the 85 Stevens plants throughout the South. Despite these hardships, many workers have met in weekly meetings and are now on the verge of creating a viable local. White workers have begun to reevaluate their traditional fears and racist notions and have moved toward the ACTWU's bi-racial, militant posture. In doing so they have begun to challenge the essence of Southern history.

Toward a Marxian Framework

A new generation of opportunistic black politicians have been elevated to hegemonic political positions within the black community, largely due to their clientage relationships with fundamental regional bourgeois interests. The black petty bourgeoisie provided critical financial support to black constitutional reformers —Martin Luther King, Jr., Andrew Young and other members of the Southern Christian Leadership Conference; James Farmer, Floyd McKissick and many participants in C.O.R.E.; Jesse Jackson and John Lewis. But as the political struggle gained major successes at the expense of segregation, black radicals like Malcolm X, the Student Non-Violent Coordinating Committee (S.N.C.C.) and theoreticians like James Boggs pointed the way toward social revolution—a frightening specter of permanent struggle and cultural transformation which neither the black petty boureoisie nor the white capitalist economic and political establishment could accept. The popular, massive struggles in the streets died down gradually as the political system granted certain concessions to the black petty bourgeoisie—and after many important black radicals were imprisoned, bought out or assassinated.

The cultural rationale for the state with Southern society is subtle. There exists the need within civil society to provide legitimacy for the new directions the Southern bourgeoisie have taken within the past decade—the acceptance of Civil Rights legislation, the integration of many public schools, the influx of heavy industry and the demise of agrarian political influence in state legislatures. The New South's creed is explained to the people through expanded educational institutions, through the promulgation of electronic media, cultural journals, new newspapers and the arts. The New South's aesthetics negate, or attempt to replace, the Afro-American cultural heritage and the *weltanschauung* of the new urban working class. Accomplished behind the rhetoric of reform the state expands its influence into every aspect of cultural life, solely to frustrate the protest impulse evident within many phases of Afro-American Southern culture.

This cultural impact within black civil society has been equally reactionary. Despite the continued rhetorical use of the word 'Black' most black social and intellectual leaders in the South have quietly accommodated themselves to the new capitalist realities and "New South" political leadership. On college campuses, radical black professors and administrators are being fired; black studies programs are abandoned; fraternity and sorority life has replaced an interest in political discussions. Clothing styles, mannerisms of speech and habits changed overnight. Afro-hair styles and dashikis are being rapidly abandoned for bleached hair, surreal clothing and high heels. The blues and jazz, once an integral part of the political struggle of the sixties, is replaced by blatantly sexist disco. Numerous black activist journals and community newspapers initiated in the sixties have been forced to close for economic reasons.

Perhaps the strongest single cultural change has occurred

within the relations between men and women. The Civil Rights era in the South was a period of expanded gender-role freedom. Women like Rosa Parks of Montgomery and Fannie Lou Hamer of Mississippi assumed leadership roles in desegregation struggles, black women of all ages ran for office, organized voter registration campaigns, gave political speeches and raised funds for civil rights activities. During recent years, however, an overwhelmingly black male caste seized the newly available state and county political offices. Southern black males have down played legislatures. Black politicians have not campaigned for expanded state-supported abortion facilities—for example, only in 1976 did abortion clinics open in Alabama, West Virginia and Mississippi. According to a recent issue of *Family Planning Perspectives,* however, less than one sixth of all women needing abortions and birth control services in 1976 could obtain treatment in Missippi, Alabama, Louisiana and Arkansas.

Traditional social conditions of Southern black women since segregation have reverted to the pre-1960 conditions. Despite federal programs in health care, many Black Belt counties have infant mortality rates in excess of 50 per 1,000 births each year. Sixty-five percent of blacks in Black Belt regions live below the poverty level, in states where legislatures seldom provide funds for day care for working mothers and grant minimal aid to dependent children. No Deep South state legislature has ratified the Equal Rights Amendment, and the traditional chauvinism inherent in the Southern ethos finds new expressions within black middle class-sponsored beauty pageants and debutante balls.

The expansion of the state and the preeminence of the bourgeoisie within Southern civil society have sparked a demise in the real cultural and intellectual creativity and status of the region. The South's aggressive economic structure, from slave labor to entrepreneurial capitalism, has contributed to what journalist W.J. Cash termed the "savage ideal." The culture of the white bourgeoisie, its love of material possessions, its lack of humanism and gross disrespect for life and ecology has encouraged widespread social violence and a backward intellectual climate. More people are murdered per thousand in Savannah and Montgomery per year, for example, than in New York or Watts. The incidence of rape increased over 41 percent in North Carolina between 1969 and 1973, and increased by significant amounts in almost every

Southern state. The "mind" of the South increasingly represents the dregs of American academic and cultural achievement. In 1970 the South had only five percent of the nation's leading graduate schools, according to a national survey. In spite of Wallace's expansion of state-supported educational institutions, Alabama ranks at the very bottom of every national scale for education. The traditional Black Southern college, the backbone of black education in the South, suffers from declining enrollments and severe financial difficulties, largely because of the desegregation of the region's major white state-supported institutions. Many white and black radicals have fled to the North and the West Coast in search of better working conditions, a freer academic climate and higher salaries.

The possibilities for social change within the South's political economy depend primarily upon the success of black activists and intellectuals in reeducating the dispossessed, black working people and the poor toward the political consciousness of struggle. Recently Ron Daniels and the National Black Political Assembly (N.B.P.A.) have moved toward creating a progressive "Southern strategy," picking up where S.N.C.C. had left off ten years ago. Presently, however, black politics in the South is still markedly to the right of national black politics. The March, 1976, Cincinnati convention of the Assembly was notable for its absence of Southern black delegates. Excepting Virginia and Louisiana, no more than one dozen Southern delegates out of almost one thousand attended the convention. There was little interest in the black South for the third party liberal candidacy of former Minnesota Senator Eugene McCarthy.

All historical analogies have at best a limited value, since history in essence is constantly dialectical. Each successive human struggle is fought on a shifting material base, on a different cultural terrain, for different political ideals. Any comparative study of reaction and revolution can only assist us in unearthing the contours of our past, as well as in understanding the limitations and possibilities for the future.

The history of humanity is no tidy series of predictable events, moving inextricably toward an inevitable social revolution or political upheaval. The Civil Rights Movement as a series of political confrontations between black folk and an archaic social institution was predictable but not inevitable. The present period of reaction in the South, caused by many subjective and objective conditions, cannot be understood outside of the important positive achievements of black people in previous decades. Jim Crow will never return as it once existed, nor will its crude indignities which crushed the humanity of its master class. In spite of contradictory leaders, compromising politicians and an affluent petty bourgeois strata, the black majority will never retreat fundamentally from the very substantial gains achieved during the 1950s and 1960s. The old tradition of community organizing, picketing, boycotting and rallying still exists and many blacks were too young to participate actively in the movement seem now to be interested in reestablishing its activist ethos, if not its original organizational forms.

The next movement in the South must be grounded within a Marxian framework if it hopes to successfully combat racism. Southern community organizers and black political activists have begun to realize the profound, historic symbiotic relationship between capitalist economic development and white racism. A principled struggle against the residual structures of segregated society can become the basis for a deeper conflict against cultural underdevelopment and expanding economic exploitation. The future struggle against the causes of racism must be channelled through new, practical political institutions that owe their perspectives to a materialist analysis of Southern life and labor. It seems probably that this depressing and immensely contradictory period will produce the groundings for an even more successful democratic movement against economic inequality in the next decade.

A Death in the New South

I listened to the telephone receiver in disbelief. A gruff police sergeant with a heavy Southern accent informed me that Lieutenant Michael Etchinson, my wife's brother, had been murdered.

Michael was a police officer in Monroe, Georgia, a small town in Walton County, located in the piedmont upcountry of the northern section of the state. He and another officer were engaged in a high speed automobile chase of a mentally deranged white man. The white man had just had a violent argument with his wife, and he had panicked when he was stopped by the first police officer. As the man's automobile crashed into a ravine, Michael leaped from his squad car. The man grabbed a hunting rifle from his car and shot Michael squarely in the forehead. Strangely, an autopsy indicated four separate bullet wounds in his body.

Michael's funeral was held three days later, and it revealed much about the unresolved tensions and feelings between blacks and whites within this very typical, small Southern town. The white mayor and white chief of police spoke briefly from the pulpit, praising Michael's commitment to law and his love for his neighbors. Michael had no enemies, they said; all law abiding citizens of Monroe respected and admired their token black policeman.

153

Nevertheless almost every white person at the funeral was either a police officer or a local political official. Michael had no close white friends, nor had his family. The black community turned out to bear witness for one of their own sons; the whites were respectfully silent, but no more than that.

The local newspaper established a fund for Michael's widow and four year old son. Letters and telegrams from the office of Governor George Busbee, local political officials and neighbors expressing sympathy arrived at the Etchinson home and at the home of Michael's mother. The black neighborhood Michael lived in decided to change its name to Etchinson. At the burial services, several hundred policemen came to show their respect.

Michael Etchinson was never popular with the fragile Negro middle class within Monroe. Several members of the local N.A.A.C.P. attempted to frame several trumped-up charges against him less than one year ago. And it was not an uncommon sentiment among many blacks that Lt. Etchinson presented more of a problem than the white policemen, because of his intolerance of black-on-black crime.

Once Michael arrested a white youth, the son of an influential and wealthy Bourbon aristocrat. The white elite made threats against Michael in the police office for having the audacity of arresting one of their own. His commitment to apply the law fairly regardless of race and class made him one of the town's most unpopular figures.

Only one week before his death, I spent several hours talking with Michael about life in his town. He told me that even before his appointment as lieutenant that a number of violent threats had been made against his life. His wife, Robbie, received several crank telephone calls saying that her husband would be attacked. A number of blacks resented Michael's decision to join the police department. Not long before, the Etchinsons' family dog was mysteriously poisoned. Michael was convinced that he would not live out the year.

"Nothing has really changed in Monroe," he told me. "Nothing's ever going to change here." Michael loved his community, and was a gospel-believing, faithful church member. Unlike many young men of both races he had decided not to move to Atlanta for a higher paying salary. But during his short life of twenty six years, very little had occurred to alter the realities of racism in Monroe.

Monroe is a typical model for the average Southern town. A casual drive through the residential area is like a return to a motion picture backlot of *Gone with the Wind*. Stately brick mansions with tall white columns grace the narrow streets that lead into the business district. Less well-to-do families manage to get by in ranch style houses or in the refurbished, late-Victorian houses in the city. The entire economic structure of the community—the banks, clothing factories, grocery stores, loan agencies, two cotton mills and the yo-yo factory—are owned and run by whites. A private school, established in 1969, perpetuates the cultural values of segregation among the children of the upper classes.

The black population is dispersed in small pockets throughout the town in the typical Southern residential pattern. Many black families were dispossessed from their farms in Walton County and have resettled in low income, government houses. Many blacks occupy menial positions at the cotton mills and clothing factories, and provide a ready supply of cheap labor. Except for their small churches, Monroe blacks own virtually nothing of real value except their own labor power.

A not-so-subtle form of servitude exists throughout the community. At one downtown service station, for example, several black men work for the station's proprietor six days a week from dawn to after dusk. The owner pays his workers extremely low salaries. Yet he maintains a pseudo-close relationship with his black workers, by advancing money for a home mortgage, paying for a spouse's dental or hospital bills and so forth. In this manner, the black employees are "beholding" or in debt to their employer, and remain in perpetual bondage to him. They are economically unable to leave him, but cannot really afford to stay with him.

A blend of white racism, paternalism, the threat of rape and sadism constitutes the culture of the town. Throughout Monroe's history, wealthy white businessmen and landowners sexually exploited black women and destroyed black families. One such incident led to the brutal, unsolved murder of four black people.

In late July, 1946, a black veteran was lynched along with his wife and two other blacks. The black G.I.'s wife was the object of sexual advances by a local white man, which sparked a fight between the two men. The white ended up in the hospital, and the Negro was arrested for assault and battery. Outraged white citizens demanded the immediate release of the black veteran in order for vigilante justice to take over. Subsequently, the black man was freed by the police, and his wife, another black man and black woman were delivered to the lynching party.

It was during the heated summer electoral campaign of the Georgia "Wild Man," old Gene Talmadge, and racist rhetoric was in the air throughout Walton County. Some white citizens were disgusted and outraged by the lunchings but feared that their racist neighbors would ostracize them. The N.A.A.C.P. entered the county, investigated the murders and turned over the names of seven participants in the lynching party to the F.B.I. and the Georgia Bureau of Investigation. Walter White, then the Secretary of the N.A.A.C.P., authorized a reward of ten thousand dollars for evidence leading to the arrest and conviction of these men.

Despite the efforts of the N.A.A.C.P. and Southern liberals, which raised the reward total to over one hundred thousand dollars, the murderers were never arrested or tried. One white man was beaten severely for testifying before a federal grand jury in the case. Walter White later reflected that "a reign of terror and fear swept over Walton County and effectively shut the mouths of both whites and Negroes." Local police and the F.B.I. did absolutely nothing.

Racism was, and is, ingrained into the realities of existence in Monroe. My wife recalls that Jim Crow was an integral part of all social relations. The downtown stores allowed blacks to shop, but refused to allow Negro patrons to drink from the "whites only" water fountain. When a black attempted to eat pastries at the local bakery, the white waiter poured catsup over their heads and food. The churches are today still as segregated as they were thirty years ago. There were informal boycotts of segregationist merchants, but few dramatic racial confrontations occurred in the town. As in the majority of small Southern cities, the forms of segregation have mostly disappeared, but the character of white racism has deepened.

It was this environment in which Michael Etchinson was born, worked and died. Neither Michael, nor most of Monroe's black community, are fooled by the "Disneyland image" of Plains or the *nouveau riche* allure of Atlanta and Miami for becoming the essence of their lives. The racially deferential society which has warped black consciousness, retarded black economic development and reinforced white racism still is the heart of Southern life.

For all of Miss Lillian's sweet homilies about her "good negras," Billy Carter's sick jokes about the "nigger in the woodpile" provide the intellectual basis for the Southern white mentality.

For every Andrew Young and Julian Bond, there are hundreds and thousands of black workers and former sharecroppers who barely survive. Michael understood that for all the talk of progress and civil rights, the material basis of racism and the basic lack of human rights continued to divide his community and his region.

We shall miss Michael. But his vision of an end to racism and exploitation provides the impetus for continuing black struggles in the South.

Tuskegee and the Politics of Illusion

Introduction

There are two statues in Macon County, Alabama: the first is an old Confederate War Monument, situated on the town square in central Tuskegee, surrounded by the major commercial district of the county. The second, at a distance of less than two miles from the center of town, is located on the campus of Tuskegee Institute, in the shadow of the new college chapel. Beneath several impressive, spreading ferns stands the statue of Booker T. Washington, the famous black educator, lifting the veil of ignorance from the face of a black slave. It is of this famous yet ambiguous statue that Ralph Ellison wrote poignantly that it was impossible to tell whether the veil was being lifted or being lowered.[1]

Both statues represent two historical, opposing social forces which have dominated the cultural terrain and general civil societal formations of central and southern Alabama for four generations—the defeated, white racists who reconquered the governments of state and local communities after the Compromise of 1877, and the aspiring black intelligentsia, whose political horizons were first sketched by the "wizard of Tuskegee," Booker T. Washington. Both sculptured symbols represent a profound interdependency. The Negro academic strata Washington created and inspired could not exist without key compromises in politics to the white establishment. Yet, the white dominated economic base would collapse without the continued economic support of the black petty bourgeoisie. Both statues represent, as it were, two central elements of the bitter drama which is Southern history and politics. Neither could have existed in the twentieth century without the other; therein lies the central burden of Southern politics.

The possible outline for transcending the tragedy of Tuskegee's political past was offered in Charles V. Hamilton and Stokely Carmichael's best seller, *Black Power.* Devoting an entire chapter to Tuskegee, Alabama, the authors claimed correctly that the city and county were "undoubtedly one of the most significant areas in the history of the black man in this country."[2] Ten years ago, blacks within the county had refused to use their newly won electoral majority to create the politics of Black Power, preferring instead to employ the "politics of deference" and bi-racial government to achieve their limited goals. However, Hamilton and Carmichael's interpretations do not adequately explain what happened after 1967: with the election of a majority-black county and city government, a prominent, aggressive black mayor and the retreat of many whites from the vicinity, serious political and economic contradictions still threaten the existence of Macon County. To understand why "black politics" failed within this Black Belt, Southern county, it is essential that the entire historical traditions and class structure of black and white Tuskegee be critically reexamined. By unearthing the past, we can more clearly discern the historical terrain upon which future Black Belt political struggles will be fought.

Origin of Accommodation

The politics of accommodation, or "deference," underscores the entire historical experience of Macon County and Tuskegee since the Civil War. The lack of honesty and representation with black controlled municipal government today is a culmination of the turbulent political legacy of the postbellum South. Since the establishment of Tuskegee as a center for cotton speculators, planters and struggling black artisans, political *mauvaise voi* and segregation between the races have been the cornerstones of the society and its political economy. The founding of Tuskegee Institute and the Veterans Administration Hospital, the creation of the Tuskegee Civic Association and the local chapter of the N.A.A.C.P., and the violent desegregation of the town's public school system were events which were played out upon these deeply rooted, historical conditions.

It was not "Black Power" which aided in the creation of Tuskegee Institute in 1881, as Carmichael and Hamilton claimed, but rather an accommodation of selfish interests on both sides of the color line.[3] During the election of 1880, Colonel Wilbur F. Foster, a crusty, Confederate war veteran, was a Democratic candidate for the Alabama legislature, representing Macon County. Foster and his close white political associate, Arthur L. Brooks, also a candidate for the state legislature, needed substantial votes from the black community to carry their districts. Both white politicians went to Lewis Adams, a former slave who had learned the art of tinsmithing and shoemaking, to see if he could use his influence in favor of their candidacies. According to local legend, Adams and other black Republicans agreed to support the Bourbon Democratic ticket on the promise that the politicians would secure passage of a bill establishing a black normal college near Tuskegee.

In the important election of 1880, Democrats finally achieved total control over the Black Belt, receiving almost twice as many black votes for governor as they had received in 1874. Foster and Brooks won by handsome margins, thanks to black Tuskegee's support. In gratitude, by early 1881 the House by a margin of 48 to 20 and the Senate by 21 to 7 approved the creation of a black institution, which became Tuskegee Institute.

What Lewis Adams and other black Republicans and independents who voted for Brooks, Foster and the entire Democratic ticket could not observe, however, were the whites' selfish, private interests in establishing a black college. Arthur Brooks was then publisher of the *Tuskegee Macon Mail* and a former county superintendent of schools. Brooks used his position as newspaper publisher and as the county's most influential lawyer to get white businessmen to see the advantages of a local black school. Some black families had fled the county in the late seventies, when white racism was especially harsh. Formerly one of the wealthiest small towns in the state and a center for cotton marketing, Tuskegee's population was declining and white merchants were suffering through a major recession. The white students who went to the Alabama Conference Female College and to Park High School did not generate enough capital. White merchants, former slaveowners and educators alike concluded that an all-black industrial and normal college within Macon County would put money in their pockets. The quality of black education itself was, at best, a "separate and unequal" consideration.

A second reason for the consummation of the deal between Foster, Brooks and the black community was political. By agreeing to support the candidates of the Democratic Party, blacks were casting their ballots for economic conservatism and "white supremacy." Despite the important gain of Tuskegee Institute, the black community effectively disbanded their political organizations to accommodate themselves to the political hegemony of paternal racists like Foster and Brooks. Within a decade, blacks in Tuskegee and throughout Black Belt Alabama would become increasingly disenfranchised, lynched without trial and brutally assaulted, largely because they lacked an effective political organization.

The historical importance of this political compromise which created Tuskegee Institute, and in turn a large black academic, petty bourgeoisie, cannot be overestimated. The Bourbon Democrats were the major architects of Jim Crow legislation and racist, Southern Progressivism through the early 1900s. Without strong black support in Macon County and elsewhere, Alabama white Populists would have won an overwhelming victory during the critical gubernatorial contest of 1892. Black votes favoring the "white supremacy" party were 3 to 1 over the Populist ticket. As in the recent election of 1976, the black vote throughout the cotton belt/plantation South gave white Democratic candidates a narrow margin of victory.[5] These Democratic candidates whom Tuskegee blacks voted for were ultimately the very same political elite who drafted the Alabama state constitution of 1901 which virtually eliminated all black electoral political participation until the late fifties.

The political isolation of Macon County whites from electoral politics was a gradual phenomena, beginning markedly in 1948. After the Second World War, white Democrats within Black Belt counties became increasingly alienated from national Democratic politics, due to their growing alliance with Northern black voters.

Harry Truman was not even on the ballot in Alabama in 1948. Black Belt Democrats abandoned their party in droves to cast their ballots for Strom Thurmond. Democratic voting percentages in nearby Dallas County declined from 45% in 1952 to 11% in 1964, and from 58% to 8% during the same period in Wilcox County. In 1968 and 1972 Macon County whites cast their votes overwhelmingly for George Wallace, American Independent Party candidates, and Richard M. Nixon, respectively. By 1976 local whites refused to follow their governor, Wallace, back into the Democratic Party by supporting Jimmy Carter. This fierce, white political movement on the right within the Black Belt has not been translated into many municipal positions or county offices for local whites, because blacks still vote in sufficiently large numbers to defeat many of them. Nevertheless, at the statewide level, ultra-conservative, white politicians control most major contests. Without the black vote, Ford carried Alabama's electorate by a margin of 56 percent to 44 percent. Within Macon County, Ford carried the white vote by a margin of about three to one.[6]

As whites retreated from electoral forms of government they re-established themselves within the confines of a separate sub-society. Significant numbers of white merchants, businessmen and land owners continued to own valuable property in town but moved to new homes in Auburn or built new homes in Franklin or Notasulga, two small communities in Northern Macon County. Those remaining whites who continued to live in Tuskegee gradually accepted the integration of the downtown shopping area and restaurants as inevitable, but in certain ways they have retreated from other social contacts with blacks. Macon County Academy was established a decade ago to accommodate the white children of Tuskegee, because white parents refused to accept the desegregation of the public schools. No black people nor news reporters are encouraged to visit the segregated school grounds, and the Academy has no black children in attendance. White churches in Tuskegee are still strictly segregated. Many whites have even gradually stopped reading the *Tuskegee News* because of its wide coverage of black events, and recently initated an alternative newspaper, located in Notasulga. Whites still own almost all the major businesses and both banks in the downtown area. Young black children and most Tuskegee students know little of the traumatic selective buying campaign during the late fifties. In short, whites still dominate the basic means of production and commercial exchange within the county and have moved prudently from open challenges in municipal political society to a subtle, segregated civil society which serves as the central organizational vehicle for the white community. The interests of local white voters have shifted away from community political questions, which they can no longer control, to state and national political forms, which they still control successfully. *De jure* segregation has ended, but *de facto* segregation and an ongoing culture of white racism remain unchallenged.

Just as important as the political metamorphosis was the drastic transformation of the rural economic strucutre. Tuskegee is representative of a more profound, region-wide transition from a cotton producing economy to an agribusiness and light industrial economic base. Large numbers of rural blacks who worked as farm laborers lost their jobs with the introduction of modern agricultural equipment and labor saving machinery. In 1940, 6,162 were employed in agriculture in Macon County, but by 1960 only 1,729 people were working. Ten years later only 299 farm employees remained.[7] The number of farm proprietors in Macon County declined from 1,635 in 1959 to 1,181 in 1969. Three hundred eighty-eight farmers were forced to work a minimum of 100 days annually to supplement their incomes. Almost half of all farmers found employment off their land at least a portion of the year. However, the real value of farm products sold during the period increased by 147.2 percent from 1959 to 1974, at a rate almost twice the national average. This economic paradox indicates a general consolidation of small, private, black-owned farms under the control of agribusiness and the erosion of a rural black working class.[8]

The city of Tuskegee and the surrounding suburbs experienced a population and economic boom at the expense of the countryside and neighboring rural communities. The number of manufacturing employees in Macon County increased from 252 to 925 between 1940 and 1970, and the capital value of industries rose to over $5.4 million by 1972. The demographic statistics of Macon County and Tuskegee illustrate a general population decline throughout the rural areas and an increase within the city of Tuskegee:[9]

	1920	1970
Macon County total population	23,561	24,840
Little Texas-Society Hill District	2,920	1,724
Notasulga District	3,148	2,862
Tuskegee and Suburbs	6,425	15,934

The major increase in urbanization occurred during the turbulent decade of the sixties. Large numbers of rural black families, dispossessed from their farms, travelled into town in search of regular employment. With the staff expansion of both the Institute and the Veteran's Administration Hospital, many black farmers sold their property and purchased or rented homes near or in Tuskegee. The migration into the town more than balanced an out-migration of many whites who left the area after desegregation.

Macon County Population[10]

Census	Total Pop.	Urban Pop.	Rural Pop.	Percent Urban Pop.
1960	26,717	3,561	23,156	13.3
1970	24,841	11,209	13,471	44.4

The white citizens of Tuskegee are mostly the descendants of the affluent class of Bourbon planters, bankers and cotton buyers who made their wealth off the systematic exploitation of black slaves. It was this comfortable class of white citizens who, in 1895, organized a lynch mob and chased a black man, Thomas A. Harris, out of the city for establishing a law practice.[11] It was the children of the Bourbon elite who in 1957 encouraged the state legislature to gerrymander all but ten black voters outside the municipal boundaries to preserve the hegemony of white elected officials.[12] And after all the bloody struggles toward integration, their worldview has changed remarkably little. The grey statue of the stern, Confederate warrior, rifle in hand, symbolically facing north, represents the last generation of a dying, segregationist culture.

Black Petty Bourgeois Politics, Southern-Style

Tuskegee's present black petty bourgeoisie is still essentially an academic elite. Tuskegee Institute employs over 350 full-time professors, several hundred administrators, staff personnel and other technical workers.[13] The Veterans Administration Hospital, founded immediately after World War I amid a political struggle of major proportions involving the federal government, local whites and Tuskegee's black educators, for salaries of doctors, interns, nurses, staff and administrators. This professional strata of predominantly middle class, upwardly mobile blacks constitute perhaps three thousand people out of the county's total population of about 26,000. Yet, it is this black elite that directs the total political and cultural life of the black community. Within this strata were the members of the Tuskegee Men's Club, which in 1941 became the Tuskegee Civic Association. From its demands for integration and civil rights came the selective buying campaign of 1957-1960. The black middle class donated thousands of dollars to support the legal battle against the gerrymandering of the city, leading to the famous *Gomillion vs. Lightfoot* Supreme Court decision of 1960. This group inspired thousands of Tuskegee students to join the N.A.A.C.P. and sent representatives to the marches in Selma, Jackson and Washington, D.C. But history's victories impose a special burden upon any group, and especially upon the black petty bourgeoisie. By 1972, after the election of Johnny Ford, a native black Tuskegeean, there seemed to be no more political worlds to conquer. White Macon County residents had retreated into their private, segregated world, and no longer deprived blacks of their Constitutional rights. For the majority of blacks within this academic elite, the goal of "Black faces in high places" connoted an end to concerted political struggles.[14]

The central illusion which plagued black middle class Tuskegeeans was the continued belief that fundamental political power could be found within electoral politics. The struggle for Black Power, as it was initially understood by even the most militant students and members of S.N.C.C., was the struggle to achieve "majority rule": total black representation on the City Council, a black mayor and a black state representative. Even among the more conservative members of the Macon County Democratic Club, a black organization which in the sixties vehemently opposed Black Power and the "majority rule" concept, civil rights connoted equal representation within electoral political forms and an end to official discriminatory practices. This illusion finds its origins in the black political ideology of black Reconstruction and the period of the Foster, Brooks and Adams compromise which established Tuskegee Institute. Bourbon Democrats controlled the government and the court system of Tuskegee, but they also controlled the basic means of production as well as many cultural institutions. What blacks failed to comprehend during their lengthy political struggle of civil rights was that the electoral domination of the white merchant class represented their general hegemony over the entire structure of the total society. The ideology of white racism as it was manifested within civil society was by far the most important superstructural element of white rule within Macon County. Elected political positions did not create the political economy of racism; rather, the reverse is true.[15]

Since black politicians and the middle class had defined freedom as the integration of state institutions, blacks anxiously expanded governmental services once in office. A bureaucratization of the Movement occurred: Johnny Ford and other lesser-known participants in the civil rights activities either won election or appointment to city or county offices. Through his support for President Richard Nixon, Johnny Ford was able to obtain a $5.3 million federal grant for a new sewage system. The size of the municipal police force expanded to 34, an amazingly high number of policemen for a town of less than 12,000. The police budget rose accordingly to $400,000 annually. The Mayor's salary was increased to $15,000 per year, a higher amount than a salary of most mayors of cities twice the size of Tuskegee. In April 1969, a Model Cities Program was launched. Model Cities initiated an Economic Development Office which attempted to attract outside investment into the town and increase local employment opportunities. Its Summer Youth Employment project provided scores of jobs for black youths between the ages of 16 to 22 years of age. Through Model Cities and the Community Development Corporation, Tuskegee and Macon County benefited from ongoing federal appropriations during the eight years of the Nixon-Ford administration, a period when most black communities were losing such programs.[16]

As Tuskegee's economic climate seemed to prosper into the

early seventies, the enthusiasm of the Movement and its altruism declined. Few students took an active interest in local politics after 1972. Campus fraternity and sorority life became more popular as a new generation of black undergraduates came to campus, students who had taken no part in the desegregation campaigns of the fifties and Black Power demonstrations and take-overs of the sixties. The black academic petty bourgeoisie became direction-less; having achieved all its major goals in the last decade, its desire for renewed political involvement evaporated once more. Never-theless, among elements of the small working class within the poorer east end communities of Black Tuskegee and even among elements of the black middle class, a sense of unrest and malaise persisted. Something was wrong within Tuskegee's society, but what was it? No one was quite sure. A number of black profes-sionals were disturbed when one disgruntled black Tuskegeean, a resident of 41 years, wrote to the *Montgomery Advertiser-Alabama Journal* on January 30, 1977, that "All of the money coming into this town from the government for help has gone in the pockets of the elected few." The vision of a black government in Tuskegee had turned into a political nightmare. "We put Black[s] in office downtown," the man observed, "and look what they have done."[17]

The rapid expansion of bureaucratic forms within local government and the increase of expenditures by the federal, state and city agencies created major social dilemmas by the middle and late seventies. Rising black sociopolitical expectations, particu-larly among the members of the black petty bourgeoisie could not be maintained except through deficit spending on the part of the city government. Local bureaucrats understood that only through the expansion of the city's tax base, that is, through the introduction of heavy industry and finance capital, could the local governmental services and new agencies be maintained. The major issue of the 1976 mayoral campaign was the question of municipal solvency. Running against two blacks in his bid for reelection, Ford insisted that the city government could continue to provide the needed community services which had begun in the late sixties and early seventies without a major revision in the local tax structure. The government of Tuskegee, Ford's supporters argued, was in the black, literally and figuratively: the politics of Black Power had triumphed in Macon County.

During the summer months, the mayoral campaign became as

bitter as Ford's initial campaign in 1972. Spending thousands of dollars more than both of his opponents combined, Ford repeatedly used the two local newspapers and the radio stations to promote himself. At one point, Ford delivered a prayer over the radio in a paid advertisement, asking black Tuskegeeans to vote for him. In response, opponent Willie Whitehead asserted that Ford's high personal salary was indicative of the city's general mismanagement and "lack of conservatism." "This government should have more to show for the millions of dollars given it by the federal government," Whitehead argued. "This should be evidenced by having paved streets, sidewalks and the elimination of blight from the communities." Tony Haygood, the 24 year old son of one of the city's most influential black ministers, directly charged the Ford administration with complete incompetency. "City services have suffered not because the city did not have the money, but because money was improperly spent and wasted."[18]

By the week before the election, many residents called the election a stand-off. Some of Ford's supporters, worried about the election's outcome, then resorted to a Watergate-style campaign. In the newspapers and on the radio, Ford advocates charged that the Haygoods were attempting to "re-enslave" local citizens by initiating "one family control in Tuskegee and Macon County."[19] Black oil refiner and Republican Charles Wallace and other local black businessmen pooled several thousand dollars to fund a public fish fry for the incumbent.

On a hot Sunday afternoon, August 8, over three thousand Tuskegee residents drove or rode buses, free of charge, to the mamouth feast given by Ford and his petty bourgeois supporters.[20] Not unlike the days of the Bourbon Democrats, when plantation owners gave a free chicken away to each black male supporter, black voters marched off to the polls two days later and gave Johnny Ford a commanding victory of 58 percent of the total vote. Observers noted privately that Ford's black supporters spent more money for his fish fry feast that Sunday afternoon than did both Whitehead and Haygood in their entire campaigns.[21]

Three short and safe weeks after Ford's reelection, the Tuskegee City Council was forced to borrow $150,000 from a white-owned bank. Mrs. Mildred Moore, the city clerk-treasurer, told the *Tuskegee News* that the city had only $16,000 in remaining funds, and that it could not borrow money from its utilities department.

The mayor was not immediately available for comment. During the campaign, the mayor had mentioned that "we may borrow in order to get through this 1976 program year." Nevertheless, the economic health of Tuskegee was excellent, Ford reiterated. Tuskegee "is richer than it has ever been because we have cut our debt . . . down to $30,000."[22]

The residents of Tuskegee received another shock several weeks before Christmas, when the mayor and the newly elected council moved to enact two new taxes: a one cent sales tax and an occupational tax, depositing one percent of any employee's salary earned within the city limits into the town treasury. The one cent sales tax made Tuskegee's tax rate seven cents on the dollar. Both taxes were scheduled to take effect on January 1, 1977. Overnight, popular support for the mayor, particularly among the poor and students, completely evaporated.[23] Students were angered that the occupational tax would be levied against their federally-sponsored grants. Lower income people claimed an inability to pay the occupational tax. At one fiery town meetng on February 8, one irrate citizen called the Ford-sponsored taxes "unchristianlike." Student government leaders challenged the political decisions of the bureaucrats and elected officials at city hall as other students had done a decade before—except that this time it was black against black.[24]

Ford initially refused to tolerate even mild criticisms of the new taxes. When J.J. Johnson, *News* staff writer, urged in a signed editorial a repeal of the occupational tax and reviewed Ford's less than candid role as a candidate in misleading his supporters, Ford responded with an amazingly vitriolic statement. "I consider this a personal attack upon my character," the mayor wrote the *News,* "and will consider any future such assertions by you as libelous and subject to legal action." Threatened by a massive public rejection of his fiscal programs, Ford found it necessary to repeat that despite the city's "cash flow problem," Tuskegee "still is not broke." "I will not be intimidated by you," the mayor declared angrily.[25]

The severe criticism from all levels of Tuskegee society and Representative Thomas Reed's opposition doomed the one percent occupational tax within two months. On March 8, the town council's five members and the mayor unanimously voted to kill the tax, and asked local employers to return all fees deducted from employees' paychecks since January 1. *News* editor Stan Voit observed that the "unworkable, unpopular" tax was supported by "few people outside of the Mayor and Council. . . . "[26]

The occupational tax confrontation was the first major political battle that Ford had lost in five years as mayor of Tuskegee. But few of Ford's pet bourgeois opponents had observed that a black-controlled government had generally failed to solve the pressing economic and political problems which confronted the community, exactly as the white-controlled government had failed in previous administrations. Blacks running for elective offices placated the community with fish fries, full promises and fat salaries for themselves, but had failed to discern the long-term problems of the county and city. Politics was in its nature the problem facing the black community, but electoral politics did not provide any lasting solutions.

More significantly, most black Democrats and elected officials had ignored the central political problem of the seventies in the South—the subordination of the municipal and county governments to the initiatives of the state government. Macon County whites no longer control Tuskegee's government, but the victory of integrationist politics at the local level forced white Democratic politicians to move the decision-making or prerogative powers from the county courthouse level to the capital at Montgomery. At the state level, Dudley Perry, the former campaign manager for Wallace in the North Carolina Democratic Primary in 1976, represents Macon County's eighty-three percent black majority in the State Senate. Institutions in politics and education in Macon County have become vitally dependent upon state loans and subsidies. One example of a state power was illustrated last August when the State Senate recessed for the year without appropriating $1.2 million for Tuskegee Institute. The college administration was caught completely unprepared for this crisis—President Luther Foster was enroute to Taiwan on a tour. The administration decided to defer ten percent of all faculty salaries over the amount of nine thousand dollars until the state agreed to give Tuskegee its traditional grant. Ironically, it was Perry and not Reed or Ford who engineered the bill through the Senate in February 1977. The appropriation would probably not have passed without the expressed approval of Wallace, who for reasons of his own has usually supported Tuskegee Institute.[27]

Without an independent political party and devoid of the

critical political perspective, the black petty bourgeoisie of Tuskegee finds itself in a position of municipal power which means increasingly very little. Macon County blacks are represented in Congress, for example, by Representative Bill Nichols, a conservative, white Democrat of the "States-Rights" variety who has changed his position not one inch from the era of sit-ins and freedom rides. Every black elected official in Macon County argues that a compromise of interests with the white-controlled state legislature is essential for the economic development of the Tuskegee black community. Out of selfish political interests, the Wallace-Democratic Party and Macon County black Democrats have moved into a political alliance of sorts. In January 1977, on the anniversary of the birth of Dr. Martin Luther King, Jr., Wallace was the featured speaker at the Alabama Conference of Black Mayors, hosted by Johnny Ford. This political detente between former segregationists and the leaders of the Movement for civil rights is a logical, and unfortunately, a necessary consummation of class interests, working to the detriment of the real interests of the black community.[28]

Southern Black Entrepreneurs

The business community of Tuskegee has been dominated traditionally by white merchants, bankers and entrepreneurs. Although a small number of black artisans like Lewis Adams were allowed to practice their trades, black business was never a vital factor in the economic base of the city. The Movement and the impetus toward desegregation created a limited number of economic opportunities for Afro-Americans within Macon County, and the foundations for a growing black entrepreneurial/petty bourgeoisie were created, about a decade ago. The handful of black small businessmen in Tuskegee had fewer illusions than their counterparts on the campus about the importance of gaining a certain number of black elected officials in restructuring the local social and economic order. Culturally, unlike the integrationist-minded campus elite, the black entrepreneurs did not identify desegregation per se as being vital to their interests; after all, it was segregation itself which limited white competition within the Negro community and allowed the black merchant to control his own neighborhood. Nevertheless, black entrepreneurs were experiencing their own set of problems for which traditional economic theories could not account.

The academic black elite began to shop regularly in Auburn and Montgomery after the major stores and shopping centers were desegregated a decade ago. This took a certain amount of business away from aspiring black capitalists who, sometimes after graduating from Tuskegee Institute attempted without success to put some principles of the master into practice within Macon County. Black groceries, usually the "mom-and-pop" variety, were unable to receive credit from white Tuskegee banks. Some black merchants were forced to allow their customers certain conveniences which white merchants would often refuse, such as extended credit and check cashing facilities. The number of black business ventures which had failed mounted in the mid-seventies. The high tax rate of the county did not attract many prospective middle-level businesses, and created in effect a market where the only attractive resource was cheap, black labor power.[29]

Black entrepreneurs understood that the depleted local economy and the strained political climate were ultimately bad for business, but have not as yet come up with a viable solution to restructure the economic and social forms within society to their advantage. In the tradition of Booker T. Washington, some black businessmen looked to what might be termed an "African solution" to the problems of Tuskegee. A small group of black entrepreneurs in the lumber processing and home building trades were accompanied by attorney Fred Grey, the defender of Rosa Parks, in investigating the possibility of creating an Afro-American business concession within the interior of Liberia. Travelling to Liberia five years ago, the small group of Tuskegeeans met with African government officials and discussed the details concerning the cutting and processing of African timber for distribution and sale in the United States. For a variety of economic reasons, the black businessmen decided against the African project. Remarkably, a similar solution to Tuskegee's dependency upon white capitalism was first suggested by Emmett J. Scott, the private secretary of Booker T. Washington, six decades ago.

In 1914 Scott became a member of the Board of Directors of the African Union Company of Brooklyn, New York, an organization of black businessmen and professionals who sought to develop private enterprise in colonial Africa. Scott was involved in the Company's scheme of transporting mahogany timber from the Gold Coast for sale in the United States under the direction of black Americans. Joseph Jones, the secretary and general sales manager of the Company, wrote numerous letters to Scott informing him of the organization's purchases of mahogany logs, timber cutting procedures and projected plans for allowing Africans themselves to hold stock.[30] Films of the Tuskegee campus and of Washington's economic achievements were shown at Company meetings in the Gold Coast.[31]   Both Scott and the black businessmen of Tuskegee today were unsuccessful in turning African timber into American capital.

Tuskegee's black entrepreneurs have attempted to initiate other money making institutions. A large number of black appointed and elected officials, including state Representative Thomas Reed, believed that a dog track would provide the boost the region needed. As owner of several fried chicken fast food shops in downtown Tuskegee and at the Institute, Reed championed the concept among other black small businessmen. Reed pushed a bill through the lower house establishing a dog track in Macon County in early 1975, but state Senator Perry blocked the proposal in the Senate. According to the State Attorney General's Office and F.B.I. records, Reed and a close associate of Mayor Ford, Ron Williams, attempted to persuade Perry to support the bill. Supposedly, Perry was offered as much as $50,000 annually to sit as a dog racing commission attorney, if he in turn worked for the bill's passage in the Senate. Reed was accused subsequently of bribery in the incident, but many black Macon County residents were convinced that the charges were groundless. After two well publicized mistrials, Reed was finally convicted in Montgomery County Circuit Court in July 1977, "of attempting to bribe" and fined $500, but was not found guilty of bribery. Attorney General Bill Baxley subsequently cited Reed's conviction "as being an abridgement of 'moral turpitude.' " However, Reed was allowed to complete his term of office. The proposed dog track scheme, once supported by the major elements of Tuskegee's political and business elite within the black community now appears dead.[32]

Another less controversial economic proposal which would expand the black economic base of the region is the construction of an oil refinery. Mayor Ford brought Charles Wallace, a black businessman, to Tuskegee to establish a proposed $300 million refinery in northern Macon County. Through extensive Small Business Administration Loans and conservative political contacts, Wallace has become one of the wealthiest black businessmen in the country. Wallace's fortune was made initially as a fuel oil delivery company owner, supplying major government facilities in the New York and New Jersey area. The entrance of Charles Wallace into the political economy of Macon County has already had a deep effect upon electoral politics: certainly without Wallace's generous assistance, Ford might not have won re-election. Wallace also was a central element in the developing economic detente between black integrationist leaders of the previous decade and the George Wallace-segregationists who control the state bureaucracy in Montgomery. Wallace admitted recently that both "Southern militant blacks" and Governor George Wallace were strong supporters of his refinery project. "They were all fighting each other in the fifties but they all joined together for the ground breaking of my new refinery at Tuskegee," he states. Wallace's projected refinery is still mostly on the drawing boards, however, and has not yet helped the struggling economic picture for black Tuskegee.[33]

The local government and public school system have been plagued recently by charges of mismanagement and outright corruption. In November 1977, the F.B.I. charged Ezra Echols, Jr., the accountant of the Tuskegee Housing Authority, with embezzlement of over $250,000. A Montgomery grand jury charged that Echols had written unauthorized checks to himself, deposited Housing Authority money into his personal account, and diverted the rental receipts. A "mysterious fire in early 1975 destroyed some key records just prior to a scheduled audit," reported the *News*, but sufficient evidence remained to charge Echols with 39 separate counts of embezzlements.[34] During the same month, the *News* disclosed that a special appropriation of $250,000 from the state of the Macon County Board of Education was "apparently spent for purposes other than those the money was intended for."[35] Sheriff Lucius Amerson was indicted three times on different charges in 1977 alone. One grand jury charged Amerson with embezzlement "in connection with the sale of stock in a proposed motel venture five years before. Some charges against the black sheriff were dismissed by State Attorney General Baxley, but a trial on other charges remained possible.[36] Burglaries and other petty crimes increased with urbanization, and most town residents blamed "inadequate police protection and patrolling" of local communities. In October 1977, Tuskegee police staged a "sick-in," demanding a pay increase of 25 percent, which further alienated black taxpayers from the all-black police force and local government.[37]

The past history of struggle against racism and political injustice has been all but forgotten. Only traces of the rural blues culture exist, as disco music and popular forms of urban culture projected on television and local black-oriented radio stations assumed primary popular influence. In a large public rally in the center of town, Mayor Ford and representatives of Motown records and Governor Wallace proclaimed June 25, 1977 to be "Commodores day," named for a nationally known black musical group from Tuskegee Institute. The old town square was renamed "Commodores Square," as a portion of Martin Luther King highway was renamed for the black recording artists.[38] Several Tuskegee fraternities decided to refurbish the square and the crumbling Confederate War monument. After quietly receiving permission from the local chapter of the Daughters of the Confederacy, the black undergraduates eagerly placed neat rows of flowers at the base of the statue. The majority of Tuskegee Institute students had absolutely no knowledge or interest in the bitter desegregation efforts, mob scenes and nonviolent campaigns which had occurred at the very site which they dedicated for a disco band. For these and other reasons, native black Tuskegeeans wondered aloud whether the Movement had succeeded or failed. "What has happened to us as a community?" Guy Trammell, the youth specialist of the Tuskegee Housing Authority wrote in an open letter to the *News*. "What has happened to that community involvement" and spirit of change that "once characterized Tuskegee?"[39]

In truth, only the facade of change existed at Tuskegee. The marches, the murder of civil rights workers, and the celebrated elections of numerous black political figures had changed precious little. The pattern of accommodation, the ingrained assumptions of powerlessness on the part of the Negro petty bourgeoisie, had defined political progress in such narrow terms as to make it worthless. Both the black elite and the Bourbon aristocracy had erected their politics upon a mountain of lies and corruption, deceiving themselves and each other, generation upon generation. At the height of the Movement in 1966, Tuskegee Institute professor Arnold S. Kaufman observed that "Tuskegee has been living a lie" for almost one hundred years; "a lie made all the more dangerous by the apparent control that Negroes have secured over the political agencies of the community."[40]. Even with the complete desegregation of civil society Carmichael and Hamilton observed in *Black Power,* "the black people of Tuskegee are perpetuating a deferential society."[41] The politics of accommodation became the politics of illusion and self-deception.

But the history of this Black Belt community has not yet ended; indeed, it may have only just begun. "Tuskegee, Alabama, could be the model of Black Power," Carmichael and Hamilton insisted. "It could be the place where black people have amassed political power and used that power effectively." A new history, a new culture rooted in the rich traditions of the blues culture of rural blacks in the ethical precepts of the Civil Rights Movement could become "a phenomenon we have not experienced to date in (U.S.) society."[42] With Fanon, we can assert: "Je crois en toi, Homme."[43] Within the ashes of Martin Luther King's dream may yet a new black society emerge.

PART IV: THE STATE, RACE AND SOCIETY

PROLOGUE TO PART IV

'Conservatism' in America's politics means "Let's keep the niggers in their place." And 'liberalism' means "Let's keep the knee-grows in their place—but tell them we'll treat them a little better; let's fool them more, with more promises." With these choices, I felt that the American black man only needed to choose which one to be eaten by, the 'liberal' fox or the 'conservative' wolf—because both of them would eat him.

> Malcolm X
> *The Autobiography of*
> *Malcolm X*
> New York, 1965

A restatement of basic principles: black political activism cannot provide the basis for self-determination unless politics is defined as more than exclusively electoral participation, electoral campaigns and voter registration. Civil society or the cultural sphere assumes a role of pivotal significance within the immediate historical period; cultural activity, whether in the arts, music, education or health care, is just as important as electoral political work, and in many instances may be moreso. No political strategy for black self-determination can be achieved within an economic framework of monopoly capitalism; an economic strategy which includes black consumer and producer cooperatives, independent black workers' councils within unions and black capital investment within responsible, community-owned businesses might provide part of the basis for the gradual transition from capitalism to socialism.

Most of the public programs which have advanced the material and social prospects for blacks in the United States have been achieved by political liberals of both races. Part of the reason for this is that there are simply many more liberals than black radicals

181

and leftists, and since the New Deal of the 1930s they have held positions of political and ideological hegemony within the federal social welfare bureaucracy and throughout the black community. Liberal solutions also have an advantage over more radical alternatives because they appear to be less costly, more "responsible" and more immediately effective.

Consider the position of an unemployed black woman who has two children to clothe and feed. The classical conservative says to her: "let the free market take its course; abandon all federal government regulation of the economy; cut social welfare spending completely." The radical says, "the welfare system as it now exists is dehumanizing and degrading to poor people; the economy is structured to benefit only the capitalist class; a revolution will destroy the material foundations of inequality and provide jobs, health care and better education for the oppressed." Between these positons stands the political liberal. The liberal approaches the unemployed black woman with genuine sympathy. For her unemployment, the liberal creates C.E.T.A.; for her children, he provides Head Start and Upward Bound; for their hunger, he creates the Food Stamp program. Unlike the radical, the liberal's solutions are relatively easy to initiate and call for no political activism on the part of the recipient. The liberal uses the radical's language to achieve the conservative's aim: the preservation of the capitalist system, and the traditional ethnic/racial hierarchy within society.

The liberal's alternatives for social development are rooted in a series of tacit assumptions about the basic prospects for black life in the twenty-first century. First, they propose the concept of the universal norm: that all human beings, for better or worse, want the same things and approach life in the same way. Within this is the idea that blacks do not have a separate culture worthy of the name, and that cultural universality is a more healthy aesthetic perspective. Many radicals also accept this idea of universality as a social norm which can or should be achieved through political legislation, desegregation of traditional black communities and/or the merger of white and black cultural expressions (i.e., disco music). Recently, the chief expression of this philosophy has been the struggle of liberals, radicals and many blacks in favor of desegregated public schools through the use of "busing" and other means. Indirectly, this philosophy is used to attack the existence of traditional black colleges in the South and Black Studies curricula throughout white universities.

Second, liberals tend to deny that significant cultural and political distinctions between ethnic groups and racial groups are differences not based solely within economic stratification, but in tradition, custom, social thought and group behavior. One liberal black social scientist, William J. Wilson, argues against the continuity of ethnic rivalries between blacks as a group versus whites by describing a "declining significance of race." Other less sophisticated critics claim that Black Power politics and the Black Arts Movement in aesthetics only obscured the hardcore problems within the black community by alienating potential white allies in the cultural and political spheres. In all instances, liberal reforms on a basis of bi-racial cooperation are proposed as the means for qualitative black social development.

The period of liberal political hegemony over black people may finally be coming to a close, unfortunately about thirty years too late. Liberal reforms to the social problems of blacks provide temporary solutions to old grievances, but do not structurally transform the fundamental causes which created the problems in the first place. The totality of a problem must be revealed to those who are the objects of oppression; this liberalism cannot do, because it would speak to the inability of the dominant socio-political elites to provide long-range solutions within the capitalist system. The liberal is actually far more politically dishonest than the true conservative, since the Right has absolutely no illusions about the future inferior position of all black folks if a full-blown conservative regime achieved power. The liberals want to socialize a small portion of the process of capital accumulation in order to placate the marginal, dissident groups within the existing political economy; they are not prepared to advocate democratic socialism, and much less to prepare the path for a full cultural democracy in which blacks as a group have an independent and interdependent status with whites.

Part four is a critique of liberal programs on education and urban renewal, plus a reconsideration of William J. Wilson's "declining significance of race" thesis. It closes with a summary of the main propositions of *From the Grassroots*. The liberal "solutions" to our problems encourage cynicism and a lack of initiative among the masses of black people, since most governmental social programs operate on the basis of political self-interest. These reforms have no overall goal other than to obscure social reality. A grassroots alternative to the ideology and politics of liberalism must be rooted within the historical reality of blackness, within the perspectives of the black working class, the unemployed and the oppressed.

Black Education/Black Struggle
Problems and Prospects

The Problems

One of the decisive battlegrounds between black people and the U.S. state and civil society has been in the field of education. At the beginning of the modern Civil Rights Movement, activists in Little Rock, Arkansas and other southern towns challenged the legitimacy of segregation and white supremacy by attacking the existence of Jim Crow public schools. For many blacks, desegregated education became the vehicle through which some of their broader political demands against racism could be achieved. By the late 1960s, however, the dimensions of the black critique of U.S. education had shifted significantly. Astute observers within the black Movement began to recognize the limitations of the demand for desegregation which public schools, and the very bankrupt and backward condition of the entire educational establishment which whites had created for themselves. In *Education and Black Struggle,* edited by the Institute of the Black World, Grace Boggs observed that "the individualist, opportunist orientation of American education has been ruinous to the American community and most obviously, of course, to the black community." Children are "isolated" from one another; the "natural relationship between theory and practice" is reversed "in order to keep kids off the labor market. The natural way to learn is to be interested first and then to develop the skill to pursue your interest." Dissatisfaction with the educational status quo, combined with a desire to advance the submerged traditions of black ethnicity, culture and history within a structural form, led to a revolution in black thinking and practice in the arena of education.

By the mid-1970s, the grounds for educational struggle had shifted still further away from the clear-cut demands for "integration within white educational institutions." Generally, the major issues involving education which confronted blacks during the period were the following:

1) Desegregation. Broad elements of the political New Right had taken the question of "school busing and racial balance" and turned it into a platform for white supremacy. Should blacks continue to support in principle the desegregation of public educational institutions, especially through the use of "busing"? Were all-black public schools as the N.A.A.C.P. maintained, "inferior"?

2) Traditional Black Colleges and Universities. The desegregation of U.S. civil society and the limited reforms granted by the Johnson Administration had accelerated black enrollments at traditionally white universities and colleges. What should happen to traditional black colleges? Should they be merged with "white-sister institutions", or gradually "integrated" by white students, faculty and administrators?

3) Black Studies. After the boom period of the late 1960s, Black Studies Departments experienced drastic cutbacks and attacks from white universities. What was the philosophical basis for Black Studies in the era of expanding desegregation? What was the relationship, if any, between the general white Reaction in culture and politics during the 1970s and the decline of Black Studies during the period?

The answers to all of these questions must begin from a single observation: the dialectic of black inquiry within education must emerge out of the more fundamental dimensions of black political struggle in the real, material world. Certainly, for all their weaknesses, the Civil Rights activists in Little Rock almost three decades ago were asking the right kinds of questions. They viewed the issue of education for their children within the context of the segregated, racist society which they encountered daily. The demand for integrated education, *at that time,* constituted a political demand against the state which could not be resolved within the limitations of the Jim Crow system. The demise of Jim Crow schooling meant, in effect, a transitional blow against the entire system. Politics was in command over education.

In examining the issues of busing, the future role of traditional black universities and the necessity for Black Studies curricula within all educational institutions, *politics, not education,* must be in command of our inquiry. Our long-term objective, the struggle against the racist and capitalist state, must determine the critique and process of black educational theory and practice.

Busing—Still in Low Gear

In September, 1978, Los Angeles seemingly took its first tentative steps toward school integration. Despite a last minute legal effort by Bustop, an antibusing group, the limited desegregation plan, involving 60,000 students out of 567,000, went into effect. The majority of white children scheduled for reassignment refused to ride the buses; most transferred to private schools.

Outside the schoolhouses, business goes on as usual. An antibusing rally attracted 3,000 people the night before school began. Leading state Democrats, from Governor Jerry Brown to Los Angeles Mayor Tom Bradley oppose a massive desegregation plan, and have offered little direction against racist attacks aimed at the Mexican-American and black communities. Members of the state legislature now claim that the impact of Proposition 13 will necessitate cutting back expenditures to implement the court-ordered busing plans.

To a greater or lesser extent, this drama has been occurring in every major U.S. city during the 1970s. The characters are by now familiar to any political observer: the integrationists, led by a collection of white liberals and progressives, the N.A.A.C.P., and the bulk of the black middle class vs. the opponents of busing, consisting of the most divergent of interests from racist, blue collar workers to black nationalists, Maoists and Republicans, the white middle class and President Carter himself. The complex case of Los Angeles cannot be understood outside its historical context and then, only as a single example of the historical inability of minorities to force racial reforms within contemporary,"democratic" U.S.A.

For all its glitter and gold, greater Los Angeles remains what it was at its origins: a conservative, isolationist cow town. Carey McWilliams once described the city as "the seacoast of Iowa," in that most of its immigrants before and since World War II have been Anglo-Saxon, politically conservative, entrepreneurial types. Between 1940 and 1960 Southern California's population grew from 3.6 million to 9 milllion; Los Angeles became the major urban center west of Chicago. Yet, for all the outward changes, its cultural continuity remains: patriotism, Social Darwinism and private enterprise still predominate.

This is not true, of course, for the minorities. The "minorities" in Los Angeles were first the Mexican-Americans or Chicanos. Historically they have been forced into inferior, low paying jobs and confined to the *barrio,* or ghetto. Mexican-American children were initially denied schools, and subsequently assigned to a system of segregated, inferior schools.

The majority of blacks in Los Angeles arrived after World War II, and, like the Mexican-Americans, they were relegated to second class citizenship. During the 1950s and 1960s, the minority groups gradually became the majority population within the public school system. Despite the rapid population growth of the non-whites, the Anglo community and its conservative value system still dominated the educational, cultural and economic structure of the city.

The struggle for school desegregation in Los Angeles grew out of the Civil Rights Movement. In 1962, several integrationist organizations, including the N.A.A.C.P. and C.O.R.E., asked the school board to initiate a small program of desegregation, which included the develpoment of magnet schools that would attract an integrated student population.

The school board took a strong stand against busing and even claimed that the city "had no segregation." After the Watts racial outburst of 1965, frustrated civil rights groups took their case to court.

Black lawyers pointed out that about 40 percent of all black elementary school children attended schools that were 90 percent or more black in 1965. Virtually all Los Angeles blacks attended schools with a black majority student population. Segregation in the "city of Angels" was worse than Mississippi. After a two month trial in 1968, the California Superior Court ordered the city to desegregate.

But it was not until 1976 when the case had gone all the way to the California Supreme Court that a comprehensive desegregation plan involving busing was initiated. The city's token program is now in effect. Unlike Boston, there is relatively little violence connected with busing and desegregation in general, but the majority of whites strongly oppose even this modest plan.

Another major U.S. city that has experienced the busing battle is the "capital of the New South," Atlanta, Georgia. Atlanta has a long history of segregation. Despite its image (Mayor Maynard Jackson calls it the "city too busy to hate"), racial equality and economic self-sufficiency for blacks have been elusive goals. Its department stores, restaurants and businesses were desegregated only after bitter political campaigns. Residential zoning patterns were based exclusively on race.

The Atlanta school system reflected the racial segregation found in the rest of the city's cultural, social and economic relations. In the 1950's the school system was almost three-quarters white, but almost completely segregated. During the 1960's thousands of middle class whites purchased homes in Atlanta suburbs to escape the threat of integrated neighborhoods and schools. The school administration remained politically conservative and predominantly white, while the pupils and parents became mostly black. By the mid-1970s about 80 percent of the children attending Atlanta public schools were black. The basic pattern of segregation, however, remained the same.

The strategy of the black middle class in Atlanta was identical to its position elsewhere: complete desegregation of city and suburban schools using busing as the means for integration. The Nixon Administration's Department of Health, Education and Welfare suggested that minimal integration could be achieved through the pairing of neighborhood schools and no busing. The white religious community, business, labor and municipal government voiced their unrelenting opposition to court-ordered busing.

In 1970, N.A.A.C.P. lawyer Howard Moore proposed an alternative to busing: black community control of Atlanta schools. Moore also advocated the hiring of additional black administrators and teachers, plus a general upgrading of conditions and facilities within black schools. Moore's proposal was bitterly denounced by local N.A.A.C.P. leaders at the time. But the demographic and political realities for desegregation grew smaller every year.

Finally in 1973 the N.A.A.C.P. Atlanta branch officially adopted Moore's approach. The N.A.A.C.P. chapter halted its legal suit against the school board when over half the system's administrative positions went to black educators. Roy Wilkins and other N.A.A.C.P. leaders denounced the "Atlanta Compromise" and suspended the local leadership from the organization.

It has become fashionable in liberal political circles to condemn the "Atlanta Compromise" for its acceptance of racial segregation. This criticism misses the point: increased mandatory busing inside Atlant's city limits would simply accelerate "white flight" to the suburbs. A comprehensive desegregation plan involving Atlanta's white suburban schools is not desired by the school board, the overwhelming majority of white, or a substantial percentage of black Atlantans.

We have reached a point when we must realistically evaluate the failure of certain struggles for desegregation.

First, the problem of "white flight": In Los Angeles, for example, a large majority of white studnets now live in the San Fernando Valley. In the rest of the city black and Mexican-American student populations are 65 to 70 percent. Demographically, school integration has become increasingly more difficult with residential segregation. White parents often oppose busing because of the genuine inconveniences involved as much as their opposition to allowing their children to attend primarily non-white schools.

Secondly, integrationists ignore the problem of ethnicity and culture. Most Chicano students are from bilingual homes, and would prefer an education that reinforces Mexican-American language, culture and history. The same could be said for many black families who have grown to maturity in the post Black Power period.

Third, and most central, is integration itself an ideal that is politically realistic or even desirable from the perspective of the nonwhite community? Are financial costs, the extensive political and legal battles, in the final analysis, worth the final goal?

Evidence increasingly suggests that new approaches are needed. The "Atlanta Compromise" may provide the foundation for one such approach, but other educational priorities are also essential.

The principle of community control of schools must be explored as an important method for improving the educational process within urban black communities. Major cities like New York, which have had community school districts for nine years, have never actually had community control *per se*. Local school boards have few official powers, and the state legislature carefully circumscribed the authority of local school administrators. Real community control, where the final educational authority actually resides in the black community, could mean the beginning of a healthier, more productive and challenging atmosphere in the public schools.

Community-controlled schools, progressive black administrators, plus massive, new federal expenditures in the form of outright grants and low interest loans to such schools, could produce an educational experience for black children superior in most respects to a suburban, white school. The choice of setting linguistic and ethnic curriculum standards would remain in our own hands, as would our children's futures.

In certain circumstances, busing may be the only way to improve the quality of education for black and Hispanic children. In the majority of urban centers like Atlanta, however, the reverse seems to be the case. We need not destroy black schools and universities that have already proven their effectiveness in order to achieve a real departure from second class education. An all-black school, provided with good learning facilities, dedicated black educators, and controlled locally by black parents, is not an inferior school.

Despite the desire to repeat tactics from previous Civil Rights struggles, it is essential to consider the kind of realistic alternatives to school desegregation that can benefit nonwhite children *now*. It has become imperative for nonwhite educators to restructure their priorities, by looking at potential educational values and resources within our own communities that can improve our public schools.

Unless this occurs, the quality of minority education will continue to decline, since white opposition to busing and desegregation is not likely to diminish in the near future.

The Attempt to Destroy Black Universities

In May, 1978, U.S. District Court Judge Frank M. Johnson handed down a decision that ultimately may have greater adverse effects than the *Bakke* or *Weber* cases on black higher education and affirmative action. Johnson ruled that Alabama State University, a predominantly black school, was guilty of 'reverse racial discrimination' against its white faculty and staff members. Former Alabama State professor Charles R. Craig successfully sued the university for back pay, reinstatement and $11,000 in damages.

Johnson ruled that the decison included all past, present and future white employees at Alabama State, and whites who have applied or will apply for jobs there. Johnson, a liberal Republican who consistently supported desegregation, prison reform and Civil Rights with Alabama, angered and shocked many of his middle class black admirers. In the decision he implied that traditionally black colleges like Alabama State no longer have a place within American education., "Nondiscriminatory hiring practices will in time result in a work force more or less representative of the racial composition of the population . . . from which employees are hired," Johnson stated. Translated, this means that since Auburn University must accommodate nonwhites, that Alabama A and M, Alabama State and other schools must open their doors to whites.

The politics of desegregation force many liberals, both white and black, to support Johnson's position. "Black institutions must face the fact (that) they can't have it both ways," stated Nathaniel Jones, the general counsel for the N.A.A.C.P. to the *New York Times.* "They have to adhere to the same laws and principles that apply to white state institutions." Speaking more directly, John Porter, the director of the Alabama Commission on Higher Education, observed that Johnson's decision means that Alabama State "will no longer be a black institution." Logically, these liberals welcome the time when a college or university will not be distinguished as a "white" or a "black" institution. Unfortunately, they do not recognize Johnson's decision for what it is—the continuation of a liberal assault against black education.

There are 107 historically black colleges and universities, including private two-year and four-year institutions, graduate and professional schools. Since 1965 these schools have awarded 300,000 undergraduate, graduate and professional school degrees. Some of these schools, like Alabama State, suffer from a lack of internal democracy. Johnson was correct in asserting that Alabama State President Levi Watkins, a black supporter of Governor George Wallace, "maintains a dictatorial grip over the internal life of the university." Yet Watkins is not the issue nor is academic advancement for white professionals within predominantly black intellectual centers; the real question here is whether the black community, existing within an overtly and covertly racist state and society, has the right to establish and to defend its academic institutions.

What is the case for the continued necessity of the black university? From this perspective, a strong one:

1) After a brief period of liberalization, white colleges are closing the door to black faculty, administrators and students. In 1974-75, for exmaple, 7.5 percent of all freshman at medical schools were black. By 1976-77, the figure was 6.8 percent; it is lower today. One in seven black students who entered white medical schools in 1974-75 were forced to repeat the first year, a higher percentage than for whites. While universities like the University of California at Berkeley have aggressively limited the number of tenure-track black faculty and have denied tenure to blacks in disproportionate numbers. Black undergraduate enrollment at Berkeley dropped from 1400 in 1972 to 700 in 1977, and is projected at roughly 350 by 1983. A Supreme Court decision that favors Bakke will only accelerate this reaction to the black presence on white campuses.

2) Black schools have traditionally accepted students with lower grade point averages and test scores than white institutions. At Tuskegee Institute, for instance, the average student in my department scored lower than 350 on both the mathematics and verbal tests on the S.A.T., the basic entrance examination for college admission. White administrators, suffering from a tradition of racial bias, would view these black students academic needs in a a radically different manner from that of a black perspective. The relationship between black professors and black students is usually more positive and stimulating than between white professors and

black students. Neither Judge Johnson nor the N.A.A.C.P. recognize that both black students and black professors deliberately desire and choose to be within a black academic environment.

3) Black universities have been, and will continue to be, the center for black intellectual achievement. Sixty-two percent of all black M.D.s and 73 percent of all black Ph.D.s received their undergraduate training at black colleges. Over 80 percent of all black veterinarians in the country have been products of Tuskegee Institute. Over 80 percent of all black physicians and dentists were trained at Howard University and Meharry. Integrating these institutions will, on balance, produce negative returns for black people.

Black Studies and Black Struggles

As Black Studies gradually emerged in the decade of the 1960s it represented an expression of political dissent and cultural protest within the contextual framework of the white U.S. educational system. Our methodological approach toward understanding black history, literature, music and aesthetics was the basis for rejecting white educational values, theories and standards. At its peak of popularity during these years the basic Black Studies curriculum represented a much needed antidote to the traditional thought processes of white America. Racist America, having failed to liberate its own nascent humanity through its own educational institutions, was pronounced dead, intellectually and spiritually. Black Studies was at a philosophical level the beginning of an alternative to the bankruptcy of white capitalist America's educational systems.

The political meaning and content of Black Studies, apart from its educational value, was the critical element of its development. Like the Black Power Movement of the 1960s and the subsequent reemergence of modern Pan-Africanism, Black Studies acquired a popular constituency among black students, a series of national spokespersons (Lerone Bennett, Chancelor Williams, Vincent Harding, Harold Cruse, etc.) and access to the major media through a number of scholarly journals *(Journal of Black Studies, Black Scholar, Black Worlds,* etc.) and regional conferences. A new generation of black history scholars followed the footsteps of W.E.B. DuBois and Carter G. Woodson, establishing the foundations for a genuine black nationalist-oriented historiography. Black literary criticism moved beyond the intellectual impass presented by the works of J. Saunders Redding into the exploration of a true Black Aesthetic.

What many failed to grasp early in the 1970s is becoming abundantly clear with the passage of time: any struggle to advance the cause of Black Studies could *progress and regress* simultaneously at a number of levels. That is, once Black Studies was viewed as a potentially subversive political expression which undermined white aesthetic and political hegemony, white civil society launched a counter-attack against its leaders (black writers, artists, intellectuals), its cadres (black college and high school professors/teachers) and its constituency (millions of black students). This white assault was, to a certain extent, planned and carried out from the very earliest stages of the Black Studies Movement. Semi-competent black instructors were sometimes selected deliberately over better qualified black applicants by white administrators in order to degrade the quality of Black Studies. With the onset of *Bakke,* white administrators could argue cogently that Black Studies faculties had to hire white professors and graduate students, to avoid the charge of "reverse discrimination." Often black faculty were hired by white universities at non-tenure track positions; when the faculty members resigned or were subsequently released, their former positions simply dissolved. The numbers of black students admitted to white universities declined as foundation grants and federal assistance for many minority undergraduates was largely cut.

This frontal white counter-assault against Black Studies was somewhat effective. After rising dramatically, the numbers of Black Studies Departments peaked in the early 1970s and began to decline throughout the decade. There were a number of gifted black faculty who had risen to national prominence during the Black Studies phenomenon, and were swiftly silenced by a combination of fear, economic insolvency and a fervent desire for acceptance within the white academic hierarchy. Some black intellectuals such as Ishmael Reed and Harry Edwards were simply denied tenure on blatantly racist grounds. Others quietly accommodated themselves to the neo-conservative winds of change and tactfully altered their stances on academic and secular issues.

On the whole, however, Black Studies has not only survived,

but is even progressing. The literacy, historiographic and theoretical achievements of the new generation of Black scholar/activists still remains and thrives. The body of literature on Black Studies continues to grow and develop. Hundreds of thousands of black youth have been influenced by our approach to life and letters, and will in turn reach out to others beyond the university, into the black community. Many Black Studies faculty advanced into political positions which had structural influence upon the total direction of the U.S. educational systems, such as former H.E.W. under-secretary of education, Mary Berry. This achievement of black educational excellence and black thought has found a permanent place within the theoretical and practical developments of contemporary black educational institutions.

Partially in response to the achievements of Black Studies, white capitalist society has escallated its attack against black education as a whole on two distinct fronts. The first I have already discussed. Federal and state governments, most private foundations and educational systems are attacking the legitimacy and even necessity of the traditional black college. White faculty have successfully sued black colleges in federal courts on the grounds of "reverse discrimination." As the overall job market for white educators declined, more opportunistic whites pushed into traditionally all-black universities, demanding their equal share of policy making positions, tenure and all other privileges. White undergraduate students are attending black colleges in steadily increasing numbers as tuition and inflation rates force broad sectors of the white petty bourgeoisie to seek alternatives to white university education.

The results are devastating for the prospects of Black Studies ten years hence: a relative decline in the growth of black undergraduate student enrollment; a real decline in the numbers of black students attending all-black universities; a loss of significant political/educationl power through the nominal control of black universities; and the firing or dismissal of large numbers of black faculty and administrators. Since the majority of black activist/scholars are still at relatively early stages of their academic careers, their positions would be most vulnerable to the white "reverse discrimination" assault. The traditional black colleges educate about one half of all black students and employ hundreds of faculty who advocate the basic principles of Black Studies research and scholarship. The projected loss of almost *one half* of all predominately black colleges by *1990* indicates a serious reduction in the potential centers of educational power through which Black Studies can be explored and extended by black intellectuals.

The second attack, aimed most directly against black children in public elementary and secondary schools, is the policy of school integration through the imposition of federal government guidelines. Substantial elements of the black middle class, as well as the N.A.A.C.P., actively support this assault. These interests located within the white liberal and black leadership organizations argue that a quality education for black children cannot take place within an all-black environment; by extension, any field of study or scholarship that concentrates exclusively on the black experience and aimed primarily for black people. At least since the *Brown* decision of 1954, the N.A.A.C.P. has unerringly followed a mistaken path that equates integration with the struggle for black equality. The two principles involved (integration vs. the struggle against white racism) are not the same; *indeed today they have become virtually contradictory.*

Illustrating the current plight of the N.A.A.C.P. leadership was an address on education given in Washington, D.C. by Executive Secretary Benjamin Hooks in March, 1979. Speaking at the eighth annual communications conference at Howard University, Hooks argued that all-black colleges should be viewed as a thing of the past. "I reject out-of-hand a separate but equal policy," he declared. "I believe all colleges should be integrated." Hooks insisted that the enrollment of large numbersof whites in traditional black universities would "strengthen" them.

Repudiating Hooks' remarks, Howard students insisted that the N.A.A.C.P. leadership would ultimately destroy the unique character and quality that a black university setting provides. "We believe that the N.A.A.C.P. has disenfranchised the black community," one black journalism student wrote. "It has traded its shield and sword for a tin cup and organ grinder." Objectively, Hooks made no critical distinction between a "segregated school"—one in which blacks are unwillingly and forcibly placed —and a deliberately, positive black school in which the majority of administrators, faculty and pupils are of a single cultural and ethnic background. Integrated education without the prerequisites for a black academic agenda in the arts, literature and in leadership, is not a quality education for our children—it is a step backward.

not a quality education for our children—it is a step backward.

Black Studies, and more generally the totality of Black Education, is the major prerequisite for the struggle for true cultural democracy and economic equality in the United States. Until black peoples' separate sense of their own historical and cultural traditions is reinforced systematically, and unless we develop a critical theory of liberation largely upon the basis of black knowledge, our material realities, and thought, we cannot achieve any measure of independence outside white, capitalist America. We cannot seriously expect our historic oppressors to educate ourselves and our children toward a goal of black cultural integrity and economic equality. The pursuit of Black Studies in a racist society expresses a de facto failure of U.S. culture and "democracy," revealing the dictatorship of a biased, narrow-minded white cultural elite which still determines the developmental path of U.S. educational systems. Our struggle for Black Studies must become a transitional step toward our larger struggle to replace the entire educational framework of white America with a system of ethics and cultural values which will genuinely promote all the diversity and integral richness of humanity.

The Prospects

In 1979 the leaders of black and white America celebrated the twenty-fifth anniversary of the *Brown* Supreme Court decision which technically outlawed "separate but equal" education. President Carter and prominent representatives from the black elite applauded the ruling by noting the "progress" achieved by blacks since 1954. Other more progressive but less prominent blacks called the anniversary a "day of shame," observing the lack of real progress made in establishing quality education for black children and students across the nation. Beyond the spectre of *Bakke* and *Weber* resides the likelihood of even greater cutbacks in minority spending, the reduction of affirmative action programs in higher education and the closing of many all-black educational institutions.

W.E.B. DuBois viewed the *Brown* decision with a great deal of initial optimism. In an essay for the *Guardian,* published on May 31, 1954, he argued that the ruling had made the formerly "impossible goal" of "equality between black and white Americans" a real possibility in the future. "We rejoice and tell the world, and by so doing admit that heretofore this nation has not been a free democracy . . ." Nevertheless, DuBois also recognized that the desegregation of public educational facilities was not the major basis for the construction of a quality education for black people in the United States.

The meaning of the mature scholar's thoughts on black education and black struggle are summarized in one of his final speeches given in the United States. At Johnson C. Smith University in Charlotte, North Carolina, on April 2, 1960. DuBois delivered perhaps his most thoughtful critique of the role of desegregation within an overall strategy for improving the quality of black education. He was, incidentally, 92 years old at the time.

In the essay, "Whither Now and Why," DuBois observes that with the successes of the early Civil Rights Movement and the *Brown* decision, it might mean that blacks would cease to appreciate and understand their own culture. "Manifestly this would not be satisfactory," he insisted. "As I have said before," the final settlement of the racial problem will not occur by "getting rid of the Negro race . . . forgetting the slave trade and slavery . . . (and) the whole cultural history of Africans in the world."

"No!" he exclaimed. "What I have been fighting for and am still fighting for is the possibility of black folk and their cultural patterns existing in America without discrimination, and on terms of equality." Desegregation should not mean cultural assimilation. "If we take this attitude, we have got to do so consciously and deliberately."

The thesis of DuBois appeared to many to be on both sides of the desegregation question. One one hand DuBois insisted that blacks must not refuse to attend formerly white colleges and schools. "We must accept equality," he stated flatly, " or die." On the other hand, he reiterated his love for black culture and ethnicity which had guided his entire career as a scholar and pioneer in African research and Pan-Africanist politics. "What we must do," DuBois reasoned, "is to lay down a line of thought and action that will accomplish two things: the utter disappearance of color discrimination in American life and the preservation of African history and culture as a valuable contribution to modern civilization."

In the speech, DuBois predicted that by the year 2000 that

there would probably be "no school segregation on the basis of race." Implicit in his remarks is the idea that parents of black children had to pressure white universities, schools and public officials to create affirmative action programs and policies for admission of minorities. Simultaneously, DuBois argued for the continued existence of "black Parent-Teacher Associations," to "carry the burden . . . left by the public schools." Black private colleges had to remain black on a voluntary basis. Black families must be encouraged to assume an active, leadership role in the educational process. The purpose of black education was to promote the continued development and existence of black American culture and ethnicity *and* bring about a greater democratic movement within the state and society as a whole.

DuBois' approach reflects the "duality" expressed early in his *Souls of Black Folks,* first published in 1903. The tactics appropriate to integration and black separatism were essential in an overall strategy toward black education. This platform of DuBois appeared contradictory to the majority of his black and white critics, because they missed the central contradiction of Afro-American life—that black people were blacks and Americans. Any realistic strategy for black educational development must incorporate the cultural factor of black ethnicity and uniqueness with the political factor for the need to struggle for full and uncompromised rights within predominately white academic institutions.

As we consider the legacy of the *Brown* decision, we would do well to learn from DuBois' observations. Quality education for black people will be achieved not by desegregation alone. Community-controlled public schools within the black community are essential, but not sufficient in themselves. The guaranteed existence and upgrading of traditional black universities is part of the solution, but not by itself. We should applaud the meaning of the *Brown* decision, recognizing the benefits it created as well as its many unsolved problems, while also insisting upon the continued necessity and the right of the black community to maintain all-black educational institutions on a voluntary basis.

On Black Urban Development
Notes on the National Crisis

For generations, 14th Street was known as Washington, D.C.'s "black downtown district." Several hundred black-operated stores, news stands and automobile dealers thrived along the boulevard that connected the black community of central D.C. with the more affluent white sections of the city. Fourteenth Street was, and remains today, the headquarters for the Association of the Study of Afro-American Life and History, the major black historical research organization in the country.

On the night of April 4, 1968, Washington, D.C. experienced its worst race riot since 1919. Dozens of black owned businesses were burned to the ground, hundreds more were looted. Policemen fought in the blazing streets with black teenagers and young men who were bitter and alienated from the pervasive system of white rule. Fourteenth Street and the black community that developed immediately around it was destroyed as a viable neighborhood.

Today, despite federal government platitudes about urban development and revenue sharing, Fourteenth Street looks like a small disaster area. At Fourteenth Street and U Streets the prostitutes and "snowbirds" or cocaine addicts and pushers are the only black entrepreneurs who are earning a profit by plying their trade. Empty storefronts, broken glass windows and bricked-up entrances now have become commonplace.

The worst aspects of urban decay always involve the problem of housing. Both the government and private enterprise have done little to solve the overcrowded, depressed living conditions of grassroots black people. Columbia Heights Village, a subsidized housing development for lower and middle income groups was built in the 1970s, but there were only 405 apartments available for over 8,000 applicants. One community activist, George E. Storey, stated in 1978 that "waiting for the federal government to do something about Fourteenth Street is like waiting on the day when you take your last breath."

The housing dilemma, along with the larger issue of urban decay and inner-city unemployment, is a problem that faces almost every major black and working class community. Black and poor people are often forced into substandard housing projects in crime-infested neighborhoods, communities long abandoned by the white upper and middle classes. As a result, statistics indicate clearly that grassroots black people pay a substantially higher percentage of their total incomes for the homes they purchase than do the wealthy. In all respects, black people are being systematically ripped off by the housing industry, by most mortgage and finance agencies, by the government and by private landlords—and little is being done by anyone to halt the process of exploitation.

Black people who can afford the down payments for a home normally finance their houses by a mortgage with a lending or mortgage institution. Despite federal laws banning racial discrimination, most houses normally available to Afro-Americans are within predominately or exclusively lower-income areas. The economic viability of such areas, as in access to new jobs, etc., is almost nonexistent. Thus, mortgage payments consume a higher percentage of a black family's income than do similar mortgages for whites. According to the U.S. Department of Commerce, mortgaged property accounts for about 20 percent of the typical black wage earner's income, but only 18 percent of the white wage earner's income. About one third of all black families spend between one-fourth to over one-half of their total income each month to pay for mortgage notes. In contrast, only 13 percent of all white families pay this high percentage for mortgages on homes.

For renters, racial discrimination in housing becomes more exploitative. In urban areas like Washington, D.C., an average black person earning less than $5,000 per year will spend one-third to one-half of his or her income solely for monthly rent. About half of all black renters spend at least one-fourth of their total income on rent, whereas whites can afford to spend a lower percentage. Black urban housing also tends to be older and more in need of repair than white-owned housing. About 70 percent of all black renters live in houses that are over twenty-five years old.

Embarassed by the situation in Washington, D.C., and by other deteriorating urban centers such as the South Bronx, the Carter Administration sought to develop a low cost urban renewal program. Aware that Carter's 1976 political support among blacks and working people in urban areas had dropped significantly during the first year in office, Administration aides promised to rectify the situation. Thus, on March 27, 1978, Carter announced his long awaited "comprehensive national urban policy."

Carter's program involving housing and the larger aspects of urban economic development were a mirror image of the non-solutions generated by the Great Society liberal bureaucrats under Lyndon Johnson in the 1960s. As nostalgia, such plans are interesting enough, but are deliberately out of touch with the real crisis which faces lower income and black people. A step-by-step analysis of the "national urban policy" reveals serious problems and a pro-capitalist and elitist, "let them eat cake" attitude toward the oppressed.

First, Carter proposed a "shakeup" in the economic sphere. As an incentive for small businessmen to return to the urban areas, Carter has created the Urban Development Bank, which would guarantee loans up to $11 billion over the next four years to inner city firms. Two federal agencies would supervise an additional $275 million in direct grants to private enterprise. An investment tax credit of 15 percent would increase investment from the private sector, create new jobs and a more vigorous urban economy. The black population will be able to afford better homes and the general quality of life will somehow improve.

Problems: Tax incentives provide increased profits, but they do not create new jobs. Very few financial institutions pay substantial local taxes in cities. Instead of channelling billions of dollars to the wealthy, the federal government should advance programs that directly aid the unemployed, the poor and black home owners in ghetto areas. Even the liberal Establishment recognized the bankruptcy of Carter's proposal. Harvard law professor Lance Liebman commented in the *New York Times* recently that Carter's Urban Development Bank is poorly conceived and pathetically inadequate. "The bank would commit Federal money, but would supply none of the other ingredients of economic success—no market for the products, no transportation facilities, no labor supply, no reductions in local taxes, no improvements in neighborhood security."

Second, Carter called for a job program for the urban unemployed. Black youth would be hired for street maintenance and other public works projects. Problems: Carter allocated only $3 billion over the next three years for public works jobs. Only 54,000 people would be hired—leaving no new programs to assist the hardcore unemployed. According to Carter's 1978 statistics, at least 6,090,000 people were unemployed. An effective employment strategy would have to be financed by a commitment of at least $20 billion over the next two years. Most of the money would come, obviously, from a major structural reduction in defense spending.

Third, Carter recommended "something for everyone" in his new program, wrote Liebman: "for mayors, for governors, for neighborhood leaders who want to be mayors and governors; for rich and poor cities; for labor leaders, day care center proprietors, deliverers of hot food to the aged." By giving these various constituencies his official sanction, Carter played the dangerous game of giving new hope and life to those who have experienced very little positive assistance form the federal government.

Problems: Behind the florid rhetoric, nothing changes. Despite the fanfare and the massive news coverage, only $734 million of new Federal funds were allotted to the old urban programs already in existence. The sad situation under Nixon and Ford of allowing cities to rot away, of tolerating high rents for urban residents did not change.

Carter said nothing at all about the high cost of black housing, for both apartment residents and for mortgaged home owners. Carter's plans provided only $150 million for social services, for instance, when a figure ten times that size would still be insufficient.

What would an alternative transitional program for housing

look like, a proposal that the majority of Afro-American people could support and benefit from? Such an agenda might include the following:

—A merger of housing struggles with the long range fight for economic democracy and consumer rights. The struggle for lower utility rates and ultimately, direct popular control over power companies, is directly related to the issue of adequate living conditions and housing.

—An end to the standard mortgage interest deduction on federal income taxes. This is a tax dodge of the middle class, the deduction which allows most of the whites in the U.S. to escape the ever increasing costs of housing. The majority of black people do not own their own homes, and under the present economic system, they never will. 66 percent of all Afro-American families earning less than $5,000 a year live in rented dwellings. Only half of all blacks who earn between $7,000 and $15,000 yearly live in their own homes. About 70 percent of all whites who earn between $7,000 to $15,000, however, own their own homes. The result is ultimately an unfair tax advantage for the mostly white, mostly upper income classes.

—Substantial federal subsidies to small minority owned and operated contractors and local builders, especially in rural areas and in the inner cities. Priority should be placed on construction of apartment dwellings under cooperative management.

—Substantial federal tax deductions for families living in apartment housing characterized as lower income or lower middle-income.

—Reduced ceilings on interest rates charged on mortgages, established by local and/or state governments.

—A national policy of housing expropriation: the federal and municipal governments would claim and restore private housing in minority areas, especially housing over twenty years old. The proprietor would be paid in federal bonds redeemable at a modest percent over a period of years. Properties would be transferred to neighborhood directed cooperatives and local non-profit agencies for management. To be effective, housing expropriation would have to be financed by a federal governmental commitment of at least $15-20 billion.

This initial sketch of possible housing strategies should not in itself provide a lasting solution to the housing question. Only through a general redistribution of the wealth and a fundamental transformation of the U.S. private enterprise system will popular democracy become a reality in Clinton Hill and in our own communities. The future existence of black communities in this country will be determined by our ability to come up with basic, anticapitalist alternatives and political demands to initiate a new struggle for equality in housing conditions and in urban renewal.

The Continuing Burden of Race
Wilson's *Declining Significance of Race*

It is possible to conceive of any social fact as a natural phenomenon without implying that it is an inseparable function of social organization. Probably intolerance is as old as human society, but race prejudice has developed only recently in Western society... The problem of racial exploitation, then, will most probably be settled as part of the world proletarian struggle for democracy; every advance of the masses will be an actual or potential advance for the colored people.

Oliver Cromwell Cox
Caste, Class and Race
New York, 1970

Introduction

Once every other year or so a controversial study on race relations, Afro-American history or black culture appears. During the Montgomery Bus Boycott in the early stages of the Civil Rights Movement, Kenneth Stampp's *The Peculiar Institution* was published. The book reviewed the history of black people in slavery and concluded that black men "are simply white men with black skins," nothing more or less. In the 1960s historian Stanley M. Elkins' *Slavery* attracted critical acclaim for its "Sambo thesis," the idea that through a series of cultural "shocks" Afro-Americans had completely lost their identity and ability to actively resist oppression. Several years ago two economic historians Robert Fogel and Stanley Engerman won academic honors for *Time on the Cross*, a historical study which argued that blacks actually weren't too badly off in bondage, and that their white masters deeply cared about their family stability and general welfare. In each of these instances, black historians and researchers ultimately responded to these works by white scholars in a critical fashion, forcing them to rethink many of their peculiar opinions and mistaken assumptions about black life, thought and culture.

Since the publication of E. Franklin's *Black Bourgeoisie,* however, no significant work of sociology has received such a controversial reception as that of University of Chicago professor Wlliam J. Wilson. Raising simultaneously a chorus of praises and scorn, his book, *The Declining Significance of Race,* became one of the decade's noteworthy political issues. Black sociologists, historians and economists disputed its methodology, contested its theories and rejected its conclusions. Panels at black academic workshops and conferences discussed the book's implications for governmental policy-making related to blacks. On the other side of the color line, *The Declining Significance of Race* usually received generous and even enthusiastic accolades as a survey of black America. Like Elkins, Fogel and Engerman, Wilson achieved the questionable distinction of having alienated an entire generation of black intellectuals. Not one of his opponents could accuse him openly of racism, however; Wilson was black, politically liberal and had a reputation as a fair and even creative scholar. Rather than retreating before the black academic assault, Wilson simply chose to hold his ground.

The Declining Significance of Race has been reviewed countless times, and has been the recipient of considerable sympathetic support from left and liberal intellectuals who disagreed with the book's thesis and conclusions. In one important review, noted sociologist Pierre L. van den Berghe called Wilson's study an "important" work which was "the butt of political invective" and "ideological abuse." In his opinion, the book was "highly unpopular (because) it clashes head on with the interest of the black middle class which has a vested interest in the perpetuation of a racial definition of the situation. Wilson's position . . . is characterized by black 'radicals' as conservative, when, in fact, its implications are far more radical than the self-serving line defended by the black profiteers of apartheid and 'affirmative action'." Van den Berghe concludes that the author must "be commended for his intellectual courage and integrity." Black intellectuals of similar persuasion have accused their colleagues of "Mau-Mau" tactics and phony "blacker-than-thou" posturing against the book. Wilson must be given a democratic right to express his opinions and the findings of his research, they insist. The *cause celebre* must be granted the very freedoms which other black intellectuals, in an earlier period of U.S. history, had been grievously denied.

Any critique of this book must involve two issues, not wholly unrelated. The first is a consideration of the book itself, and its merits as a piece of research and sociology. Second, we must also examine the significance of the political debate surrounding the book. This critique takes the position that the idea of "race's declining significance" has great ideological appeal to numerous vested interests within the existing white elites in government, business and academic institutions. The question of continued white racism versus the lack of adequate capitalist economic mobility for blacks is in reality the heart of the entire controversy.

A Critique of *Declining Significance*

Wilson begins his work by considering the general development and character of the black experience within U.S. economic and social institutions. Briefly, he argues that there have been three basic phases of black social development. The first and historically the longest period was that of the antebellum South, the world of the masters and slaves. Drawing heavily upon the recent historical studies of Marxist Eugene D. Genovese, Wilson accepts the theory that "by the end of the eighteenth century, the southern slave-holders had clearly established their hegemony" over both race's economic, cultural and social relations. (p. 10) Despite feeble attempts at resistance, blacks developed a "close symbiotic relationship" with white racists which did not "threaten the norms of racial inequality." (p. 35) "The slaves' reliance on their masters for protection established a pattern of group dependency that was to persist several decades after slavery ended." (p. 36) Wilson accepts that passive model for black antebellum existence, whereby the slave is isolated from having the decisive role in creating his own cultural norms, values and politics.

The second phase of black social development includes the antebellum period in the North, and the entire Jim Crow years from 1865 until 1945 throughout the country. Wilson resorts to an economic determinist position to explain the creation of a split labor market and the continuation of white racism within all social relations. The "white working-class," rather than the owners of capital, was responsible for the "elaborate system of Jim Crow segregation that was reinforced by an ideology of biological racism." (p. 61) According to Wilson, the emergence of industrial capitalism gave birth to a white proletariat, which was able to transform its "labor power into increasing political power." Modern white racism resulted partially from the inability of black workers to make the successful transition to capitalist affluence during the epoch of Jim Crow. Wilson writes that "there is, in fact, little empirical support for the Marxist's contention that the capitalist class attempted to isolate the black labor force by imposing a system of racial stratification both in and outside of industries." (p. 83)

The third phase of black development occurred after World War II, in the Civil Rights and Black Power Movements. The major characteristics of this period are a collapse of white racism in economic relations, the concentration of electoral political power in metropolitan areas by black middle class politicians, and the creation of a growing class division between upper and lower income groups within the black population as a whole. In Wilson's opinion, corporations have been primarily responsible for the "elimination of race in labor-management strife." Black youth are being recruited in steadily increasing numbers into corporate positions. The "movement of blacks from the rural South to industrial centers" was the beginning of greater economic opportunity and achievement for the budding black middle class. The only group which has not been able to progress economically has been the "black lower class." (pp. 99-100) He concludes that "given the structural changes in the American economy and the recent political changes that prohibit racial discrimination, the life chances of individual blacks seem indeed to be based far more on their present economic class position than on their status as (blacks)." (p. 111)

The immediate projection for black social development that Wilson proposes is one which minimizes race at the expense of economic categories. The expansion of the capitalist economic system has benefitted first, the white working class during the period 1865-1945, and subsequently the black middle classes. The task for the future, Wilson implies, is to find a "capitalist solution" to the problems of the black lower economic groups. This would involve going "beyond the limits of ethnic and racial discrimination by directly confronting the pervasive and destructive features of class subordination." (p. 154) The means for achieving lower class development would be a combination of government intervention and an expansion of incentives for private enterprise to provide jobs for the poor. Wilson essentially says that the black middle class has solved most, if not all, of its socioeconomic problems through upward mobility within capitalism; the same struggle must be waged for black lower income groups along similar lines of economic development. Race "declines in significance" and economic questions take the central place in our analysis of the black community.

The most glaring weakness of the book is its conceptual failure in approaching Afro-American history. Through each phase of black social development, Wilson accepts the view of blacks-as-objects of oppression rather than as active participants in their own history. Like other sociologists of the Chicago school, notably Robert Park, Wilson cannot conceive of an autonomous black culture with its own sense of aesthetics, religion, political ideas and economic inclinations. His description of the antebellum period is essentially a top-down approach which negates the reciprocity of values and interests between masters and slaves. During the Reconstruction and strict segregation era, the white working class was not uniformly racist; there were frequent instances of black-white alliances within politics and labor. Wilson's book is devoid of any appreciation for the permanent social movement of black people against all aspects of white oppression, and the line of continuity between Frederick Douglass and Martin Delany, W.E.B DuBois and Marcus Garvey, Martin Luther King and Malcolm X. Any sociological study that claims to examine the evolution of blackness without also exploring black social protest thought and activism cannot really speak accurately to our history.

Wilson's chief contribution to the discussion about black-white relations is his extensive use of economic data. Throughout the book, Wilson attacks the "class interpretation" of "classical Marxism," yet places all of his major discussion about the evolution of the black community as a function of the immediate class changes within the capitalist economy. But what is "class" according to Wilson? After some hesitation, he explains that class "means any group of people who have more or less similar goods, services, or skills to offer for income . . . and who therefore receive similar financial remuneration in the market place." In other words, Wilson's theoretical basis for class is a function of income level.

There are many problems with this kind of an approach toward describing black social development. It ignores the role of consciousness and cultural phenomena within income groups which can, in turn, produce a "radical chic" within elements of the capitalist class and an antiunion "Archie Bunker" within sectors of the white working class. When income levels are not adjusted to the rate of inflation, which Wilson does not do, a false perception of rapid economic growth appears within the data on blacks in the U.S. since 1945. Although the percentage of black women's incomes compared to white women's has risen from 49 percent in 1953 to 98 percent in 1974, this is not an indication of a "relaxation of racial tensions" in the private sector; what has occurred instead is a structural change of many black women from working as household domestics and in agriculture to clerical and industrial working class positions of employment. This produces a statistical rise in income, but in terms of the entire political economy, black women still remain at the very bottom. The statistical rise in all black incomes after the Great Depression does not occur because "the center of racial conflict has shifted from the industrial sector," but because blacks moved from a rural, self-sufficient but "cash poor" economic status into industries and lower-to-middle level jobs in the public sector. The result is that blacks as a group are still behind whites; no amount of statistical doubletalk will obscure this fundamental fact.

For Marxists, class does not directly connote income, but rather the position of a group relative to the means of production; the class status is defined by whether a group sells its labor power for a wage in order to live, or owns the productive process. Class is also influenced by other important factors, such as race. Using these criteria, instead of Wilson's, one concludes that the oppression of blacks has intensified in recent history. The great black middle class which Wilson repeatedly refers to is at best a small "elite." Compared to whites, black businessmen control a steadily shrinking economic market for their products. In ideological terms, black workers and executives alike identify their interests along racial lines, and usually act accordingly, since the historical development of race relations has been predicated upon both the group's lower position within the economic structure and by the permanent ideological and cultural barrier of race between themselves and whites as a group.

If Wilson had approached the problem of racism as a partial byproduct of *capitalist development* within cultural and political relations, then he would be forced to admit that there can be no "decline in the significance of race" until the basic ownership of the economic system is made more democratic. Socialism is no guarantee that racial relations would become egalitarian, but it would provide the basic economic security and democratic reallocation of public services which are essential for a decent, humane way of life. Under these material conditions, race might simply become an element of human diversity and aesthetic value, rather than a continuing burden of economic bondage.

The Political Implications

Unlike other controversial scholarly works, *The Declining Significance of Race* does not merit the passionate defenses and assaults it has generated within social science circles. Considered solely on its fundamentals, its scholarship and its originality, it is neither clearly left nor right, anti-black separatist or pro-integrationist. It is quite simply mediocre. The debate about Wilson has less to do with the book itself as it does with the tenor of the times, the current state of Black America and the role of social analysis and research within any historical period.

In Part III of this book I have described the period of the 1970s as "the Reaction." Any sociologist, including Wilson, implicitly understands the meaning of the phrase from the vantage point of Black people. Since the demise of Black Power and the social activism which characterized the Civil Rights Movement, the reaction of whites of all income groups, cultural backgrounds and political loyalties against black society has become increasingly worse. In politics, the reaction is characterized by the law suits of Alan Bakke and Brian Weber against the principle of affirmative action; the passage of Proposition Thirteen in California and subsequent taxpayer "revolts" which, in turn, lead to a reduction of black employment within the public sector; the rebirth of the Ku Klux Klan and racial violence in the South.

Many of these problems were to be expected. After every social movement of historical importance there has been a subsequent period of cultural retrenchment and economic conservatism by the ruling elites. What is unusual about the most recent reaction is that it has generated an intellectual movement against the perceived "privileges" of minority groups which were achieved in the 1960s. The principle thrust of this movement has been the efforts of politically conservative social scientists and humanists to undermine affirmative action based on the criteria of race. For example, the Committee on Academic Non-Discrimination and Integrity was formed to oppose the ideal of "group rights" over the "meritocratic" ideal of "individual freedom." Historians Daniel Boorstin and Oscar Handlin, sociologist Nathan Glazer, economist Milton Friedman and political ideologue Sidney Hook joined over 500 other intellectuals in the Committee. The group argues bluntly in the words of Glazer, that "affirmative action" is an attempt to "undermine the very foundations of our society." In its media campaign against special treatment for blacks, the Committee has described all racial quotas as "unjust, discriminatory and evil." According to George Roche, racial quotas merely advance "the minority member (who) doesn't have what it takes. Even the minority member who earns his competence will surely be undermined as a result."

Theoretically, intellectuals have published books which do not specifically attack the use of affirmative action for blacks as a group, but nevertheless postulate the thesis that *race* per se is no longer as viable a category for sociological research and policy making as it once was. These studies presuppose that the ideological and economic origins of racism have been sharply reduced, and that other social categories have replaced race as the critical determinant in U.S. social reality.

One school of thought argues that caste, rather than race, is the feature which distinguishes black-white relations. Professor John U. Ogbu, a Nigerian social anthropologist, takes this approach in his study *Minority Education and Caste: The American System in Cross-Cultural Perspective.* Ogbu examines the reasons given for lower academic performance of black students, and rejects the reasons usually given by black educators: that white institutions structurally deny the validity of the black cultural experience; and that ghetto schools are usually deficient in physical and financial resources compared to white schools. "Caste, rather than race," Ogbu claims, sets a common tradition for an inferior education. The victim of white institutional racism thus becomes the creator of his own oppression. "Black students neither make sufficient efforts in their studies," he concludes, "nor match their aspirations with accomplishments."

Other recent schools of sociological thought approach the question of black oppression somewhat differently. Professor Robin M. Williams, Jr., writes that most ethnic and racial confrontations in U.S. society are ultimately resolved without violence. A concomitant proposition of his book, *Mutual Accommodation: Ethnic Conflict and Cooperation,* is that racial prejudice among whites has sharply dropped. His empirical data argues for the achievement of "social maturity" at the expense of special treatment or compensatory provisions for minority groups. Professor H. Edward Ransford carries this notion of black progress in the 1970s in his work, *Race and Class in American Society: Black, Chicano and Anglo.* Blacks suffer not from social distance or inequality, but because of a lack of competitive status vis a vis the white middle class. Ransford insists that racial barriers and stratification no longer describe the black experience, given the relative rise of educational and economic opportunity for blacks. Any reaction by whites against blacks today is not "racism," he suggests, but the social stress resulting from threats to their educational, economic, cultural and political posture. In short, racism is again not the basic problem, for either blacks or whites.

When *The Declining Significance of Race* appeared, therefore, it presented nothing new—that is, its social analysis which minimized the role of racism within the composition of black economic and cultural life was not original. Others in the field of sociology had said as much in other ways, and will assuredly continue to do so. What was surprising to black academicians was, first, its lack of scholarly subtlety, the clear and unequivocal break from race that it proposed. Let us consider what would have occurred had Wilson selected the title, "The Increasing Significance of Class." The manuscript would have been published, but few people outside of the field of sociology would have noticed. The fierce criticism from black researchers, social scientists and activists would have been virtually nonexistent. Wilson set the entire tone for the debate by choosing "race" as the central focus for discussion. In doing so, he sold many more copies of the book; he won the fierce loyalty of conservative and liberal educators and their black allies; he earned the wrath of black intellectuals and social activists.

More important were the social implications of Wilson's study for public policies affecting blacks. White intellectuals were looking for a theoretical framework to justify their assault against affirmative action, and *The Declining Significance of Race* provided them with new academic ammunition. Wilson clearly states (p. 110) that "affirmative action programs are not designed to deal with the problem of the disproportionate concentration of blacks in the low-wage labor market." Racism as a problem "in the economic order [has] declined," while "there has been a gradual shift of racial conflict from the economic to the sociopolitical order." (p. 111) Wilson observes that "the more educated blacks continue to experience a faster rate of job advancement than their white counterparts." Thus, "at this point there is every reason to believe that talented and educated blacks . . . will continue to enjoy the advantages and privileges of their class status." (p. 153) Wilson evidently believes that any additional expansion of special programs, such as those created by the Association of American Medical Colleges to increase black enrollment at white institutions, merely obscure and perpetuate the greater problem of class oppression for lower income groups. "In the final analysis," he concludes, "the challenge of economic dislocation in modern industrial society calls for public policy programs to attack inequality on a broad class front," going beyond the "limits" of "racial discrimination."

In its popular context, Wilson was understood as saying: 1) that racial prejudice and discrimination were no longer major problems within the capitalist economic system; 2) that affirmative action programs for blacks were no longer necessary, and were in fact destructive to the black group's own best interests; and 3) that economic development along liberal, welfare capitalist lines could alleviate any residual dilemmas with which blacks were afflicted. Race had "declined in significance" for public policy making. In the future, federal bureaucrats at the Department of Health, Education and Welfare could concentrate their corrective efforts toward "poorly trained and educationally limited blacks of the inner city," rather than toward blacks as a group. In effect, this approach minimizes the continuing burden of racism as the major feature in all black peoples' lives, regardless of their economic status, cultural achievement and educational mobility. Wilson's thesis serves to perpetuate racism by transferring the historic guilt of whites as a group toward another criterion, namely the lack of adequate economic mobility for some blacks.

W.E.B. DuBois once observed that "all literature is," in the last analysis, "propaganda." Sociological studies do not exist in an empirical void, but either concur with or deny the existing socio-economic reality. All academic work, directly or indirectly, perpetuates existing social dogma or raised questions about it. Theoretical work draws its basis from existing cultural and social norms, but attempts to project solutions to existing human problems. By any measure, *The Declining Significance of Race* prepares the way for a white reaction against black folks as a group and blackness in general. It is "propaganda," in DuBois' sense, of the white ruling elites in economics, culture and politics. On these grounds alone it deserves our critical examination and a decent hearing. Beyond that, it has earned nothing else.

Black Politics and the
Pursuit of Human Equality

The decade of the seventies has given birth to two compli-mentary illusions regarding black folk in the U.S.—the illusion of black empowerment through the institutions of electoral politics, and the illusion of black economic achievement within the con-textual framework of advanced capitalism. Both illusions are rein-forced by the hegemony of the ruling elites, by the dominant social forces which control the economic order. Both illusions speak to the bankruptcy of black activist leadership, because contemporary black leaders are often among the most vocal advocates of the rhetoric of black success. Any discussion about the prospect for black politics in the next decade must begin with a reconsideration of these illusions.

By most standards, the years 1960 to 1974 were a dynamic period of political achievement and economic growth for most black people. The percentage of black income to white income at all levels rose from 56% to about 63%. The number of black banks rose dramatically, as politicians on all ends of the political spectrum, from Richard Nixon to Hubert Humphrey, advanced the notion of "black power" as "black capitalism." The federal govern-ment initiated affirmative action guidelines which forced hundreds of businesses with federal contracts to hire specific numbers of minority people. The number of black elected officials more than doubled within eight years, as thousands of black activists in the movement became part of local, state and federal bureaucracies. Blacks acquired new leverage within society, as thousands of black men and women were hired in the media, artistic and cultural institutions. The greatest achievement in politics, the destruction of the Jim Crow system of racial segregation, the American *apartheid,* broke the continuity of eighty years of Southern history and white racist mentality.

By the initial years of the 1970s, a period of acute social retrenchment and political reaction, the national media began to run highly publicized essays on the birth of a new U.S. elite—"the black bourgeoisie." Pointing to the rapid increase in overall black income levels, social commentators observed that the Negro had at long last achieved economic parity with white Americans. Discrimination aimed against all blacks, solely on the basis of color, was fading from the political and cultural arena. New black millionaires were spotlighted in magazines; black faces on television began to appear in rapidly increasing numbers.

Within any illusion, there is an element of truth. Black political and economic achievements during this period of history were limited, but real. Yet the *limits* of black advancement, especially within the pursuit of economic equality, have seldom been discussed openly by bourgeois economists and social scientists, bourgeois politicians and corporate executives. Let us consider, first of all, the question of black economic development, and secondly, how limited economic achievements for some helped to create the illusion of group advancement at all income levels.

What is the reality behind the economic illusion? First, at almost all income levels, the ratio of black wealth to white wealth is less than 40 percent. By "wealth," I mean the total accumulation of capital, real estate, property, liquid and non-liquid assets. White families earning annual incomes of under $2,500 had accumulated an average net wealth of $10,700 in 1971. The figure for blacks that year was $2,100, roughly twenty percent of the white wealth figure. More significantly, the wealth to income ratio for whites was over 7 to 1, while the black wealth to income ratio was 1.5 to 1. Moving up the economic scale, the condition of black families tended to get somewhat worse. Between the $10,000 to $14,999 income per year level, the net wealth for white families was $24,000 in 1971, compared with $8,600 for blacks. The wealth to income ratio for whites was something in excess of 2 to 1, while the ratio for blacks was much less than 1 to 1. For income groups earning $20,000 and above annually, black net wealth was $30,000 on average, while white net wealth was over $101,000.

Also significant is the breakdown of net wealth accumulation and distribution. The average black family has a net wealth, covering all assets, of about $3,800. This includes approximately $2,100 equity in a home, $309 equity in an automobile and $450 equity in real estate. The majority of black families own no stocks, government bonds or securities. The typical bank account of an average black family amounts to less than $300, compared to $3000 for the average white family.

Obviously it is difficult and perhaps a bit misleading to isolate economic statistics to discuss the "average black family." For example, only about one third of all black families own their own home; so statistics on home equity therefore cannot accurately indicate the real economic prospects for the other two thirds of black U.S. families who rent their homes. Nevertheless, statistics like these are of some political importance because they indicate quite clearly that: 1) black incomes have risen sharply during the Civil Rights era, but the distance between total black vs. white wealth has actually increased, 2) an analysis of income levels per se is not a very reliable tool to gauge the economic health or prosperity of most sectors of the black population; 3) racism manifests itself structurally within the marketplace as a force to negate the minimal income wage gains achieved by black people in recent years, and 4) legislation which aims at either increasing the minimum wage or creating jobs (the original Humphrey-Hawkins) does very little in addressing the basic problem of long-term, net wealth inequality.

The second economic illusion involves the continued dilemma of growing black unemployment, especially in the inner cities. Since World War II, the total percentage of U.S. workers who were unemployed officially was less than 4 percent only seven of the past 33 years. Since 1969, the official unemployment rate has seldom been below 5 percent. For black workers, unemployment rates have risen from about 8 percent to above 13 percent. Black youth have experienced staggeringly high unemployment, from 41 percent nationally to over 80 percent in some urban areas.

As a result of permanently high unemployment figures, liberal and conservative economists have tended to redefine the phrase "full employment" to mean a steadily increasing level of unemployment. For example, former Kennedy adviser Walter Heller now states that full employment should mean a stable unemployment rate of 5.5 percent. Economists within the Republican Party maintain that a jobless rate of 6 percent to 6.5 percent should be viewed as acceptable and even desirable. Most of these economists, only ten years ago, argued that a 4 percent figure was a realistic goal.

We must remember that 6 percent unemployment translates to an official unemployment rate of about 12 percent for working black and Hispanic people. According to Urban League statistics, real black adult unemployment is actually between 15 to 20 percent. About one out of five black people, in other words, cannot find employment today.

The great exception to this status of black economic inequality is the new black petty bourgeois strata or black elite. For the first time in U.S. history, a substantial number of black youth after 1940 were educated at colleges and professional schools, were the chief beneficiaries of Great Society liberal programs and became almost as upwardly mobile as their white counterparts. This generation helped to lead the struggle against *de jure* segregation because it posed a barrier to its own economic and social development; it pursued policies of affirmative action to open positions in corporate middle management, government and academics that had previously been closed to them. They did not embrace the progressive elements within Black Power and S.N.C.C., but they did produce and support the centrists and right wing leaders of the Movement— from King to Jesse Jackson to Andrew Young to John Lewis.

A profile of their success can be viewed partially in terms of a function between wealth accumulation and educational opportunity. At the level of 16 or more years of education, the disparity between black and white income drops sharply. For the typical black family whose major income provider earns $25,000 per year, is 35 years old, and has a college degree; median net wealth is $49,700. As black and white professionals rise in their respective professional careers, the distance of net wealth narrows. For black professionals earning $25,000 per year, between the ages of 55 to 64, median net wealth accumulated is $103,000, about 86 percent of white net wealth,which is at $120,000. As this black elite acquires advanced academic degrees and competes for positions nearly on equal terms with their white counterparts, the character of their wealth also changes. The majority of black wealth is in nonliquid assets, such as real estate; but greater numbers of black professionals are purchasing stocks and government bonds, taking advantage of high interest rates.

What has occurred therefore is not the 1968 prediction of the Kerner Commission, which warned of the development of "two nations, one black and one white." Instead, within the black community, we are observing a unique class phenomenon—the evolution of at least two distinctly different communities, with different educational backgrounds, with conflicting cultural interests, with fundamentally conflicting economic interest. The first group, perhaps 5 to 10 percent which exerts hegemony over the second, is the professional black elite—college-trained home owners competitive with white professionals, owners of property, limited but steadily increasing wealth and secure within the system of private enterprise. The second group, which is numerically dominant, is educated at a high school level or less, is not as competitive with whites in the work place, has experienced a rise in annual income levels but continues to fall behind in terms of actual wealth accumulated, is a real victim of inflation, has virtually no cash reserves or investments whatsoever, and has little faith in the basic social and economic institutions of capitalist society. A potential "third group," which has grown into the millions of peoples in recent decades, is the black underclass, or *declasse*,— characterized by its permanently unemployed status, economic poverty, lack of a stable home environment, functional illiteracy and are the victims of robbery, rape and other criminal activity within the black community. A consideration of this black *declasse* is beyond the scope of this book. Let us observe here that the existence of this class is a product largely of the widespread, permanent unemployment within black cities at levels of 15 to 20 percent, as well as a product of the gradual destruction of traditional social and cultural institutions within black communities that had existed during the age of segregation, and have since either disappeared or have been reduced in importance.

Differing economic interests do not translate immediately into different political forces. If this were true, political scientists could turn their discipline over to the computers and elections could be predicted before hand on a net income or net wealth accumulation scale. Blacks who were able to vote between 1880 to 1940 overwhelmingly chose Republican politicians, on ideological rather than purely economic grounds. Since the "Second New Deal," blacks at all income levels have tended to vote for Democrats, whether the candidates were perceived as being liberals or conservatives on economic policy. The essential question for all blacks has always been the question of race, and whether the white candidate seeking their votes was an opponent or supporter of civil rights legislation, affirmative action, open housing and school desegregation. Because racial oppression is so overwhelming against black people in this country, the primary response of black voters to all political questions is 'what does it mean for our race'—or 'will black folk benefit materially, socially and so forth?'

Contrary to the predictions of black sociologist William Wilson and the works of Nathan Glazer and Pat Moynihan, "race" has not declined in significance. It remains the *fundamental organizing theme within black culture and civil society*. What *has* occurred is a different meaning of race, and different usages for race, within the contextual framework of black politics.

The black majority, located within the working class, view themselves and their political activities through the prism of race, primarily because their children still attend largely black schools, they still live in mostly black neighborhoods, they still attend all-black civic associations, fraternal societies and churches; and because they still perceive whites as a whole discriminating against them because of their race. The black elite, on the other hand, employs race as an ideological and cultural tool to maintain and extend its own influence, its hegemony, over the bulk of working class black society. The N.A.A.C.P., for instance, projects an image of a multi-class, largely black organization; but in practice it carries out pre-corporate, pro-integrationist policies which cut against the real interests of the black majority.

The politics of the black elite can be described in two words, "equal opportunity." The new leaders of black society do not wish to transform what they view as fundamentally "a good thing." They are not interested even in structural *reforming* basic property relations. What it desires *above all else* is the *chance*, the *opportunity*, to compete for society's surplus value, the economic profits obtained from black and white workers, on a roughly equal basis with white elites. Equal opportunity within the existing status quo, to the N.A.A.C.P., means lending support to the promulgation of nuclear power plants, so long as blacks are hired as engineers and industrial workers equally. Equal opportunity in Exxon corporation means providing affirmative action gains within the corporate hierarchy for black executives and middle managers, without having an overview on the relationship between Exxon's monopoly of energy sources and the dependence of blacks on this energy.

The challenge in the 1980s for black activists and scholars, black community organizers and trade unionists, is two fold—first, we must break the hegemony of the black elite within our cultural institutions, media, economic centers and educational institutions; and secondly, we must make a case not for equal opportunity but for full equality, and for the prerequisites of equality, in every aspect of economic, social and political relations, involving not just blacks, but every U.S. citizen. This will not be an easy task.

Equality, as I am defining the term, must become the principle theoretical foundation for a new humanistic Movement within society, a movement which will stand on the shoulders of the Civil Rights Movement of the 1950s and 1960s and the Black Power Movement of the late 1960s. Equality within the mode of production means an equal share of decision making power from the shop floor of a factory to the upper echelons of the managerial elite. Equality, defined as the principle of human *fairness*, must take the place of equal opportunity, which is defined as an equal chance to become our own oppressors.

Equality must mean more than simply the attainment of full employment, the guarantee of a job for each individual. Equality must also involve the responsibility of work, of training black youth to view work as a means toward redefining themselves in relationship to their environment, and in contributing to a better kind of society for everyone. We have to teach our youth that the ultimate dehumanization is life without work; that work provides us with a way of confronting ourselves and others toward building a new world.

Equality should mean that the federal government should commit itself to the pursuit of the prerequisites of a fair and just life for all people, without turning people into dependents and nonproductive individuals. Part of the solution toward real economic equality might mean that the federal government would provide several billions of dollars in interest-free loans and outright grants to minority businessmen and contractors and to black economic cooperatives, not as a dole, but to allow them to have the prerequisites to compete more equally with larger, white-owned corporations. Cultural equality would mean in part, massive federal fiscal support to all traditionally black colleges, without federal pressure to desegregate these institutions.

Equality must revive the ideal of poverty and self sacrifice. This is in direct conflict with the natural assumption of wealth which is part of the American Dream. We cannot all be wealthy. We should not all be wealthy. In an ideally democratic society, no one should have an income or an accumulation of wealth which he does not personally need, nor acquire economic power sufficient to destroy the aspirations and lives of others. As in everything, absolute power corrupts absolutely. "If civilization is to turn out millionaires," DuBois wrote, "it will also turn out beggars and prostitutes. A simple healthy life on limited income is the only responsible ideal of civilized folk."

If we devote all our energies simply in the acquisition of individual wealth, we will neglect the ideals of philanthropy and service. It was not too many years ago that the majority of black middle class people devoted a regular portion of their incomes toward the construction of black colleges and trade schools, black churches and civic organizations. We must instill in our young adults the gift of giving toward others less fortunate within our communities. Equality must promote a certain depth of purpose, a belief in sharing and assistance.

Equality must connote, more than everything else, the construction of a sensible, democratic economic alternative for U.S. society, an alternative which socializes the accumulation of capital. We must stop thinking of ourselves as "minorities" and calling our interests "special interests," and begin to view our demands as the basis for a new beginning to the needs of the oppressed and exploited classes of the United States. As Martin Luther King wrote in 1966, "the long journey ahead requires that we emphasize the needs of all America's poor, for there is no way merely to find work, or adequate housing, or quality-integrated schools for Negroes alone. We shall eliminate unemployment for Negroes,"

Martin believed, "when we demand full and fair employment for *all*."

The central problem of the twentieth century was in large measure, as DuBois accurately termed it, the problem of the color line—the relations of the darker to the lighter races in Africa, Asia, the United States, and throughout the world. Many of the problems within societies are still racial or ethnic confrontations. But in our country, in our time, an even greater problem has emerged that underlies even the crisis of race—can we achieve real equality for all people, in every aspect of economic, social and political relations? As we destroy the economic illusions of U.S. society, the crisis of equality looms as the great unresolved riddle for democracy in the U.S. For the sake of our children, and for the future of the world, we must address the problem and master it, without uprooting the best of black cultural and social traditions which were created during the former period of segregation and inequality. We must resolve ourselves to struggle for the basic principles of fairness and equality for all people.

Postscript: Between the Races
A Parable

Two runners are on the track preparing for the first of two important races. One is black; one is white. Both have trained many years for these celebrated races. Both are looking forward to the spirited competition and to the handsome cash prize given to the victor.

Before either runner can position himself in his starting blocks, several conscientious officials run onto the field. The black runner's legs are chained together. The gun is fired suddenly and the white runner trots away. The black runner languishes far behind. He cannot stand, he can barely crawl. His muscled legs are cut and bloodied from the constant rubbing against the rusty irons.

The white runner reaches the halfway point around the track, when a sympathetic black spectator realizes the injustice of the contest. He runs down to the track, grabs a metal ball from the shot put area and gives it to the black man. The black runner smashes his shackles. He stands and begins to quickly narrow the distance between himself and his sole competitor. As the white is turning the bend toward home, the black runner is approaching the halfway point. Closer and closer he comes to the white runner. The finish tape is clearly in sight. Finally, the white runner surges forward, defeating the black runner by a few steps.

The black runner argues loudly that the race was not at all fair or sportsmanlike. The white runner disagrees: the rules of the race call for one of the runners to wear ankle irons throughout the contest. It was an unfortunate accident of fate that the black runner received the chains and that the white runner had not. But certainly, the white runner insists, rules are rules. The race was designed by fair and impartial gentlemen. The race was a national institution and public celebration, designed for the amusement and pleasure of the general public. "Surely you are not questioning the traditions, the customs and the authority of the race?" the white runner asked in amazement.

Exactly so, states the black runner. "The rules of this game must be revised. What I desire," he argues, "is equality between our races."

"Long before we began training for this race," the white runner responds, "you knew that our respective positions were to be separate but equal. Why, you know the old saying: 'We can be separate as the fingers, yet one in the hand in all matters of mutual athletics.' "

The officials of the games congregate, disagreeing amongst themselves what course of action to follow. One junior official, the sole black man, suggests cautiously that the white runner be allowed to keep the large cash purse for his victory, but that the race be declared a draw. The senior official disagrees intensely. The black runner should receive nothing, and should possibly be banned from further competition. "Indeed, he violated every code of his race by deliberately breaking his chains!" he says. The spectator who had run onto the field of play illegally had already been arrested and was in a local police station awaiting criminal charges. The black runner must be penalized in some way. Still another official believed that the white runner should donate some small portion of his prize to the black man's children and that the entire incident be erased from the official proceedings.

Finally, the perfect solution is reached. Both runners are ordered to return to the starting line for the second race. The white runner is allowed to keep both the first place prize and is declared the winner of the first race. The black runner will be neither punished nor rewarded for his actions. Henceforth, no runner will be bound by chains.

All the participants including most spectators in the stands agree that the decision is both fair and just—save the black runner. "The white runner should be penalized by wearing my chains, at least through a brief portion of the second race," he insists. "Those are the rules of the race. You said so yourself. Look at your own rulebooks, if you dare to. Either the white runner should wear these chains in this race, or I should collect the prize from the first race."

All of the officials, including the black one, disagree. "That would not be exactly fair, now would it?" he explains. "You wanted equality. You even broke your chains for equality. Now you've got it."

The black runner continues, "but those old chains bit into my legs, cutting deep wounds and leaving bruises. I may not be able to run well this time. Certainly I should be compensated in some significant way."

"There is nothing in our rulebooks about compensation to injured players," a white official interjects. "You run the race, you assume the risks. We know the rulebook; we wrote the rules for our race."

"I hate to be troublesome," the black runner persists, limping slowly back toward the starting point. "But it seems to me that the white runner could be forced to start perhaps five to ten yards behind me in the second race. My legs are swollen and still bleeding. It would only be fair."

"Of course it would be fair, my boy," a white official smiles, placing his arm around the black runner's shoulders. "But it wouldn't be equal. That's what you've been asking for all along, isn't it? All runners will be considered equal in all these future races, endowed only with their physical abilities in their pursuit of life, liberty and happiness. Besides," he adds, "there is no such thing as perfect equality between all races."

An impatient official looks at his watch. A gun is raised and fired. The second race begins.

Author's Note

Some of the essays were published without the traditional elements of academic scholarship, such as footnotes and a bibliography. Other articles were originally written for a more academic-oriented audience. I have decided to keep the footnotes for articles in which they were used, and to add a list of source materials which were helpful in the writing of the other articles.

Manning Marable
Senior Research Associate,
Africana Studies and Research Center,
Cornell University.
September 12, 1979

Footnotes and Sources

Footnotes / Anatomy of Black Politics from 1970

1. Andrew Young, "Why I Support Jimmy Carter," *The Nation* (April 3, 1976), p. 222.
2. "Turning Up For The Vote," *Focus* (October, 1976), p. 4.
3. Arthur Miller, Warren E. Miller, Alden S. Raine and Thad A. Brown, "A Major Party in Disarray: Policy Polarization in the 1972 Election," in Richard G. Niemi and Herbert Weizberg, *Controversies in American Voting Behavior* (San Francisco, 1976), p 190. Whites supported Nixon by a margin of 68 percent to 32 percent.
4. "Let Them Eat Words," *the New Republic* (September 17, 1977), p. 77.
5. Oliver W. Cromwell, "Black voter participation," *Focus,* 5, (January, 1977).
6. "Black House members re-elected," *Focus,* 4, (November, 1976).
7. Paul Abramson, *Generational Change in American Politics* (Lexington, Massachusetts, 1975), p. 51-70.
8. *Sacremento Observer,* December 9, 1976.
9. *Cleveland Call and Post,* November 20, 1976.
10. Eddie N. Williams, "Black Impact on the 1976 Elections," *Focus,* 4, (November, 1976).
11. J.K. Obatala, "How Carter should pay his Debt," *The Nation,* 223, (November 27, 1976).

12. "Publisher's Foreward," *The Review of Black Political Economy,* 7, (Fall, 1976), p. 3-4.

13. *The New Republic,* 175, (October 23, 1976); 176, (May 14, 1977); 177, (July 2, 1977); all sources listed as editorials.

14. "Let Them Eat Words," *The New Republic,* 177, (September, 17, 1977).

15. About fifty five to sixty percent of all black adults vote in a Presidential year. In off-year Congressional, state and city contests, black voting seldom rises above 40 percent.

16. Ronald Walters, "Strategy for 1976: A Black Political Party," *Black Scholar,* 7, (October, 1975), p. 13.

17. Alfred E. Osborne Jr., "A Note on Black Economic Well-Being in the North and West," *The Review of Black Political Economy,* 7, (Fall, 1976), pp. 85-92.

18. Herrington, J. Bryce, "Are Most Blacks In the Middle Class?" *Black Scholar,* 5, (February, 1974), pp. 32-33.

19. Arthur Tolson, "Historical and Modern Trends in Black Capitalism," *Black Scholar,* 6, (April, 1975), pp. 9-12.

20. Theodore Cross, *Black Capitalism* (New York, 1969); Robert L. Allen, *Black Awakening in Capitalist America* (Garden City, New York, 1969), p. 156.

21. John H. O'Connell, Jr., "Black Capitalism," *The Review of Black Political Economy,* 7, (Fall, 1976), pp. 67-84.

22. Jon Frappier, "Chase Goes to Harlem: Financing Black Capitalism," *Monthly Review,* 28, (April, 1977), p. 33.

23. Waltraud M. Kassarjian, "Blacks as Communicators and Intrepreters of Mass Communication," *Journalism Quarterly* (Summer, 1973), pp. 285-291.

24. Robert Axelrod, "Communication," *American Political Science Review,* 68, (1974), pp. 718-719; *Statistical Abstract of the United States* (Washington, D.C., 1973), p. 379.

25. Alfred E. Osborne, Jr., "A Note on Black Economic Well-Being in the North and West," *op. cit.,* pp. 32-33.

26. Eugene Smolensky, "Poverty, Propinquity and Policy," *Annals of the American Academy of Political and Social Science,* 409, (September, 1973), pp. 120-124.

27. Official unemployment rates for Mississippi are currently 5.5 percent. When one includes 1) all workers who have stopped looking for work, 2) involuntary part-time workers, and 3) full-time workers whose incomes are below the official poverty level, the "Sub-Employment Index" for rural Mississippi amounts to 42 percent. Richard J. Margolis, "Redlining Rural America," *The New Leader,* 60, (August 15, 1977), pp. 13-14.

28. Robert S. Brown, "Economics and the Black Community," *Review of*

Black Political Economy, 2, (Spring, 1975), p. 309.

29. Cathy Sedwick and Reba Williams, "Black Women and the Equal Rights Amendment," *Black Scholar,* 7, (July-August, 1976), pp. 24-29.

30. Jodie T. Allen, "The Food Stamp Program: Its History and Reform," *Public Welfare,* 35, (Summer, 1977), p. 33.

31. Lester M. Salamon, *Black-Owned Land: A Profile of a Disappearing Equity Base* (Durham, North Carolina, 1974).

32. Robert Browne, "Black Land Loss: the plight of black ownership," *Southern Exposure,* 2, (Fall, 1974), pp. 112-115.

33. Gilbert H. Caldwell, "Black Folk in White Churches,' *The Christian Century* (February 12, 1969).

34. One important example of this is Dr. Nathan Wright, a black organizer of the initial Black Power Planning Conference in 1966, who also was executive director of the Department of Urban Work of the Episcopal Diocese of Newark, New Jersey. Wright's brother, Benjamin Wright, served as Market Development Manager for Clairol, and later use his influence to obtain corporate support for subsequent Black Power meetings. The Wrights and other religious/business leaders encouraged large industries to create "a front for channeling black militancy into the arms of the corporate capitalists." Robert Allen, *Black Awakening in Capitalist America,* pp. 161-165.

35. The complex and crucial relationship between the church and state within advanced capitalism has been ignored generally by most U.S. socialists. One indication of the church's economic power is revealed in statements of corporate assets for 1975. The Southern Baptist Convention, a predominately white denomination with over 12,400,000 members, recorded greater assets than Dow Chemical, one of the largest corporations in the U.S. The United Methodist Church recorded assets for 1975 greater than the assets of the Columbia Broadcasting System, Coca Cola, J.P. Stevens, Texas Instruments and Burlington Industries *combined.* Jim Sessions, "Protestant Power and Wealth," *Southern Exposure,* 4, (1976), pp. 83-87.

36. Frantz Fanon, "The Negro and Hegel," *Black Skin, White Masks* (New York, 1967), pp. 216-222.

37. William R. Morris, "Housing: Segregation's Last Stand," *HUD Challenge* (April, 1977).

38. Thomas Bodenheimer, "The Poverty of the State," *Monthly Review,* 24, (November, 1972), pp. 7-18.

39. Dorothy Buckton James, "The Limits of Liberal Reform," *Politics and Society,* 2, (Spring, 1972), pp. 309-322.

40. Ron Walters, "Strategy for 1976: A Black Political Party," *op. cit.,* p. 16.

41. John Conyers, "Toward Black Political Empowerment: Can the System be Transformed?" *Black Scholar,* 7, (October, 1975), p. 5.

42. Jeffrey M. Elliot, "Interview with Julian Bond," *Negro History Bulletin,* 39, (September/October, 1976), pp. 608-609.

43. Mari Evans, *I Am A Black Woman* (New York, 1970), pp. 91-92.

Sources / Whither a Black Political Party

Richard Hatcher, "Black Politics in the Seventies," *Black Scholar* (September, 1972), pp. 17-22.

Manning Marable, "The Third World in Struggle: Notes on the Cincinnati Conference of the National Black Assembly," *African Youth* (Summer, 1976), pp. 34-40.

National Black Political Assembly, "National Black Agenda," news-letter, published by the Michigan Black Assembly in February, 1977.

National Black Political Assembly, *Speeches 1974 Convention* (Leadership Training Systems, 1974).

Harold W. Cruse, *The AfroAmerican Communicator,* 1, (June-July, 1979).

Footnotes / A. Philip Randolph; a political assessment

1. Irwin Silber, "Randolph: What was his Role?" *Guardian* (May, 1979).

2 Jervis Anderson's biography, *A. Philip Randolph: A Biographical Portrait* (New York, 1972), examines the black socialist's personal and political life. There are two excellent sources on the Brotherhood of Sleeping Car Porters: William H. Harris' recent study, *Keeping the Faith: A. Philip Randolph, Milton P. Webster, and the Brotherhood of Sleeping Car Porters* (Urbana, Chicago and London; 1977), and Brailsford R. Brazael, *The Brotherhood of Sleeping Car Porters: Its Origin and Development* (New York, 1946). Theodore Kornweibel's Ph.D. dis-sertation, "The *Messenger* Magazine, 1917-1928" (Ph.D. dissertation, Yale University, 1971), examines Randolph's early years as a political activist.

The list of popular and scholarly articles published about Randolph or his role in the black Movement are almost endless. See, for example, L.W. Thomas, "Three Negroes Receive 1964 Presidential Freedom Medal," *Negro History Bulletin* (December, 1964), pp. 58-59; M. Kempton, "A. Philip Randolph," *New Republic* (July 6, 1963), pp. 15-17; Arna Bontemps, "Most Dangerous Negro in America," *Negro Digest* (September, 1961), pp. 3-8; John Henrik Clarke, "Portrait of an Afro-American Radical," *Negro Digest* (March, 1967), pp. 16-23; A. Morrison, "A. Philip Randolph: Dean of Negro Leaders," *Ebony* (November, 1958), pp. 102-104.

3. Philip S. Foner, *Organized Labor and the Black Worker, 1619-1973* New York, 1974), pp. 129-135.

4. *Ibid.*, pp. 169-172.

5. *Ibid.*, pp. 164-166, 171-172.

6. *Ibid.*, pp. 147-160.

7. J. Anderson, *A. Philip Randolph*, pp. 32, 50, 51, 52.

8. *Ibid.*, pp. 76-77; W. Harris, *Keeping the Faith*, pp. 28-29. In 1944 Randolph commented that his "extensive reading of Socialist literature" was one of the "fundamental forces that had shaped his life." The Socialist Party theorists and authors he named included Morris Hillquit, Algernon Lee, Norman Thomas, Frank Crosswaith and Eugene V. Debs. Until 1964, when he voted for Lyndon Johnson, he had consistently endorsed the Socialist Party ticket. J. Anderson, *A. Philip Randolph*, p. 343.

9. J. Anderson, *A. Philip Randolph*, pp. 79-82.

10. *Ibid.*, pp. 48, 59.

11. Editorial, "Some Negro Ministers," *Messenger* (March, 1920), p. 3.

12. J. Anderson, *A. Philip Randolph*, p. 25. Randolph stopped attending church within a year after his arrival in Harlem in 1911. But in December, 1957, the Reverend Richard Allen Hildebrand, an AME minister in Harlem received a request from Randolph to become a member of his church. Randolph seldom attended, if ever; nevertheless, he probably rested somewhat easier with the spiritual knowledge that he was a member.

13. J. Anderson, *A. Philip Randolph*, pp. 97-98.

14. *Ibid.*, pp. 107-109.

15. "The Bolsheviki," *Messenger* (January, 1918), p. 7.

16. "The Russian Triumph," *Messenger* (March, 1920), pp. 3-4. Randolph's mechanistic, economic determinism is evident in his faulty commentary on the Bolsheviks and the coming U.S. revolution. "The Government of the United States . . . is located in Wall Street. When the large combinations of wealth—the trusts, monopolies and cartels are broken up . . . a new government will then spring forth just as the Soviet Government was an inevitable consequence of the breaking up of the great estates of Russia and assign the land to the peasants, and the factories to

the workers. It is as impossible to have a political machine which does not reflect the economic organization of a country, as it is to make a sewing machine grind flour." "The Negro Radicals," *Messenger* (October, 1919), p. 17.

17. Editorial, *Messenger* (September, 1919), pp. 9-10.

18. J. Anderson, *A. Philip Randolph,* pp. 92-96.

19. "When British Capitalism Falls," *Messenger* (March, 1920), p. 3.

20. One of DuBois' most controversial prowar editorials was "Close Ranks," published in the July, 1918, issue of the *Crisis.* He argued, "Let us, while this war lasts, forget our social grievances and close our ranks shoulder to shoulder with our white fellow citizens and the allied nations that are fighting for democracy."

21. Chandler Owen, "The Failure of the Negro Leaders," *Messenger* (January, 1918), p. 23.

22. Randolph. W.E.B. Dubois," *Messenger* (July, 1918), pp. 27-28; Editorial, *Messenger* (March, 1919), pp. 21-22.

23. W.E.B. DuBois, "Socialism is Too Narrow for Negroes," *Socialist Call* (january 21, 1912); DuBois, "A Field for Socialists," *New Review* (January 11, 1913), pp. 54-57; DuBois, "Socialism and the Negro Problem,' *New Review* (February 1, 1913), pp. 138-141. This does not mean that DuBois disavowed socialism. In May, 1914, DuBois joined the editorial board of the Socialist Party's journal, *New Review.* His criticisms of some Socialist's explicitly racist platforms in the South did not lessen his intellectual commitment to socialist economic goals.

24. W.E.B. DuBois, "The Black Man and the Unions," *Crisis* (march, 1918).

25. W.E.B. DuBois, "The African Roots of the War," *Atlantic Monthly* (May, 1915), pp. 707-714.

26. W.E.B. DuBois, "The Reward," *Crisis* (26. W.E.B. DuBois, "The Reward," *Crisis* (September, 1918).

27. W.E.B. DuBois, "The World Last Month," *Crisis* (March, 1917).

28. W.E.B. DuBois, *Crisis* (September, 1917), p. 215.

29. W.E.B. DuBois, "The Negro and Radical Thought," *Crisis* (July, 1921). DuBois' attitude toward the Bolshevik revolution warms as Randolph's wanes. See DuBois' "Opinion" on Russia, *Crisis* (December, 1925), where he states, "We should stand before the astounding effort of Soviet Russia to reorganize the industrial world with an open mind and listening ears."

30. "The Crisis of the *Crisis,*" *Messenger* (July, 1919), p. 10.

31. J. Anderson, *A. Philip Randolph,* pp. 100-101; *Ibid.*, p. 10.

32. "A Record of the Darker Races," *Messenger* (September, 1920), pp. 84-85; Owen, "The Failure of the Negro Leaders," p. 23.

33. J. Anderson, *A. Philip Randolph,* pp. 115-119.

34. "W.E.B. DuBois," *Messenger* (July, 1918), p. 27.

35. J. Anderson, *A. Philip Randolph*, p. 122.

36. *Ibid.*, pp. 122-123; Tony Martin, *Race First: The Ideological and Organizational Struggles of Marcus Garvey and the Universal Negro Improvement Association* (Westport, Connecticut, 1976), pp. 9-10. On the Garvey Movement, also see Amy Jacques-Garvey editor, *The Philosophy and Opinions of Marcus Garvey*, Volumes I and II, Reprinted (New York, 1977).

37. Martin, *Race First*, p. 182. After Harrison's newspaper, *The Voice,* closed in 1919, Garvey offered him a position on the *Negro World.* During 1920-1921 Harrison was "joint editor" of the paper. Martin, *Race First*, p. 92.

38. "A Negro Party," *Messenger* (November, 1920), pp. 130-131.

39. Martin, *Race First*, p. 320.

40. "The Garvey Movement: A Promise or a Menace," *Messenger* (December, 1920), p. 171. Throughout the entire history of the *Messenger* one finds an anti-nationalist bias. Randolph and Owen even took the extreme position that the greatest danger to U.S. socialism and the trade union movement was not the racist, conservative white worker, but the Negro! "Negroes must learn to differentiate between white capitalists and white workers," the editors declared. Since they do not, "this makes the Negro both a menace to the radicals and the capitalists. For inasmuch as he thinks that all white men are his enemies, he is inclined to direct his hate at white employers as he is to direct it at white workers." In the *Messenger*'s opinion, the only hope was for organized labor to "harnass the discontent of Negroes and direct it into the working-class channels for working-class emancipation." "The Negro—A Menace to Radicalism," *Messenger* (May-June, 1919), p. 20.

41. *Ibid.*, p. 170-172.

42. Editorial, *Messenger* (November, 1922), p. 523.

43. Editorial, *Messenger* (July, 1922), p. 437.

44. A. Philip Randolph, "The Only Way to Redeem Africa," *Messenger* (January, 1923), p. 568-570, and (February, 1923), p. 612-614. DuBois' comments against the Garvey organization were provocative. He defended the *Negro World* against Attorney General Palmer's attacks during the Red Summer of 1919, and in late 1920 described Garvey as "an honest and sincere man with a tremendous vision, great dynamic force, stubborn determination and unselfish desire to serve." In 1921, he admitted that the "main lines" of the U.N.I.A.'s activities "are perfectly feasible." It was only in 1922 and 1923, when Garvey began to consider the Ku Klux Klan as a potential ally to the black liberation movement, that DuBois registered his strongest denunciations. See "Radicals," *Crisis* (December, 1919); "Marcus Garvey," a two-part essay in *Crisis*

(December, 1920) and (January, 1921); "Back to Africa," *Century Magazine* (February, 1923), pp. 539-548.

45. J. Anderson, *A. Philip Randolph*, p. 82.

46. Harold Cruse, *The Crisis of the Negro Intellectual* (New York, 1967), pp. 45, 75. At its peak in 1921, the A.B.B. had 2,500 members in 56 chapters throughout the country. It demanded th right for black self defense, "absolute race equality," a "free Africa" and political suffrage. In many respects, its platform was strikingly similar to the agendas of Malcolm X's Organization of Afro-American Unity, over forty years later. See "Cyril Briggs and the African Blood Brotherhood," W.P.A. Writers' Project Number 1, Schomberg Collection, New York Public Library.

47. *Ibid.*, p. 46.

48. The final break between the black Marxist-Leninists and Social Democrats does not come in early 1919, as many have suggested, but much later. As late as mid-1920 Briggs was a participant in Randolph's Friends of Negro Freedom. Martin, *Race First*, p. 320.

49. "The Menace of Negro Communists," *Messenger* (August, 1923), p. 784. The division between black socialists and Communists tended to be along ethnic as well as political lines. Cruse observes that "after 1919, the split among Negro Socialists tended to take a more or less American Negro vs. West Indian Negro character. The Americans, led by Randolph, refused to join the Communists, while the West Indians—Moore, Briggs and Huiswoud—did." There were several exceptions; Fort-Whiteman, an American, joined the Communists. It is interesting to note that Cruse does not fully discuss the fate of Harrison, a revolutionary socialist who abandoned the Socialist Party because of its racism and never joined the Marxist-Leninists; a black nationalist who nevertheless did not wholeheartedly embrace the Garvey phenomenon. His primary concerns were generating independent black political activity and developing a greater race-consciousness among all socialists. See H. Cruse, *The Crisis of the Negro Intellectual*, p. 118.

50. DuBois, "Socialism and the Negro," *Crisis* (October, 1921).

50. DuBois, "Socialism and the Negro," *Crisis* (October, 1921), p. 245; DuBois, "The Class Struggle," *Crisis* (August, 1921), p. 151.

51. DuBois, "Communists Boring into Negro Labor," *New York Times* (January 17, 1926), pp. 1-2.

52. Emmett J. Scott, "The Business Side of a University," *Messenger* (November, 1923), p. 864. Early in its career, the *Messenger* was not reticent in its denunciations of Moton. "Moton has neither the courage, education or the opportunity to do anything fundamental in the interest of the Negro," Randolph declared in 1919, "He counsels satisfaction, not intelligent discontent; he is ignorant of the fact that progress has taken place among any people in proportion as they have become discontented

with their position . . . ." "Robert Russa Moton," *Messenger* (July, 1919), p. 31.

53. "High Types of Negro Business Men," *Messenger* (January, 1925), p. 21.

54. 'Samuel Gompers," *Messenger* (March, 1919), p. 22; "Why Negroes Should Join the I.W.W.," *Messenger* (July, 1919), p. 8; and "Unionizing of Negro Workers," *Messenger* (October, 1919), pp. 8-10.

55. "The Knowledge Trust," *Messenger* (may, 1925), pp. 197, 209.

56. "Black Persons in Selected Professional Occupations, 1890-1970;" "Percent of Persons 5 to 20 Years Old Enrolled in School;" and "Illiteracy in the Population 14 Years Old and Over for Selected Years," in U.S. Department of Commerce, Bureau of the Census, *The Social and Economic Status of the Black Population in the United States: An Historical View, 1790-1978* (Washington, D.C., 1979), pp. 76, 89, 91.

57 Brazeal, *The Brotherhood of Sleeping Car Porters,* p. 40. At this time, Randolph also began a modest effort within the A.F.L. to drum up support for the Brotherhood's position against Pullman. See Randolph, "Case of the Pullman Porter," *American Federationist* (November, 1926), pp. 1334-1339.

58. *Ibid.,* p. 18; J. Anderson, *A. Philip Randolph,* p. 140. Crosswaith eventually became a member of New York City's Housing Authority, appointed by Mayor Fiorello LaGuardia, in the early forties. Earlier he had been a leading political opponent of Marcus Garvey, and revolutionary Socialist Party theorist.

59. J. Anderson, *A. Philip Randolph,* pp. 171-174; Harris *Keeping the Faith,* pp. 76, 78-79, 91-92. It is significant to note that DuBois had anticipated Randolph's interest in the porters by at least a decade. In a brief essay for the *New York Times,* DuBois suggested that the porters should organize as a union and strike for higher wages and better working conditions. See DuBois, "The Pullman Porter," *New York Times* (March 16, 1914), p. 5.

60. Robert L. Vann, conservative black editor of the Pittsburgh *Courier,* argued that "the company will not deal with (Randolph) because of his history as a socialist. It is known that American capital will not negotiate with socialists." *Courier* (April 14, 1927). A more fundamental reason was provided by one lower level Pullman boss to his black employees: "Remember, this is a white man's country, white people run it, will keep on running it, and this company will never sit down around the same table with Randolph as long as he's black."

61. Harris, *Keeping the Faith,* p. 110; Foner, *Organized Labor and the Black Worker,* pp. 183-184.

62. Harris, *Keeping the Faith,* p. 110; Foner, *Organized Labor and the Black Workers,* p. 185.

63. Harris, *Keeping the Faith,* p. 112.

64. *Ibid.*, pp. 113, 114.

65. Foner, *Organized Labor and the Black Worker,* p. 184.

66. J. Anderson, *A. Philip Randolph,* pp. 204-205. It should be noted as well that after 1928 Randolph remained "the dominant figure" in the Brotherhood, but no longer wielded "absolute power." Webster demanded and won the right to have all major union decisions made within the Brotherhood's Policy Committee, which he chaired. Historian William H. Harris describes Randolph as the union's "national black leader," whereas Webster was "a union organizer. Randolph thought in wider terms; he saw the problem of blacks in the totality of American society, whereas Webster thought mainly of the porters and of finding ways to improve their conditions at Pullman."

67. Ralph J. Bunche, "A Critical Analysis of the Tactics and Programs of Minority Groups," *Journal of Negro Education,* (1935), pp. 308-320; Ralph J. Bunche, "The Programs of Organizations Devoted to the Improvement of the Status of the American Negro," *Journal of Negro Education,* (1939), pp. 539-50; A. Philip Randolph, "The Trade Union Movement and the Negro," *Journal of Negro Education,* (1936), pp. 54-58; Walter Green Daniel, "A National Negro Congress," *Journal of Negro Education,* (1936); A. Philip Randolph, "Why I Would Not Stand for Re-Election as President of the National Negro Congress," *American Federationist* (July, 1940), pp. 24-25.

68. J. Anderson, *A. Philip Randolph,* p. 254.

69. *Ibid.*, pp. 254-255.

70. *Ibid.*, pp. 241-261.

71. See August Meier and Elliot Rudwick, *From Plantation to Ghetto,* Revised Edition (New York, 1970).

72. On the question of Malcolm, we confront again the inconsistencies of Randolph pertaining to black nationalism. According to one source, Randolph was "a friend and admirer of Malcolm" even during his years as minister of Harlem's temple number seven of the Nation of Islam. In 1962, Randolph invited him to serve on the Committee on Social and Economic Unity, a multiethnic coalition in Harlem. When several conservative black ministers threatened to leave when Malcolm arrived, Randolph replied that he would leave immediately if he was denied a voice on the committee. See Anderson, *A. Philip Randolph,* pp. 13-14.

73. Harold Cruse's discussion of Rustin is in his book, *Rebellion or Revolution* (New York, 1968).

74. Harold Cruse, *The Crisis of the Negro Intellectual* (New York, 1967), p. 65.

75. W.E.B. DuBois, "The Field and Function of the Negro College,' in Herbert Aptheker, ed., *The Education of Black People, Ten Critiques, 1906-1960* (New York, 1973), pp. 95-96.

Footnotes / The Cultural Dialectics of Violence

1. Anne Taylor Fleming, "The Dark Roots of Violence," *New York Times Magazine* (January 13, 1980), 38-42.
2. *Ibid.,* 38-42.
3. Harold Cruse, *The Crisis of the Negro Intellectual* (new York, 1967), 456.
4. J.H. Plumb, "Angst," *In The Light of History* (New York, 1967), 196-97.
5. See Julian Mayfield, "Challenge to Negro Leadership, The Case of Robert Williams," *Commentary* (April, 1961); Cruse, *The Crisis of the Negro Intellectual,* 347-81; H. Rap Brown, *Die, Nigger, Die* (New York, 1969).
6. Frantz Fanon, *Black Skin, White Masks* (New York, 1967); Fanon, *The Wretched of the Earth* (New York, 1960); M. Frank Wright, "Frantz Fanon: His Work in Historical Perspective," *Black Scholar,* 6 (July-August, 1975), 19-25.
7. See Robert Allen, *Black Awakening in Capitalist America* (Garden City, New York, 1970), 94-96; Eugene Genovese, *Red and Black* (New York, 1971), 143-44.
8. Vincent Harding, "Black Students and the Impossible Revolution," *Journal of Black Studies,* (September, 1970), 98-99.
9. Nguyen Khac Vien, *Tradition and Revolution in Vietnam* (Berkeley, California, 1974), 50.
10. Antonio Gramsci, "State and Civil Society," *Prison Notebooks* (New York, 1973), 258-59.
11. Eldridge Cleaver, *Soul On Ice* (New York, 1968), 12-13.
12. *Ibid.,* 13.
13. *Ibid.,* 13-14.
14. *Ibid.,* 14-15.
15. Susan Griffin, *Rape: The Power of Consciousness* (San Francisco, 1979), 86-88.
16. *Ibid.,* 88.
17. "Rape Victims," *The Sun Reporter* (January 3, 1980), 5.
18. Susan Griffin, *Rape,* 75.
19. Gramsci, *Prison Notebooks,* 407.
20. Christopher Caudwell, *Studies and Further Studies in a Dying Culture* (London and New York, 1971), 110, 122, 151.
21. Herbert Marcuse, *An Essay on Liberation* (Boston, 1969), 46-47.

Sources / Reaction: Thoughts on the Political Economy of the South Since the Civil Rights Movement

Bailey, Hugh C., *Liberalism in the New South: Southern Social Reformers and the Progressive Movement* (Coral Gables, Florida, 1969).

Bildner, Robert, "Southern Farms: A Vanishing Breed," *Southern Exposure,* 2, (Fall, 1974), pp. 72-79.

Brown, Robert, "Black Land Loss: The plight of black ownership," *Southern Exposure,* 2, (Fall, 1974), pp. 112-121.

Cruse, Harold, *Rebellion or Revolution?* (New York, 1968).

Foner, Philip Sheldon, *Organized Labor and the Black Worker 1619-1973* (New York, 1974).

Frady, Marshall, *Wallace* (New York, 1968).

Gramsci, Antonio, *Selections from the Prison Notebooks* (New York, 1971).

Janeway, Elliot, "Money and Business," *Mainliner* (September, 1976), pp. 11-13.

Key, V.O., *Southern Politics* (New York, 1949).

Lee, Emma, "J.P. Stevens' Day Will Come," *In These Times,* 2, (Fall, 1974), pp. 38-49.

Marshall, Ray, *Rural Workers in the Rural Labor Markets* (Salt Lake City, 1974).

Massey, David Dyar, "Hard Times and High Hopes: The Federal of Southern Cooperatives," *Southern Exposure,* 2, (Fall, 1974), pp. 38-49.

Roy, Donald F., "The Southern Labor Movement," in John C. McKinney and Edgar T. Thompson, ed., *The South in Continuity and Change* (Durham, 1965).

Southern Exposure, "Discrimination in the Publishing Industry Against Women and Blacks," 2, (1975), p. 80.

Tindall, George B., *The Emergence of the New South* (Baton Rouge, 1967).

Williamson, Handy, and Thompson, Noel, *An Economic Study of the Alabama Black Belt* Tuskegee Institute, Alabama, 1976).

Woodward, C. Vann, *The Origins of the New South* (Baton Rouge, 1951).

Footnotes / Tuskegee and the Politics of Illusion

1. Ralph Ellison, *Invisible Man* (New York, 1949).
2. Stokely Carmichael and Charles V. Hamilton, *Black Power: The Politics of Liberation in America* (New York, 1967), p. 122.
3. *Ibid.*, p. 126.
4. The history of Macon County is explored in a special issue of *Alabama Historical Quarterly*, 18, (Summer, 1956). Louis Harlan provides a good, brief treatment of the deal which founded Tuskegee Institute in *Booker T. Washington, The Making of a Black Leader, 1856-1901* (new York, 1972), pp. 113-115.
5. In the Alabama election of 1892, the registered white voters cast 53 percent of their votes for the Populists, 27 percent for the Democrats and 20 percent did not vote. Blacks voted 49 percent for the Democrats, 14 percent for the Populists and 36 percent did not vote. The total statewide Populist vote was 47.6 percent. J. Morgan Kousser, *The Shaping of Southern Politics: Suffrage Restriction and the Establishment of the One-Party South, 1880-1910* (new Haven and London, 1974), pp. 41-42.
6. *Tuskegee News,* November 4, 1976; Kevin P. Phillips, *The Emerging Republican Majority* (Garden City, New York, 1969), pp. 209-232.
7. Handy Williamson and Noel A.D. Thompson, *An Economic Study of the Alabama Black Belt* (Tuskegee Institute, Alabama, 1975), p. 104.
8. U.S. Department of Commerce, *Census of Agriculture* (Washington, D.C., 1972), *Ibid.*
9. U.S. Department of Commerce, *Census of Population, 1970* (Washington, D.C., 1972).
10. *Ibid.*, Williamson and Thompson, *An Economic Study, passim.*
11. Harlan, *Booker T. Washington, op. cit.,* pp. 171-175.
12. Stokely Carmichael and Charles V. Hamilton, *Black Power,* p. 133.
13. The Black academic elites' median salary is several thousand dollars higher than that of the majority of rural whites and working class blacks, but it is not in most repects an overwhelming, annual income. By both regional and national standards, faculty salaries at Tuskegee Institute are rather low. The median Tuskegee faculty salary for the 1975-76 academic year was $12,500, compared to $16,600 at nearby Auburn University and $13,800 at Alabama A&M. Instructor's salaries at Tuskegee Institute averaged $10,000 during the last academic year. Considering that the average yearly cost of living for a family of four in the nonmetropolitan South for the year 1975 was estimated by the federal government to be $19,800, Tuskegee's academic elite do not have significant surplus capital for major investments outside of food, educa-

tion, clothing, shelter, transportation and a minimal amount for conspicuous consumption. These figures also provide an explanation for the lack of a taxation base for increased governmental services and higher bureaucratic costs and salaries which the Ford administration became noted for. See the *Bulletin of the American Association of University Professors* (Summer, 1976).

14. One is constantly reminded of Booker T. Washington's joke about Macon County's political economy: "I went to the black belt of the South, inhabited almost exclusively by Negroes and mules." The entire physical culture of the population, black and white, is rooted in the soil: even today, many Tuskegeeans cultivate sizeable vegetable gardens in their backyards. The town itself is barely a generation removed from a rugged, agricultural economy and the plantation itself.

15. A critical discussion on the relationship between political society, and especially electoral political institutions, and civil society is presented in Antonio Gramsci, "State and Civil Society," in *Selections from the Prison Notebooks* (New York, 1973), pp. 206-276.

16. *Tuskegee News,* April 17, 1969; *the Model Cities Experience: Tuskegee, Alabama, 1968-1975* (Tuskegee, 1975).

17. Letters to the Editor, *Montegomery Advertiser-Alabama Journal,* January 30, 1977.

18. *Tuskegee News,* July 15, 1976.

19. *Tuskegee News,* August 5, 1976. In most Southern small towns, the black ministerial elite has served as the black intelligentsia as well as the central political vehicle for the entire black community. This has not been true for Tuskegee, because of the existence of a well educated, academic black petty bourgeoisie strata. Relations between town and gown blacks were always at best rocky, even during the pre-Populist period. As early as 1884, one local black minister of the A.M.E.Z. Church, the Reverend P.J. McFintosh, referred sarcastically to Tuskegee Institute as "the beacon light on yonder hill, kept in a blaze by $3,000 annually poured into the furnace by a Southern legislature." *Tuskegee News,* September 25, 1884.

20. *Tuskegee News,* August 5, 1976.

21. *Tuskegee News,* August 12, 1976.

22. *Tuskegee News,* August 26, 1976.

23. *Tuskegee News, December 30, 1976.*

24. *Tuskegee News,* February 10, 1977; *Tuskegee Voice,* February 12, 1977.

25. *Tuskegee News,* February 24, 1977.

26. *Tuskegee News,* March 3, 1977.

27. *Tuskegee News,* January 20, 1977. Since the middle fifties, Governor George Wallace attempted to identify his political interests with the

interests of Tuskegee Institute. Wallace achieved his initial national exposure by refusing to desegregate the University of Alabama, on the grounds that state assisted institutions like Tuskegee Institute already existed for young black students. Marshal Frady, *Wallace* (New York, 1975).

28. *Tuskegee News,* January 14, 1977.

29. *Tuskegee News,* September 8, 1977.

30. Joseph Jones to Emmett J. Scott, May 14, 1914; Jones to Scott, May 18, 1914; Jones to Scott, June 29, 1914; Scott to Jones, August 13, 1914; Jones to Scott, September 24, 1914. Cpy of "Weekly Report on Mahogany," no date but probably 1914; letter to Directors of Company discussing the amount of stock Africans should be permitted to purchase, May 14, 1915; Scott to Jones, May 18, 1915. All letters are in the Booker T. Washington Collection, Container 9, Library of Congress, Washington, D.C.

31. Charles W. Chappelle to Jones, no date; Jones to Scott, August 15, 1915; August 17, 1915; August 25, 1915. Letters are in the Washington Collection, Container 9, Library of Congress.

32. *Tuskegee News,* December 16, 1976; "Baxley Rules Reed out," *The Tuskegee News,* October 27, 1977.

33. *Tuskegee Voice,* March 5, 1977.

34. Stan Voit, "Money misuse chard made," *Tuskegee News,* November

34. Stan Voit, "Money misuse charge made," *Tuskegee News,* November 24, 1977.

35. Stan Voit, "Audit explains school money," *Tuskegee News,* November 24, 1977.

36. "Charges Dropped, but Amerson, Young and Baxley keep talking." *Tuskegee News,* December 1, 1977.

37. Stan Voit, "Police didn't have total banking," Editorial, *Tuskegee News,* October 27, 1977.

38. "Commodores, Tuskegee musicians to be honored on Saturday," *Tuskegee News,* June 23, 1977.

39. "The Way I See It," *Tuskegee News,* October 27, 1977.

40 Arnold S. Kaufman, "Murder in Tuskegee: Day of Wrath in Model

40. Arnold S. Kaufman, "Murder in Tuskegee: Day of Wrath in Model Town," *The Nation* (January 31, 1966), 119.

41. Carmichael and Hamilton, *Black Power,* p. 143.

42. *Ibid.*, p. 144.

43. Frantz Fanon, Introduction, *Peau Noire, masques blancs* (Paris, 1952).

Sources / The Continuing Burden of Race; Wilson's *Declining Significance of Race*

Harold M. Baron, *The Demand for Black Labor: Historical Notes on the Political Economy of Racism* Somerville, Massachusetts: New England Free Press, 1971).

Barbara Caress, "The Myth of Reverse Discrimination," *Politics and Education,* 1, (1977), p. 10.

Nathan Glazer, *Affirmative Discrimination: Ethnic Inequality and Public Policy* (New York: Basic Books, 1976).

H. Edward Ransford, *Race and Class in American Society: Black, Chicano, Anglo* (Cambridge, Massachusetts: Schenkman Publishing Company, 1977).

John U. Ogbu, *Minority Education and Caste: The American System in Cross-Cultural Perspective* (New York, Academic Press, 1978).

Barbara Page, "The Assault on Affirmative Action," *Politics and Education,* 1, (1977), pp. 31-38.

James P. Smith and Finis Welch, *1978 Race Differrences in Earnings: A Survey and New Evidence* (Santa Monica, California: The Rand Corporation, 1978).

"The Social and Economic Status of the Black Population in the United States: an Historical View, 1790-1978," Series P-23, Number 80 (Washington, D.C.: Government Printing Office, 1979).

Pierre van den Berghe, Review of *The Declining Significance of Race,* in *Sociology and Social Research,* Volume 63, Number 1, (1978), pp. 154-156.

Robin M. Williams, Jr., *Mutual Accommodation: Ethnic Conflict and Cooperation* (Minneapolis, Minnesota: University of Minnesota Press, 1977).

William J. Wilson, Peter I. Rose and Stanley Rothman, editors, *Through Different Eyes, Black and White Perspectives on American Race Relations* (London, Oxford and New York: Oxford University Press, 1973).

William J. Wilson, *Declining Significance of Race, Blacks and Changing American Institutions* (Chicago: The University of Chicago Press, 1978).

Other Titles by South End Press

Southern Africa

U.S. Military Involvement in Southern Africa / W. Mass ACAS. Documents the role of the U.S. government and multinationals within the overall Western strategy of economically and militarily supporting the white-minority rule in southern Africa—focuses on how the U.S. has systematically violated the U.N. arms embargo.

Ba Ye Zwa / Judy Seidman. A penetrating portrait of life under apartheid. Through drawings, poems, folk songs, newspaper clippings, and narrative Seidman presents a seldom seen picture of South African black culture.

United States

They Should Have Served that Cup of Coffee / ed. by Dick Cluster. A collection of engaging and serious essays and interviews by activists in the Civil Rights, Women's, Gay, Anti-War and Soldiers' movements; and in the Black Panther Party and the League of Revolutionary Black Workers.

Indignant Heart; a black worker's journal / Charles Denby. Denby's life in the oppressive South and in the auto factories of Detroit. He talks about every mass movement in the U.S. in the last 25 years. *go on to next page*

Chains of Change / Mel King. King, a black community leader in Boston, puts forth a vision and a strategy for how the Black community in Boston can fight against the "New Reconstruction" of Black dependence on the white power structure, and can lead the way in the struggles of all peoples to gain genuine decentralized control of their lives.

Conversations in Maine / James & Grace Lee Boggs; Freddy & Lyman Paine. On the Maine coast since 1968, four people have come together to ask the question: Why hasn't there been a socialist revolution in the U.S.? Their discussions present diverse proposals for socialist strategy and commitment for a fulfilling society.

Politics

Ecology As Politics / Andre Gorz. In his first English-speaking work since the widely acclaimed *Socialism and Revolution*, Gorz examines the relationship between ecology and politics—between ecological balance and our economic and political structures. A major premise of the book is that we cannot avoid the political nature of ecological issues. At the same time, the ecological movement is not an end in itself, but a stage in the larger struggle. Gorz shows that technology which has at its base the domination of nature can only lead to the domination of people; and he shows that only a fundamental restructuring of technology and society can reduce waste and inequality.

The Politics of Eurocommunism / ed. by Carl Boggs & David Plotke. A collection of essays by Marxist activists and scholars from Spain, France, Italy, and the U.S. The contributors address critical questions raised by Eurocommunism: Do the Communist Parties of Western Europe represent the interests of working people? Is it possible to achieve socialism through parliamentary means? This book also contains sections on the emergence of the women's struggle for liberation and how this struggle has affected the communist parties, the implications of Eurocommunism for the left in the U.S., and original documents from Italy, Spain, and France.

The Political Economy of Human Rights (2 volumes) / Noam Chomsky & Edward Herman. *The Washington Connection and Third World Fascism (vol. I)* documents the complicity of the U.S. government, corporate establishment, and the media in Latin Amerian, and African repression and torture.
After the Cataclysm: Postwar Indochina and the Reconstruction of Imperial Ideology (vol. II) gives a detailed account of postwar Vietnam, Cambodia, and Laos, and the media's rehabilitation of the bruised doctrinal system of the imperial powers.

Between Labor and Capital; a political controversy series / ed. by Pat Walker. Is there a middle class between capital and labor? This controversy is based on a lead piece by Barbara and John Ehrenreich who argue that there is a professional and managerial class (PMC).

The Crisis in the Working Class; an argument for creating a new labor movement / John McDermott. A straightforward, down to earth look at the position of workers in the U.S. today. Mc-Dermott begins with a telling indictment of trade unionism as it has been practiced in the U.S. in recent years. We are led back through one hundred years of American labor history, reliving the lives of Frederick Douglass, Eugene Debs, and others, as well as great movements, such as the American Railway Union and the I.W.W. The history is vivid and detailed, and throughout, the author does not lose sight of its relevance to the present. He describes a new stage of U.S. capitalism—collectivized capital—and presents a proposal for working class organization today.

Write to us for a catalogue of our other titles:
P.O. 68 Astor Station, Boston, MA 02123

South End Press

South End Press is committed to publishing books which aid people's day-to-day struggle to control their own lives. Our primary emphasis is on the United States—its political and economic systems, its history and culture—and on strategies for its transformation.